B.M. Jain was formerly Professor and Senior Research Scientist in Political Science at South Asia Studies Centre, University of Rajasthan in India; Visiting Professor in Asian and Asian American Studies at State University of New York, Binghamton, NY and Visiting Professor, The UNESCO Chair of Philosophy for Peace, Jaume 1 University at Castellon, Spain.

INDIA IN THE NEW SOUTH ASIA

Strategic, Military and Economic Concerns in the Age of Nuclear Diplomacy

B.M. JAIN

Viva Books

New Delhi | Mumbai | Chennai | Kolkata | Bengaluru | Hyderabad | Kochi | Guwahati

First Indian Edition 2011

VIVA BOOKS PRIVATE LIMITED

- 4737/23 Ansari Road, Daryaganj, New Delhi 110 002
  E-mail: vivadelhi@vivagroupindia.net, Tel. 42242200
- 76, Service Industries, Shirvane, Sector 1, Nerul, Navi Mumbai 400 706
  E-mail: vivamumbai@vivagroupindia.net, Tel. 27721273, 27721274
- Jamals Fazal Chambers, 26 Greams Road, Chennai 600 006
  E-mail: vivachennai@vivagroupindia.net, Tel. 28290304, 28294241
- B-103, Jindal Towers, 21/1A/3 Darga Road, Kolkata 700 017
  E-mail: vivakolkata@vivagroupindia.net, Tel. 22836381, 22816713
- 7, Sovereign Park Apartments, 56-58, K. R. Road, Basavanagudi, Bengaluru 560 004
  E-mail: vivabangalore@vivagroupindia.net, Tel. 26607409, 26607410
- 101-102 Mughal Marc Aptt., 3-4-637 to 641, Narayanguda, Hyderabad 500 029
  E-mail: vivahyderabad@vivagroupindia.net, Tel. 27564481, 27564482
- First Floor, Beevi Towers, SRM Road, Kaloor, Kochi 682 018, Kerala
  E-mail: vivakochi@vivagroupindia.net, Tel: 0484-2403055, 2403056
- 232, GNB Road, Beside UCO Bank, Silpukhuri, Guwahati 781 003
  E-mail: vivaguwahati@vivagroupindia.net, Tel: 0361-2666386

Published by arrangement with

I. B. Tauris & Co. Ltd.
6 Salem Road, London W2 4BU
175 Fifth Avene, New York NY10010
www.ibtauris.com

ISBN : 978-81-309-1784-9

Published by Vinod Vasishtha for Viva Books Private Limited, 4737/23, Ansari Road, Daryaganj New Delhi - 110 002. Printed and bound by Gopsons Papers Limited, Noida.

To My Late Parents

CONTENTS

LIST OF ACRONYMS

ADB	Asian Development Bank
AHWR	Advanced Heavy Water Reactor
AJTs	Advanced Jet Trainers
APEC	Asia Pacific Economic Cooperation
APHC	All Party Hurriyat Conference
ARF	ASEAN Regional Forum
ASEAN	Association of South East Asian Nations
ASEM	Asia-Europe Annual Meeting
ASLV	Advanced Satellite Launch Vehicle
AWACS	Airborne Warning and Control System
BARC	Bhabha Atomic Research Centre
BBC	British Broadcasting Corporation
BIMSTEC	Bay of Bengal Initiative for Multi-Sectoral Technical and Economic Cooperation
BJP	Bharatiya Janata Party
BDR	Bangladesh Rifles
CAR	Central Asian Region
CAS	Central Asian States
CBMs	Confidence-Building Measures
CCP	Central Communist Party
CCS	Cabinet Committee on Security
CD	Conference on Disarmament
CENTO	Central Treaty Organization
CIS	Commonwealth of Independent States
CPI	Communist Party of India
CPI (M)	Communist Party of India (Marxist)
CTBT	Comprehensive Test Ban Treaty
DAE	Department of Atomic Energy
DMK	Dravida Munnetra Kazhagam
DoS	Department of Space
DPG	Defence Policy Group

DRDO	Defence Research and Development Organization
EAS	East Asia Summit
ENR	Enrichment and Reprocessing
EU	European Union
EUMA	End-Use Monitoring Agreement
FBTR	Fast Breeder Test Reactor
FBR	Fast Breeder Reactor
FDI	Foreign Direct Investment
FMCT	Fissile Material Cut Off Treaty
FMF	Foreign Military Financing
FMS	Foreign Miltary Sales
FOC	Foreign Office Consultations
FTA	Free Trade Agreement
G-4	A formal group of four middle-tier powers: Brazil, Germany, India, and Japan.
G-8	A group of top 8 industrial countries consisting of Canada, France, Germany, Italy, Japan, Russia, United Kingdom and United States
G-15	A group of 19 developing countries from Asia, Africa and Latin America
G-22	A group of 22 developing countries
G-77	A group of 133 developing nations
GDP	Gross Domestic Product
GSLV	Geo-Synchronous Satellite Launch Vehicle
HuJI	Harkat-ul-Jihad-al-Islami (terrorist group)
IAEA	International Atomic Energy Agency
IAF	Indian Air Force
IBSA	India, Brazil and South Africa
ICBM	Intercontinental Ballistic Missile
ICC	International Criminal Court
IGG	Inter-governmental Group
IGMDP	Integrated Guided Missile Development Programme
IIGs	Indian Insurgent Groups
IMF	International Monetary Fund
IPKF	Indian Peacekeeping Force
IPR	Intellectual Property Rights
ISI	Inter-Services Intelligence
ISRO	Indian Space Research Organization
JeM	Jaish-e-Mohammed
JMB	Jama'atul Mujahideen Bangladesh
JKLF	Jammu and Kashmir Liberation Front

JWG	Joint Working Group
LAC	Line of Actual Control
LCA	Light Combat Aircraft
LeT	Lashkar-e-Taiba
LoC	Line of Control
LTTE	Liberation Tigers of Tamil Eelam
MAD	Mutual Assured Destruction
MEA	Ministry of External Affairs
MoI	Memorandum of Intent
MoU	Memoranda of Understanding
MFN	Most Favoured Nation
MNNA	Major Non -NATO Ally
NAM	Non-Aligned Movement
NATO	North Atlantic Treaty Organization
NCA	Nuclear Command Authority
NDA	National Democratic Alliance
NGOs	Non Governmental Organizations
NMD	National Missile Defence
NNPA	Nuclear Non-Proliferation Act
NPP	Nuclear Power Project
NPT	Non-Proliferation Treaty
NRC	Nuclear Regulatory Commission
NSAB	National Security Advisory Board
NSCN	National Socialist Council of Nagaland
NSG	Nuclear Suppliers Group
NSSP	Next Steps in Strategic Partnership
NTB	Nuclear Test Ban
OIC	Organization of Islamic Countries
ONGC	Oil and Natural Gas Commission
PAEC	Pakistan Atomic Energy Commission
PAK	Pakistan Administered Kashmir
PDP	People's Democratic Party
PoK	Pakistan-occupied Kashmir
PFBR	Prototype Fast Breeder Reactor
PHWR	Pressurized Heavy Water Reactor
PRC	People's Republic of China
PSLV	Polar Satellite Launch Vehicle
PWR	Pressurized Water Reactor
R&D	Research And Development
RAPS	Rajasthan Atomic Power Station
SAARC	South Asian Association for Regional Cooperation

SAFTA	South Asian Free Trade Area
SAPTA	South Asia Preferential Trade Agreement
SCO	Shanghai Cooperation Organization
SEATO	South East Asian Treaty Organization
TAPS	Tarapur Atomic Power Station
TSA	Technology Safeguards Agreement
UF	United Front
ULFA	United Liberation Front of Assam
UML	Unified Marxist Leninist
UN	United Nations
UPA	United Progressive Alliance
USSR	Union of Soviet Socialist Republics
WTO	World Trade Organization

ACKNOWLEDGEMENTS

My thanks go out to all those colleagues and friends who have richly contributed to this book project in several ways, although it is not possible to mention all of them individually.

I owe my special thanks to Shalendra D. Sharma, Professor, University of San Francisco, California, and Kevin Clements, Professor and Director, Centre for Peace and Conflict Studies, University of Otago, New Zealand, who wrote endorsements for the book despite their numerous prior commitments.

I have immensely profited from the comments, observations, and suggestions of Sumit Ganguly (Indiana University, Bloomington), Patrick James (USC, Los Angeles), T. V. Paul (McGill University, Montreal), and Luc Reychler (Leuven, Belgium). I am grateful to all of them.

I am thankful to students I taught at SUNY, Binghamton, New York, and Jaume 1 University, Castellón, Spain, for prodding me into writing this book while I was teaching a course on India and South Asia, and Regional Peace and Conflict.

I express my deep gratitude to Joanna Godfrey, editor at I. B. Tauris, London. This book would not have been possible without her amazing patience, understanding, and cooperation. I owe my thanks to Maria Marsh for her valuable editorial advice at the final stage of the book, and also to Rasna Dhillon who was instrumental in launching this book project.

I thank my daughter, Romi, and son, Rahul, who have been part of the project right from its inception. My daughter Romi, during her MBA studies at SFSU, San Francisco, did meticulous proofreading with incisive comments and useful suggestions despite being unusually busy with her studies. My son, Rahul, went through the entire typescript to ensure the accuracy of facts and figures. Last but not least, my heartfelt thanks to my wife, Manju, whose unfailing support and encouragement made it possible to complete this project.

PREFACE

The debate about the new South Asia is essentially a byproduct of the daunting challenges confronting the region in the aftermath of the 9/11 and the recent onset of the era of economic globalization. Prior to the tragic events of 9/11, the world was rapidly becoming United States-centric. But things began changing when non-state actors directly challenged the military, economic, and technological dominance of the United States as an invulnerable world hyper-superpower. Non-state actors have sent out a loud and clear message to world chanceries that it is now geopsychology rather than geopolitics or geoeconomics that will be a decisive factor in shaping the nature and pattern of international relations.

Hardcore conservatives believed that command of the world would rest in the unipolar system led by the United States. Perhaps, policymakers and strategic-affairs pundits failed to grasp the potency and value of a geopsychology that could erupt like a volcano at any moment. Today, the tough wars that America has been fighting in Iraq and Afghanistan are the manifestation of an inbred geopsychology of regimes that are deadly opposed to the plundering of their national resources (oil and natural gas), assailment of their religious tenets and cultural values, and violation of their territorial sovereignty and integrity.

It is the inherent salience of geopsychology that has prodded me to undertake this re-evaluation of old security paradigms, primarily based on the geopolitics of theories of international relations. I am amazed that while billions of dollars are squandered on defence and security studies in Western universities and think tanks, none of them seems to have paid serious attention to the imperative of studying geopsychology as an independent branch of research in order to understand the dynamics of violence, ethnic conflicts, and civil wars in many troubled parts of the world. Power operators and foreign-policy conductors, churning through rigorous studies at their world-class research institutes, rely heavily upon conventional wisdom and knowledge because they lack the aid of a geopsychological barometer with which to make an accurate diagnosis.

My research interest in South Asian domestic and foreign policies has spanned more than three decades and has convinced me beyond any shadow of a doubt that world-class universities need to open new research centres to conduct rigorous studies on the particularities of the geopsychologies of the ruling classes and influential sectors of society in volatile regions. There is a categorical need to find answers to nuclear proliferation, arms development, jihads, and bloody violence.

The rational-choice model is no longer germaine to analyses of foreign behaviour and the security policies of ruling elites who are strongly preconditioned by their geopsychological approaches to international relations. Therefore, solutions must be discovered in the geopsychology of power wielders who are capable of manoeuvring political and strategic decisions in their favour. A modest attempt in this regard has been made in this book. I have arrived at the broad conclusion that no region other than South Asia has become a captive of the geopsychological impulses of the ruling classes—civilian and military—which have mastered the art of manipulating mass psychology.

In a broad sense, geopolitics and geopsychology are intertwined and interconnected in South Asia in terms of history, socio-cultural structures, psychology, and strategic thought. No geopolitical formulations, both in theory and practice, are meaningful in terms of goals and interests unless they are structured on the perceptions and responses of the broad populace. This poses a real challenge to strategic planners and public decision-makers. It is important to take into account the inbred geopsychological orientation of political leadership, nurtured in a long historical process of mutual suspicion and hatred, while evaluating the policy decisions of New Delhi and Islamabad regarding, for example, central issues such as Kashmir, cross-border terrorism, and nuclear proliferation.

In envisioning a new South Asia, it is categorically important to see how the enduring hostility between India and Pakistan may be put to an end. The single biggest challenge facing the region is how to change the old mindsets of leaders, including civilian and military bureaucrats, who are stumbling blocks in the creation of a secure, stable, and peaceful South Asia. To that end, the geopsychology of accommodation on shared interests and threats needs to be cultivated through the cultural socialization of the ruling classes, including religious leaders, intellectuals, and media personnel.

Furthermore, at the core of an integrated South Asia are a common perception of threat, common political values, and common strategic interests, which are crucial for the development of a well-coordinated strategy to fight the common enemy of terror. The problem is further compounded by the fractured geopsychology of the region's national elites who are relentlessly engaged in projecting the other side as the source of all problems. Their motivation is to exploit mass psychology to widen their political base and capture and consolidate power.

In this book, I have tried to examine military, security, and strategic issues in South Asia in the context of the two nuclear-armed states—India and Pakistan—whose congenital antagonism has helped sharpen the geopsychology of mutual hatred. This has made it extremely difficult to keep the region tension-free, which is essential for peace, stability, and economic development.

I concede that geopsychology has its limitations as an approach to and a tool of the analysis of foreign and security policies. However, what I argue is that it should not be ignored as an analytical framework, alongside other analytical tools, when the world faces new threats and challenges whose roots lie in the geopsychology of state and non-state actors, especially in volatile regions such as South Asia and the Middle East. Undeniably, security and peace structures are embedded in the mental make-up of these actors. Without this understanding, threat perceptions and security challenges–military and non-military–cannot be effectively dealt with in this age of globalization.

I have explained in this book that though studies in geopsychology first began in Germany in the 1930s, and were later advanced by an anthropologist and a psychologist in the West, they did not attract most research scholars. Perhaps, the central reason was the onset of Cold War politics between the two superpowers that prodded international-relations scholars to develop a host of theories and models in order to understand the nature of the international system and the foreign-policy behaviour of international actors. With the end of the Cold War paradigm, eminent scholars of international relations theories, such as Robert Keohane, John Mearsheimer, Joseph Nye, G. John Ikenberry, and John Lewis Gaddis, came up with new concepts, models, and formulations. Their writings are devoted to analyzing the nature of power in an increasingly interdependent world. Joseph Nye's recent work on soft power is a major contribution to evolving a peaceful world order through the instrumentality of 'attractiveness' (in a country's culture and political ideals) and 'cooptation'.

The use of soft power is a categorical necessity to enlist the support of anti-United States countries in the Muslim world whose inbred psychology is not to surrender to the United States unless the latter hears and treats them with due respect. At least in some respects, Nye's work comes closer to the understanding of the geopsychological impulses of those countries whose national pride has been bruised and whose religious and ethical tenets have been attacked with disdain and arrogance.

In chapter one I attempt to explain the threat perceptions of South Asian leaders as well as their defence and security perspectives and approaches within the geopsychological paradigm. I also explain that the projection of India as a regional hegemon by the smaller countries of South Asia is rooted in their deeply entrenched fear and distrust of India.

In chapter two I re-evaluate the geopolitical shift in South Asia and its broader ramifications both regionally and internationally. A new trend of forging strategic partnerships between medium and major powers, especially in the aftermath of 9/11, speaks of a fundamental change in global and regional security contours. The chapter further addresses how strategic partnerships could contribute to fostering a peaceful and secure global political order to enable regional actors to deliver the basic "political goods" in terms of internal security, political stability, economic development, and communitarian harmony.

In chapter three I examine various phases in the evolution of India's nuclear policy since the early 1940s in order to identify the reasons behind occasional shifts in India's nuclear policy. It is an uncontestable fact that India's first nuclear explosion in May 1974 introduced a nuclear arms race in South Asia by prompting Pakistan into developing its nuclear programme with outside assistance, notably from China. This is evident from the fact that Pakistan conducted six nuclear-weapons tests in response to India's five nuclear tests. Thus, the nuclear factor has fundamentally altered the security and strategic environment in South Asia. In view of the changing security contours, the chapter also focuses on India's nuclear doctrine to reassess whether India can be a stabilizing factor so far as regional and global peace and security are concerned.

Chapter four deals with the dynamics of India–Pakistan relations within the framework of geopsychology and psychocultural prophylaxis, to analyse not only the persistence of India–Pakistan hostility over Kashmir and cross-border terrorism, but also the resolution of peripheral bilateral issues such as the Siachen Glacier, Sir Creek, and the Tulbul Project.

Chapter five explores and evaluates India's political, economic, defence, security, and strategic relations with Nepal, Sri Lanka, and Bangladesh in light of the unprecedented political developments that have recently taken place in these countries. The chapter postulates challenges to and opportunities for India with the abolition of a 240-year-old monarchy in Nepal, the regime change under the leadership of Ms. Sheikh Hasina in Bangladesh, and the May 2009 end of more than two decades of ethnic conflict in Sri Lanka. These developments have multiple implications for India's defence, security, strategic, and economic interests in the region and beyond.

Chapter six examines the waxing importance for the United States of South Asia in the post-9/11 security and strategic environment. It is argued, on the one hand, that the tragic terrorist attacks on the United States greatly enhanced Pakistan's strategic importance as key partner in the global war on terror. On the other hand, India's emergence as a global power is perceived by the United States as a counterweight to China. The chapter also discusses the problematic issues and disturbing trends in United States–South Asia equations.

In chapter seven I examine China's increasing security and strategic engagement in the South Asia region and India's responses in order to judge the manifold ramifications of a paradigm shift in Beijing's policy in the post-Soviet era. The chapter also discusses China's perception of threat and its notion of the new world order and makes an objective assessment of what China's future behaviour may be in South Asia. The chapter also focuses on the implications of the military-strategic nexus between Beijing and Islamabad, and China's arms transfer to Sri Lanka and Bangladesh, which not only affect the multifaceted India–China relationship, but also regional peace and stability.

B. M. Jain

1

SOUTH ASIA IN THE GLOBAL AGE

Globalists are faced with the problem of evolving and articulating a new paradigm in order to explain the complex nature of the interconnected and interdependent world order. The chapter argues that the era of globalization has opened up new opportunities as well as novel challenges so far as the post-9/11 world order is concerned. Inevitably, in this era 'more and more nations are striving to join global networks of information, commerce and cooperative security because their economic well-being and national survival increasingly depend on it'.[1] More importantly, a shift in the 'global centre of political gravity' from the North-centric order to the Asia Pacific region has necessitated rethinking old security paradigms in the current international system. A mix of geoeconomic and geostrategic factors, propelled by increasing global cooperation, is likely to force public decision makers to refashion their countries' policies as well as to work out new strategies in accordance with the ongoing trend of globalization and regionalization.[2] It means that the dominant–dominated power structure is drawing to a close.

As part of the globalization trend, regional integration in economic, political, security and cultural terms has become an increasingly dominant feature among countries belonging to a specific region in order to protect and promote their commonly shared interests. Initially, the drive toward new regionalism was a reaction to the pressing need to address common problems confronting populaces, and a desire among regional actors for regional economic integration on the model of the European Economic Community (now the European Union). Lately, regional trade patterns have assumed varied forms in different parts of the world. For example, unfair 'trade protectionism' is practised by Western countries against developing nations. Trade arrangements within the European Union are feverishly opposed by Third World nations, which support and advocate a non-discriminatory trade regime. Slowly but surely, growing economic regionalism in Asia has had a profound impact on the current international system in terms of trade, investment, and transfer of capital-intensive technology.[3]

In the process of democratic globalization, democrats across the world are faced with the onerous task of promoting political pluralism and civil society in order to help build a free and democratic world. Nearly four dozen countries are still far from becoming democratic. There is a widely shared belief that radical militancy, intolerance, and violation of human rights are on rise in those societies where democratic institutions have not been allowed to grow and flourish or have been sabotaged by ruling elites.

Democratization of societies is one of the hallmarks of the globalization phenomenon. New waves of globalization, on the one hand, and an increasing trend toward regionalization, on the other, have become irreversible. Though the ongoing processes of globalization and regionalization, primarily in the economic sense, may appear paradoxical, in reality, they are complementary processes in the quest to establish an integrated and equitable international political and economic order based on notions of democracy, freedom, equality, and rule of law.[4]

A major challenge facing the proponents of globalization and democratization is the consolidation of democratization throughout the globe. According to some political analysts,[5] it is possible if societies are remade according to democratic values and norms.

Against this background, it is indispensable for South Asia to redefine itself in the new global age. New insights, new ideas, and new concepts are imperative to grapple with complex problems of a vast magnitude—including the 'tyranny of oil'[6]—facing South Asia, a peculiar region in terms of history, culture, psychology, and strategic thought.

In the recent globalization discourse, both empirical and normative arguments in favour of building a peaceful, democratic, and stable world order through a broad political and societal transformation have caught the attention of public-policy makers globally. Moreover, global civil society has acquired an added significance in peace-building initiatives as the world is faced with the threat of terrorism on an unprecedented intensity and scale. Congruently, the old paradigms of peace building have outlived their utility. As such, key policymakers and influential think tanks are called upon to refocus on the imperative of an alternative strategic paradigm that can address new threats emanating from the 'leverage-centric' geopsychology of non-state actors who neither subscribe to the idea of a world order under international liberalism nor share the vision of a democratic society committed to communitarian peace and societal harmony. To quote Samuel R. Berger who has aptly summed up the situation: 'globalization has raised the strategic cost of indifference to local conflicts; it has raised the moral cost.'[7]

It is also 'quixotic' and 'gaseously utopian' to think of a unilateral world order under American leadership. Robert S. Litwak, while quoting former Prime Minister Tony Blair, writes, 'There is resentment of US predominance. There is fear of US unilateralism.'[8] The discourse over unilateralism versus multilateralism has created a great deal of confusion and uncertainty as the world responds to the new threats of global terrorism and separatist elements, including the unauthorized use of weapons of mass destruction. The moot question is why the United States, with its overwhelming military and technological prowess, demonstrated by its 'unconventional war strategy' of carrying out remote-controlled drone attacks on suspected militant hideouts , has failed to undermine the rock-like morale of the Taliban and al-Qaeda forces. It is also a myth that humanitarian intervention has acquired a 'mantle of international legitimacy.' On the contrary, humanitarian intervention by the great powers under the garb of UN resolutions has caused a flare-up of mass hysteria against it. This is simply local populations look upon humanitarian intervention as a veiled interference in their domestic affairs. Although local people commonly welcome humanitarian assistance operated through the United Nations, they have little faith in international actors as saviours.

Joseph Nye's work entitled *Soft Power: The Means to Success* (2005) is a significant contribution to the encouragement of peace and stability in the international order. He argues that if the United States desires to remain a sole superpower, it needs to pay attention to soft power.[9] The soft–hard power syndrome suggests that soft power can deliver maximum goods with a minimum of loss in terms of human and material resources provided it is prudently used. What is problematic is that power operators and foreign policy conductors have failed to understand the dynamics or value of employing soft power to win friends and gain public good will and sympathy. Perhaps, they understand the reified tradition of subduing their perceived adversaries through stealth. It is a patent fact that the international community is incapable of controlling hard-power operators once they firm their resolve to employ military means to achieve their narrowly structured goals and interests. This is evident from President Bush's intractable approach to the so-called rogue states without 'understanding the origins of the "rogue-state" concept and its translation into policy before 9/11.'[10]

The above viewpoint is reinforced in the work of G. John Ikenberry who has rightly argued that problems in a unipolar world led by a 'hyper-power' arise because 'hegemony and the process of socialization' go together. He raises a question, 'What do hegemonic states do when they are being hegemonic? They do it through manipulation of material incentives.'[11] Ikenberry has brilliantly explained that a 'distinctive type' of international order has been organized by the United States together with European and East Asian partners around open markets, social bargains, intergovernmental institutions, and cooperative security.[12] On the other hand, Peter J. Katzenstein holds the view that some regions in the interdependent world order have become critical in contemporary world politics.[13] If seen from this perspective, the South Asian region has acquired primacy in terms of geoculture, geopsychology, and geostrategy. It is, therefore, vitally important to analyze the potency and relevance of geopsychology in South Asia, which has been characterized as the 'most dangerous hotspot' in the world.

Geopsychology

Realists and neo-realist students of theories of international relations share the broad consensus that that there has been a cyclical change from the geopolitics paradigm of the Cold War through the primacy of geoeconomics of the post-Cold War era to the primacy of a geopsychology paradigm rooted in perceptions—false or real—images, belief systems, 'interethnic prejudices', historical experiences of national elites, and the mindsets of key players in policy decision making.[14]

Willy Hellpach, professor of psychology at the University of Heidelberg, was the first to popularize the study of geopsychology as an 'organic combination of *geopolitik* and modern psychology'.[15] Hellpach shows how space gains importance as an intellectual and psychological experience or *Raumerlebniss* shared by every human encompassed by the three dimensions of terrestrial existence. While consisting of objective and physiographic features, space nevertheless asserts itself in man's life only through individual and subjective.[16]

Therefore, the geopsychologies of national elites, especially those belonging to conflict-ridden regions such as South Asia and the Middle East, need to be taken into account. As the history of wars in these regions suggests, government leaders are driven by a deeply entrenched psychology of mutual mistrust and hatred rooted in historical processes as well as in their bitter personal experiences of the past.[17] It must also be borne in mind that there is an ineluctable interaction and interconnectedness between geopolitics and geopsychology, and between cognitive beliefs and decision-making.[18]

The geopsychological paradigm is gradually acquiring salience in a fast-globalizing world. It helps us to understand the dynamics of the post-Cold War international system in the face of nontraditional threats such as separatist movements, religious radicalism, and ethno-religious conflicts throughout the world, especially in societies in transition. International relations theorists have yet to grasp the inherent complexities behind the phenomenon of non-military threats. At best, they have studied the role of personality in the foreign, defence, and strategic policy decisions of national and international actors such as Winston Churchill, John F. Kennedy, Nikita Khrushchev, Jawaharlal Nehru, and Charles de Gaulle. But political scientists and peace theorists have scarcely paid attention to the potency and role of the geopsychological orientation of decision-makers and ruling elites who are instrumental in generating mass psychology in favour of nuclear weapons and missile-building programmes. It can best be exemplified by Pakistan's late Prime Minister Zulfikar Ali Bhutto's emotionally overcharged call to his countrymen in the wake of India's overt hand in Pakistan's dismemberment in December 1971. He announced that Pakistan must build nuclear weapons even if the people were to eat grass.[19] This example shows how mass psychology in Pakistan is systematically manipulated in favour of nuclear-weapons building.[20] In case of Iran, the nuclear programme is impelled more by Iran's 'profound distrust of outside institutions', including the United Nations, making it very difficult for the United States to denuclearize that country.[21]

Doubtless, geopsychology is rooted in history, culture, and nationalism as well as in societal traditions and values. Psychocultural perceptions, formed in the process of building nation-states, tend to influence the psyche of people living within the specific national boundaries. Cultural divergences between various ethnocultural and religious groups—for instance, between Hindus and Muslims in Pakistan, between Hindus and Buddhists in Sri Lanka, and between Buddhists and Muslims in Bangladesh—are becoming sharper because of faster communications technology and transportation, bringing individuals of diverse cultural backgrounds together. On the one hand, multicultural interaction fosters a better understanding among individuals. On the other hand, it acts as a catalyst in creating awareness of one's cultural identity, especially among minority sections of society. Consequently, it continues to foster and strengthen the subordinate–dominant relationship in society.[22]

More importantly, common ethnicity, religion, language, and culture, including marriage alliances, tend to produce group solidarity among populations who look upon 'cultural others' as a threat to their own cultural identity. In this regard, leaders in India and Pakistan with their diverse ethno-cultural backgrounds are no exception. They are engaged in a bizarre political game of blaming each other for the persistence of the adversarial relationship between them. This is evident from the cases of India and Pakistan in South Asia, and the Arabs and Israelis in the Middle East.[23] As such, these countries can scarcely provide a rational choice for a model of the decision-making process. Moreover, the geopsychology of congenital hostility—for instance between India and Pakistan—is further fuelled by an interplay of ethnic and religious forces as well as by their age-old rivalries. Consequently, imaginary threats tend to change into real ones over a period of time.[24]

The geopsychology of mutual hostility makes it even more politically difficult for government leaders in India and Pakistan to resist the heterogeneous demands of diverse ethnic and cultural groups. In effect, they resort to populist rhetoric to woo their respective populaces in order to consolidate their vote bank. Moreover, government leaders' political, cultural, and strategic decisions are narrowly structured, concentrating on a psychology of mutual animosity and hatred.[25] Unlike Singapore, South Korea, and Taiwan, India and Pakistan have remained prisoners of the past, allowing past history to consume them psychologically.[26] That is why politically motivated choices outmanoeuvre rational choices even on critical issues such as national unity and integration.[27]

In a broader sense, South Asian geopolitics and geopsychology are intertwined and interconnected, given the specific history, culture, and societal structures of the region. No geopolitical formulations, both in theory and practice, can be meaningful in terms of goals and interests unless they are structured on the perceptions and responses of the populace. It is also important to mention that the inbred geopsychological orientation of political communities and leadership, nurtured in a long historical process of mutual suspicion and hatred, needs to be taken into account when evaluating policy approaches of key decision-makers—for example, on vital issues such as the war on global terror and the regime change led by the United States in Iraq. Undoubtedly, the anti-American climate, propelled by government leaders and generated over a period of time along religious, cultural, and ethnic lines has driven the Iraqi people into opposing the presence of alien forces on their land even though they had grievously suffered at the hands of Saddam Hussein's authoritarian regime. Viewed from this perspective, the Bush administration's decision to wage war against Iraq was proved wrong, based as it was on misjudgment as well as on the flawed advice of 'policy hawks' and pro-administration think tanks that American forces would be welcomed by the Iraqi people as their saviours. It shows that policymakers and policy advisors lacked a sound understanding of the geopsychology of the Iraqi people—and the people of Iran—who are swayed by a passionate sense of nationalism and by Islamic ideology and cultural affinity.

According to the 'psychiatric school' of thought, geopsychological impulses might further provoke the populace's ire over the transfer to extra-regional powers of their country's natural resources such as oil and natural gas. In Henry Kissinger's perception, 'local conditions' are paramount in judging the psychology of a particular region.[28]

Also, still alive in Chinese minds are memories of the humiliation the Chinese endured at the hands of alien powers—British and Japanese—who treated them as 'barbarians'. This has injected into the Chinese the peculiar psychology of suspecting aliens to be enemies. Similarly, Pakistan's psychology is that India is bent upon destroying Pakistan's survival as a sovereign and independent nation. This is one of the core reasons for Pakistan's deeply entrenched psychology of hostility toward India. Over a period of time, the popular psychology becomes transformed into a fixed geopsychology through which populaces look upon their neighbours as their natural enemies. Parallel examples abound in the Middle East and the Gulf region, between Arabs and Israelis, between Iran and Iraq, between Iran and Saudi Arabia, and between Lebanon and Syria.

If viewed within the interactive geopolitical and geopsychological framework, both India and Pakistan are set to vying for power, prestige, and influence in regional and international affairs. Accordingly, there has been a perceptional shift among Pakistani rulers in the aftermath of Islamabad's attainment of nuclear parity vis-à-vis India in May 1998. Since then the realization has percolated down in the psyche of these rulers that Pakistan needs to pursue proactive diplomacy in order to expand the country's political and strategic space vis-à-vis its main adversary: India. For this reason, Pakistan's civilian and military leaders have embarked upon projecting their country's nuclear-deterrence capability as a force to be reckoned with, fully capable of challenging

India's preponderance not only in South Asia but also in the 'extended neighbourhood'. This has, in the Indian perception, upset the strategic balance in South Asia. Moreover, the enduring and protracted conflict between India and Pakistan has further undermined India's image abroad, reinforcing the Western perception that India's asymmetric conflict with Pakistan has made the latter an equal of India. It is embedded in the geopolitical structure of the region in which India and Pakistan are located.[29]

Consequently, South Asia will largely remain an arena of psychological competition between India and Pakistan. However, one should not gloss over the stark fact that India has the largest population of Muslims after Indonesia, and also has the second largest population of Shia Muslims after Iran. Hamid Ansari writes:

> Geography is relevant. Muslim countries and societies form the immediate and proximate neighbourhood of India in South, Southeast, Central, and West Asia. Contacts with countries figure prominently in our relations. These for the most part have a substantive economic content, and considerable potential in terms of our developing capabilities. They have a bearing on our strategic environment.[30]

India as an Onlooker

India's perception of South Asia has been profoundly influenced by two major events in the region: attainment of strategic parity by Pakistan in May 1998, and the 13/12/01 terrorist attacks on the Indian parliament, which shook the foundation of India's pluralist democratic order. Without exaggeration, India lost its strategic preeminence in South Asia when Islamabad responded to India's nuclear tests by conducting six nuclear-weapons tests. Not only this, Islamabad mustered the courage to defy the United States' appeal not to follow suit, ignoring Washington's threat of sanctions. On the other hand, nuclear Pakistan sent a clear signal to India that India was now no longer invulnerable, its mighty conventional military power notwithstanding. That perception further emboldened Pakistan's ruling class to bleed India by employing terrorism as an instrument of its state policy. Not surprisingly, a minuscule number of terrorists operating from Pakistani soil have held the entire subcontinent hostage to their nefarious machinations without any fear of reprisal from New Delhi. The classic case of India's inept handling of the post-26/11/08 situation is reflective of Pakistan's feeble efforts and dilatory tactics of in bringing the perpetrators to justice despite the fact that India provided dossiers of irrefutable evidence of that the terrorists originated in Pakistan. Pervez Hoodbhoy writes, 'Baitullah Mehsud's offer to jointly fight India was welcomed by the Pakistani army.'[31]

Furthermore, India has failed to convince the world community that the Mumbai attacks not only threaten peace and stability in South Asia but also jeopardise global peace and security. On the other hand, Pakistan has succeeded in promoting an image of 'relevance in geopolitics' that prevents its key strategic ally—the United States—from taking firm action against Islamabad on the cross-border terrorism issue. But Islamabad also needs to remember that 'The cancer of religious militancy has spread across Pakistan and it will take decades to fight.'[32]

Though the United States and many other Western countries have praised India's exemplary restraint while dealing with Pakistan on the issue of terrorism, they also realize that India lacks diplomatic prowess, political courage, and moral stamina to undertake concrete action against Pakistan to defend the Indian people from the terrorist threat emanating from Pakistan. If viewed from a realistic paradigm, the United States understands very well that Pakistan is fully capable of causing and sustaining inestimable damage to India because the New Delhi leadership lacks a well-defined and clearly articulated long-term strategy to blunt Pakistan-sponsored terrorists and jihadi elements who are determined to destabilize India. At the same time, the United States is unable to leverage its influence over Pakistan since the latter is fighting a war in close collaboration with American forces against the Taliban and al-Qaeda, including al-Qaeda's indigenous terrorist outfits. If seen from the standpoint of realism, India has found itself in a 'paradoxical conjunction' of power and vulnerability.

New Political Dynamics

The new South Asia apparently differs from the old South Asia of the Cold War era both from the domestic and external points of view. On the one hand, a new political swing has already begun in countries such as Nepal with the abolition of a 240-year-old monarchy under the pressure of mass mobilization against the autocratic rule of King Gyanendra who could hardly read the people's political mood. On the other hand, General (retired) Musharraf was unable to gauge the depth of the competitive politics led by the two antagonistic political heavyweights, Zardari and Sharif, who made Musharraf's political exit possible, paving the way for a transition to democracy in Pakistan.

From the external point of view, the region's geopolitical, geostrategic, and security landscape has undergone a major transformation following nuclear-weapons tests carried out by India and Pakistan in May 1998 and the 9/11 tragic events. On the one hand, these developments have contributed to enhancing Pakistan's geostrategic importance to the United States, which is fighting a global war on terror against the al-Qaeda and Taliban elements with Pakistan's military and logistical support. On the other hand, India's loss of strategic preeminence with Pakistan's attainment of nuclear parity has complicated New Delhi's relationship with Islamabad on the interconnected issues of Kashmir and cross-border terrorism, which might trigger off a nuclear exchange between them.[33]

The new South Asia has witnessed unprecedented political changes. Monarchy in Nepal has been replaced by a republican state. Pakistan has witnessed the return to a democratic regime after the long spell of the authoritarian regime of Pervez Musharraf. Bhutan has become a parliamentary democracy, reducing the king's status to that of a symbolic head of the state. The Maldives has witnessed a peaceful transformation of the old power structure with 'significant and historic' democratic elections held in October 2008, replacing the decades-old, monolithic, one-party regime led by President M. A. Gayoom. Mohamed Nasheed's new and dynamic leadership has raised hopes of a better future among the Maldivians. Also, the end of more than two decades of ethnic conflict in Sri Lanka in May 2009 heralded a new political era in Sri Lanka.

New Nepal

Nepal has witnessed major political upheavals with the abolition of a 240-year-old monarchy. It has facilitated the role of peripheral political actors now emerging as the key political stakeholders in the dynamics of political power. The tortuous political journey of the Maoists began in 1996 with the launching of a revolutionary movement in the countryside. The movement was focussed on overthrowing the monarchy, establishing Nepal as a Republican state, and ensuring socio-economic justice to the rural poor, farmers and artisans who had been living under the shadow of a feudal society in Nepal. In the more than decade-old Maoist movement, approximately fourteen thousand people have lost their lives.

With the introduction of democracy within the framework of a new constitution set up in Nepal in 1990, the Maoist rebels got the opportunity to launch the countryside movement against the monarch to broaden their political base. King Gyanendra had never dreamt, even in his wildest of wild dreams, that monarchy would be abolished once and for all. The Maoists seized on internal contradictions in Nepalese society and polity to capture power.[34] In the 2006 people's movement, supported by a seven-party alliance, including the pro-king Nepali Congress Party led by G. P. Koirala, the king had ultimately to bow to the wishes of the common people. The interim parliament passed a resolution in 2007 to abolish the monarchy and decided to hold national elections in the country in April 2008, in which the Maoists secured the highest number of parliamentary seats. Naturally, in an inevitable struggle for power among key political rivals, the ultimate choice for the position of prime minister fell on Pushpa Kamal Dahal, nicknamed Prachanda (fierce), in August 2008. Dahal's past credentials as a rebel leader, with ideological leanings toward China, were already well known.

In the new Nepal, the ultimate power shifted from the monarch to the Maoists for the first time in Nepal's history through a democratic process. The Maoists' ideological proximity to China was a cause of major concern to India. In fact, New Delhi was in favour of retaining the monarchy in coexistence with democracy in Nepal. But Indian political pundits could not anticipate the political strength of the Maoists to rule the roost in Nepal's fractured democratic polity. Rival political groups in Nepal were more concerned with grabbing power by any means than motivated by the consensual politics of working together on a new agenda of nation building. In that murky political scenario, the Maoists had a splendid opportunity to exploit the situation in their favour with a multiple agenda of ensuring social justice to the marginalized sections of society at home and assuring freedom and autonomy in conducting Nepal's foreign policy and diplomacy with the outside world. By virtue of their ideological affinity with China, the Maoists thought of China as a card to be played against India in its security and economic sectors. Chinese leaders also demonstrated their keen interest in cultivating friendship with the Maoists and CPN (UML)-led governments. Beijing came forward, offering multiple incentives, such as developing Nepal's infrastructure and expanding trade and investment ties with Kathmandu in order to scuttle India's longstanding influence over Nepal. China knew well that New Delhi had monopolized relations with Kathmandu for nearly sixty years, mainly by pumping aid into Nepal, and supporting the monarch and Nepali Congress as pillars of India's Nepal policy. But things have fundamentally changed in the new power configuration.[35] The altered political setting of the new Nepal warrants that India should change its old colonial mindset both at the political and bureaucratic level.

Undoubtedly, the Indian foreign-policy establishment, over a period of time, has earned a reputation for interfering with Nepal's domestic and external affairs while virtually treating Nepal as its subordinate partner. But new political actors in Nepalese politics have made it clear to India that they desire to base Kathmandu's relations with New Delhi on equality, mutual respect, and non-interference in each other's internal and external affairs. Furthermore, the CPN (UML)-led government in Kathmandu has made it clear to New Delhi that Nepal favours scrapping the flawed 1950 treaty along with other treaties with a view to reshaping its relations with India. However, India's back-channel diplomacy facilitated the dislodging of a nascent democratic government led by the Maoist supremo, Prachanda. The latter was forced to resign following President R. B. Yadav's blanket refusal to sack the army chief, Rookmangud Katawal, on Prachanda's recommendation. This generated a new political controversy in Nepal on the question of the civil–military relationship having spillover effects on South Asia. To substantiate this claim, it may be recalled that the Pakistani army takes vital decisions on foreign, defence, and security matters. The fate of the democratically elected rulers in Pakistan virtually depends on the support of its military and the ISI.

To drive the point home, India cannot take the new Nepalese government, led by Madhav Kumar Nepal (resigned in June 2010), for granted. India will need to redefine its policy toward a new Nepal, and will need to abandon its old hegemonic mindset by treating Nepal as an equal partner in South Asia. More particularly, India's foreign-policy establishment will also have to alter its watertight-compartment mentality, which is politically incorrect and morally indefensible. Moreover, the dominant nature of the Indian foreign-policy establishment has greatly harmed India's long-term national interests as well as quite significantly diminished its political and strategic influence over Nepal. In addition to that, China is already bolstering its strategic engagement with Nepal, which might have negative geopolitical ramifications for India. As such, Indian policy elites need to grasp both the dynamics and logic of a completely transformed Nepal, whose priorities are social good, good governance, social justice, political stability, equidistance between India and China, and resolution of bilateral issues with its neighbours on the basis of mutual respect, mutual dignity, and equality.

Democratic Pakistan?

The 9/11 tragedy made it imperative for the world community to promote political liberalism and to democratize traditional societies with a view to defeating the dark forces of terrorism and religious radicalism in favour of a secure, peaceful, and democratic world order.[36] With this goal in mind, the world community is committed to rooting out terrorism, and encouraging democratic forces through diplomatic, economic, and strategic means. The UN has been an arch supporter of 'a new wave of democracy' to help the transitional democracies to take roots. As regards the transition to democracy in Pakistan, the persisting, ineluctable military–mullah nexus raises the fundamental question of whether President Asif Ali Zardari and Prime Minister Syed Yousaf Raza Gilani are capable of exercising their political power and authority to govern the country within a consensual democratic framework. It is doubtful that ineffectual civilian leadership in Pakistan will be able to deliver on social good.

There is a widely shared perception among commentators and political analysts that the nascent democracy in Pakistan still has a long and bumpy road to travel to lift the country out of its moribund economic conditions. The question of whether the Zardari–Gilani combination is capable of exercising control over the army in order to take independent political and strategic decisions remains unanswered as yet. It merits a mention here that Prime Minister Nawaz Sharif, though elected with an overwhelming majority, faced an extraordinarily embarrassing situation when General Pervez Musharraf undertook the 'Kargil adventure' in the summer of 1999 without taking Sharif into his confidence. That military offensive against India was undertaken at a turning point when Vajpayee and Sharif had inked the historic Lahore Declaration in February 1999 to improve relations between two countries. Sharif made a disclosure to that effect in September 2007. He conceded that he had 'let down' his then Indian counterpart, Atal Bihari Vajpayee. While holding Musharraf responsible for the Kargil episode, Sharif stated that Musharraf had 'subverted' the process of improving relations with India.[37] He added: 'Kargil was a very tragic incident in the history of the relations between the two countries.'[38]

The lesson to be drawn from the Kargil conflict is that unless the military is placed under direct civilian control, the future of democracy in Pakistan appears to be bleak and uncertain. It would be fatuous to anticipate that India and Pakistan would be able to transcend their historic animosity, nurtured, sustained, and solidified by the military in a nexus with the ISI and militant groups unless Pakistan's nascent democracy takes firm roots in the country. This is the single most important challenge to nascent democracies in the new South Asia.

There is a widely held assumption among South Asian political analysts that Pakistan is heading toward becoming a failed state. Though the Zardari government managed to liberate the Swat Valley from the Taliban's control, it is an uphill task to flush out the homegrown terrorists who have found a safe haven in the tribal belt. President Zardari has publicly acknowledged that terrorist and jihadi elements, as non-state actors, pose more of an existential threat to the country's security than India. Given the enormity of the deteriorating internal security situation in Pakistan, the army might stage a comeback. In this regard, the army chief, Ashfaq Pervez Kayani, gave a clear-cut signal to President Zardari to take efficacious measures to control the chaotic internal situation or be ready to face the inevitable return of military rule in Pakistan.[39]

There is a common perception in Pakistan that the Zardari–Gilani duo has proved worse than Pervez Musharraf's regime so far as the country's internal security and economic viability are concerned. It is not merely a question of fragile democratic structure in Pakistan. Equally important is whether the two mainstream political parties—the Zardari-led PPP and Nawaz Sharif's Muslim League Party—which had initially joined hands to oust the Musharraf regime, would be able to work together toward stabilizing democracy against the possible return of military rule in Pakistan. In this regard, sequentialists argue that unless the necessary conditions and structural constraints are properly addressed, democracy cannot take firm root anywhere; on the other hand, universalists believe that democracy can take roots everywhere. But the latter have been proved wrong in case of Pakistan. In fact, critics and political analysts have been voicing their serious concerns about the erosion of the state's coercive capacity to deal with local militant groups that are directly challenging the state's legitimate authority, as manifested by the terrorist attacks against the Sri Lankan cricket team in Lahore in broad day light in March 2009.

Political pundits are now debating whether Pakistan is a failed or a wobbly state and whether India will be sucked into the region's anarchy. The Congress Party spokesperson, Manis Tiwari, described Pakistan as 'the Somalia of South Asia'. Quoting former Secretary of State Madeleine Albright, Tiwari said, 'Pakistan has become a migraine for the international community.'[40] This statement was made in the context of the Pakistan-based jihadis' threat to global security and the ceding of its territory to the Taliban. Erosion of Islamabad's political authority can be further gauged from the signing of an agreement with the Taliban, under which the latter was allowed to enforce *sharia* rule in the Swat Valley. So far as the use of Pakistani territory by jihadi non-state actors is concerned, India's familiar rhetorical stance has been to bring the perpetrators to justice and to dismantle the infrastructure of terrorism. India's External Affairs Minister, S. M Krishna, accused Pakistan of suspending the composite dialogue between New Delhi and Islamabad because Pakistan had not taken concrete steps to prosecute the perpetrators of the Mumbai blasts. Krishna admitted that India's options were limited and it would have to play a very 'patient game' with Pakistan.[41]

Bangladesh

Islamic radicalism has rapidly proliferated in Bangladesh mainly due to the political patronage of militant outfits such as HuJI, Jama'atul Mujahideen Bangladesh (JMB), and its affiliate, Jagrata Muslim Janata Bangladesh (JMJB). These forces have dealt a serious blow to Bangladesh's 'ethos and culture', especially during Begum Khalida Zia's regime. One defence analyst observes:

> HuJI is the only group with the capacity to link up with groups in India and Pakistan. It also has connections with al-Qaeda and Osama bin Laden. HuJI is prepared to carry out operations anywhere and anytime. There are a number of religious and leftist terrorist groups capable of operating within Bangladesh. This has happened because of the radicalisation of society. Bangladeshi society is under transition and is also under tremendous pressure from radical groups. This helps fringe elements to carry out terrorist attacks and to survive in society.[42]

The interim military-backed government took charge of state affairs on 11 January 2007, focusing on anti-militancy, weeding out public and private corruption, and bringing about political reforms in Bangladesh. As reported in the *Bangladesh Assessment 2008:*

> According to the Cabinet Committee on Law and Order, between January 11, 2007, and the first week of January 2008, a total of 440,684 people had been arrested on various grounds by the law-enforcement agencies. This included close to 200 politicians and businessmen who are under prosecution

> for involvement in corruption. Among them are the country's foremost leaders and members of their families, including former Prime Minister Sheikh Hasina, on charges of extorting Bangladesh Taka (BDT) 29.6 million from a private company, and Khaleda Zia, for tax evasion.[43]

The interim government in Bangladesh took a decision to hold national elections at the end of December 2008, in which the Awami League, led by Sheikh Hasina, won a landslide victory. She took the oath of office as prime minister in January 2009. She was faced with daunting challenges at home, especially on the internal security front. She assured the nation that internal security would be her top priority by sternly dealing with militant outfits, including foreign insurgents and radical elements that have illegally sought refuge in Bangladesh. Her tall claims were soon exposed when a bloody mutiny by the Bangladesh Rifles (BDR) took place in February 2009. The mutiny, the first in the country's history, sent shock waves to the newly elected democratic government of Sheikh Hasina who had to struggle hard to come to terms with BDR's mutinous forces, which killed nearly a hundred army officers.[44] The mutiny was a red signal to the government that divisions within the security forces, propped up by Islamist militants, had the courage and capacity to challenge the legitimacy of authority within democratic governance.

India's reaction to the BDR mutiny was initially well guarded, saying it was an internal affair of Bangladesh. Later on, India's External Affairs Minister Pranab Mukherjee wrote to Bangladesh Prime Minister Sheikh Hasina that India was ready to provide any form of assistance that Dhaka might require in the post-mutiny situation. Moreover, India's security concerns were also linked to it. The unsuccessful attempt to destabilize the Hasina government was also a signal to India to be on hyper-alert so far as its internal security was concerned.[45] But the irony was that India was unable to check the illegal entry of BDR personnel into its territory. The Hasina government asked the Indian government to take all possible measures to prevent their entry into Indian territory so that they might not escape legal action by Hasina's government. More significantly, Prime Minister Hasina appealed to the FBI of the United States and New Scotland Yard of the United Kingdom to assist in investigating the BDR mutiny. It was tantamount to marginalizing India's security and diplomatic role in Bangladesh, reinforcing the latter's perception of New Delhi's inability to assist in the investigation of the entire gamut of the BDR's mutinous act. From the point of view of border security, it is now seen as dangerous to assign a security role to the BDR without 'the force's complete detoxification'.[46] The trial of nearly 4,000 border guards took place in Bangladesh's special courts in November 2009.

In the wake of the BDR mutiny, there is a categorical need to undertake CBMs between India and Bangladesh in order to manage border security in the long-term national interests of both countries. In order to revitalize military cooperation, both countries have agreed to boost military and strategic CBMs in order to check the overt and covert activities of insurgents and militants who are bent upon challenging the internal security and political stability of India and Bangladesh.

Sri Lanka

The end of more than two decades of ethnic conflict in Sri Lanka following the killing of the LTTE supremo, V. Prabhakaran, and the defeat of the LTTE in May 2009, marked a new era in Sri Lankan history. The public mood across the country was jubilant when President Rajpaksa announced that the nation had won the war against the Tamil Tiger separatists. Sri Lanka offers a unique example to the world in its unbelievable accomplishment in eliminating separatist forces while ethnic and separatist movements are still going on in many parts of the world with a much greater intensity. In this long, fierce conflict, approximately seventy thousand people lost their lives and the country suffered inestimably in terms of economic development, human resources, and material progress. The woes of the country are not yet over.

Perhaps, Sri Lanka is likely to undergo major political and strategic upheavals for a host of reasons. First, at the political level, the Sri Lankan government under President Mahinda Rajpaksa will need to redress the grievances of the Sri Lankan Tamils and a large section of the Muslim community, victims of the state's discriminatory policies. Second, the end of the ethnic conflict does not signal the beginning of good governance without delivering on the aspirations and expectations of a vast majority of the disgruntled sections of Sri Lankan society. It demands a creative and visionary leadership to pursue a policy of social and political inclusiveness in order to rebuild the strangulated nation. Third, the nation's rebuilding task needs huge development assistance from donors. Also, the president is faced with the onerous task of bringing 'peace and harmony' to various groups in the country. Finally, there is a gigantic challenge before the government to help resettle the internally displaced people (IDP). The government is spending 1.7 billion rupees a month to maintain these temporary IDP welfare villages in the North. It is also feared that there are Eelamist and pro-LTTE lobbyists all over the world who might launch the campaign of subversion to destabilize the Rajpaksa government.[47]

In strategic terms, Sri Lanka will need to follow a more cautious and prudent policy while dealing with China, in general, and India, in particular. This is especially so when India seems to be unhappy over the Sri Lankan government's increasing defence and strategic engagement with China in regional affairs ever since China came forward to supply arms to Sri Lanka against the LTTE. President Rajpaksa should understand that China will ask for a bigger price for its military assistance to Sri Lanka at a critical juncture when India had refused to accede to the President's request for military hardware. In this regard, Sudha writes:

> China is all set to drop anchor at India's southern doorstep. An agreement has been finalized between Sri Lanka and China under which the latter will participate in the development of a port project at Hambantota on the island's south coast … The significance of Hambantota to China lies in its proximity to India's south coast and on the fact that it provides Beijing with a presence midway in the Indian Ocean.[48]

Idea of an Integrated South Asia

Public-policy makers and pundits of South Asian affairs are engaged in a discourse on an integrated South Asian community on the pattern of the European Union (EU). However, they need to bear in mind that even the EU took a long time in accomplishing the goal of establishing a free-trade regime and common market. Furthermore, the EU members have not yet been able to develop common security and foreign policies. In the case of South Asia, its political and economic conditions are much different from those of Europe. Despite the persisting bilateral disputes between the member countries of South Asia, several resolutions regarding the urgency of an integrated South Asia were passed at the SAARC summits. The SAARC leaders have realized that in the fast-globalizing interdependent world, South Asia cannot remain isolated in the economic and trade realm in which they have common stakes and interests.

Prime Minister A. B. Vajpayee underlined the prospect of an integrated South Asia that possesses a unique cultural identity. At the SAARC Summit held in Kathmandu in January 2002, he said:

> With a market of this size, our natural wealth, our human resources, our technical skills and our intellectual strengths, an integrated South Asia can be an economic powerhouse by using its synergies creatively in building up on the mutual complementaries of its constituent economies.[49]

The idea of an integrated South Asia sounds good in theory but is not feasible to implement in practice for a host of reasons. It is a mistaken belief that the idea of an integrated South Asia in terms of politics, economics, society, and culture can be translated into reality. How can there be a common culture, common political system, and common security arrangement, given the fact that there is an absence of convergence on security and threat perceptions among South Asian government leaders? On the contrary, they have divergent strategic perceptions. For instance, unlike India, Pakistan favours the strategic presence of China in South Asia with a clear intent to contain India. Further, small states of the region, such as Sri Lanka and Nepal, look upon India as a hegemonic power rather than a facilitator of peace and stability in the region. This perception is deeply embedded in the psyche of the national elites of most of the South Asian countries and more prominently in the Pakistani psyche.

At the core of an integrated South Asia is the sharing of common threat perceptions, political values, and strategic interests in order to evolve a common and well-coordinated strategy to fight the common enemy of terrorism. This problem is further compounded by the fractured geopsychology of the national elites of each country in the region who relentlessly engage in projecting one another as their archenemy. The motivation behind these practices is to exploit the mass psychology in order to expand the political base to capture, consolidate, and sustain power. There is a common perception among political élites in South Asia that given the abject poverty, hunger, and mass illiteracy in the feudal, backward, and straight-jacketed hierarchical societies of the region, it is much easier to manipulate mass psychology in their favour by invoking caste, cultural, racial, and religious symbols. Countless examples abound in this respect.

Divergences on political, security, and strategic perceptions among South Asian government leaders are more conspicuous and transparent than those of their counterparts in other parts of Asia. For example, while dealing with Southeast Asian countries, India is comfortable forging economic or strategic partnerships with countries such as Vietnam, Singapore, Malaysia, and Thailand. Similarly, Pakistan feels at ease entering into a military and nuclear relationship with China. Islamabad, on the other hand, is not enthusiastic about forging a strategy with New Delhi to stamp out the common threat of terror. In brief, unless South Asian countries rid themselves of mutual fear and mistrust, the idea of an integrated South Asia will remain a mirage. For that, 'liberal' and 'progressive' elements in each country of the region need to be strengthened to create momentum in integrating South Asia, at least in the economic realm.

Conclusion

In South Asia, challenges are harder to define and predict. They fundamentally emanate from militant organisations and jihadi elements operating within the region with the aim of destabilizing it, and destroying its economic and financial infrastructures. To deal with them, South Asian leaders will need to garner the political will to develop a citizen-centric cooperative security system as well as to deepen regional economic and trade engagements to build an integrated and prosperous South Asia. This is an uphill task. Without the support and confidence of the populace, the goal of a peaceful, stable, and prosperous South Asia will remain a pipedream, given the fact that militants and Taliban elements have rebounded with a greater intensity and scale. As such, South Asian ruling and non-ruling leaders from the mainstream political parties need to narrow down their political differences and personal prejudices to come up with a new action-oriented strategy to bring perpetrators of terror to justice. In envisioning a new South Asia, it is categorically important to see how the congenital hostility between India and Pakistan can be put to an end: the imperative of mutual survival makes a common defence inevitable. The single most important challenge facing the region is how to change the old mindsets of government leaders, including civilian and military bureaucrats who act as the stumbling blocks to the creation of a secure, stable, and peaceful South Asia. As a solution, the geopsychology of a positive approach needs to be cultivated through the sociocultural socialization of the ruling class and influential sections of society, based on the people-centric social good.

2

THE POST-COLD WAR GEOPOLITICAL SHIFT IN SOUTH ASIA

The geopolitical and security environment in South Asia has undergone an amorphous and ambiguous transformation with the end of the superpowers' geopolitical contest, and the occurrence of the 9/11 terrorist attacks. Optimists have interpreted the absence of the super-power rivalry as the beginning of a new era in the relationships between South Asian states. A vast majority of the scholarly community in South Asia is of the view that the post-Cold War geopolitics offers enormous opportunities to the countries of the region to refashion and rearticulate their policies in tune with the imperative of the emerging global political order.

However, fundamental uncertainties regarding its pace, scale, and direction, looming large over the region, have produced a state of inertia among South Asian states responding to geostrategic realism. South Asian policy elites are caught in the dilemma of choosing between appropriate responses and euphoric reactions to the discourses on 'the end of ideology', the end of political game rules, and the beginning of new strategic thinking. For instance, there is no clarity in terms of goals and priorities for strategic cooperation between India and the United States, between India and Russia, between India and Israel, and also between Islamabad and Washington. But do small or medium-level partners have any freedom of choice to refashion their destinies? The debate is now centred on unipolarity versus multipolarity, and more recently multipolarity versus 'multipartnership'. The question of who will be losers and who will be gainers in the new setting is not yet precisely answerable. At best, only hazy sketches are being outlined by political and strategic pundits without clarity of purpose.

Joseph S. Nye, a foreign-policy and strategic-affairs specialist, cautioned the United States in his work *The Paradox of American Power* (2003) that its 'unilateralism' and 'arrogance' might prove counterproductive in a transformed geopolitical and geopsychological environment in which the 'dark side of globalization' has made the United States vulnerable to new threats despite its being a hyper-superpower. In this regard, writes Robert S. Litwak, 'As American society and societies worldwide adopt counterterrorism measures to address new risks and uncertainties, 9/11 has an unshakable psychological, and practical impact.'[1]

Further, Joseph Nye suggests that the United States ought to choose the course of soft power (openness and persuasion) instead hard power (overwhelming military and economic strength) to realize its policy objectives. The use of 'hard power', Nye underlines, is incompatible with nation-states' geopsychological impulses.[2] Such an assessment is rooted in a dramatic geopsychological change among relatively medium and small powers, inherently opposed to the US unilateralism. Sensibilities of this nature are pervading the political scene in South Asia in which small countries such as Nepal and Sri Lanka feel themselves susceptible to the overwhelming power of India, which restricts the autonomy of their defence and security policies. This is grounded in the belief that a never-ending hostility between the two nuclear-armed nations—India and Pakistan—does not augur well for peace and stability in South Asia.

Views and arguments of this nature reflect in the writings of Stephen P. Cohen, *India: Emerging Power* (2001), George Perkovich, *India's Nuclear Bomb* (2001), John J. Mearsheimer, The *Tragedy of Great Power Politics* (2001), and Ashley J. Tellis's *Limited Conflicts under the Nuclear Umbrella* (2001). A common thread running through their writings is the salience of public and popular perceptions in decision-making processes. For instance, Perkovich talks of 'Indian polity's psyche' to emphasize the significance of national psyche in decision making. The endless 'action–reaction chain' in the context of India and Pakistan explains the deeply entrenched psychocultural divergences between the two countries, which impinge upon their geopolitical perceptions and perspectives. Minimally, a new trend is clearly visible in the Western writings that have devoted feeble attention to the persisting psychocultural peculiarities of the South Asian region, mainly among government leaders, bureaucratic elites, religious zealots, and court intellectuals.

A host of questions come to mind in making a realistic assessment of the altered geopolitical environment of the region. What is the altered character of geopolitics? [3] Does the Cold War psychology still persist between India and Pakistan? Is it true that the globalization process in the field of economy, trade, and investment has brought about a change in the old mindsets of South Asian government leaders while conducting bilateral relationships? These questions will be taken up in subsequent chapters.

This chapter primarily aims at re-evaluating the geopolitical shift in South Asia as well as its broader regional and international ramifications. A new trend of forging strategic partnerships between medium and major powers, as witnessed today in post-9/11 international relations, is an indicator of the changing global and regional security contours. The fundamental question that needs to be addressed, however, is how strategic partnerships will serve the long-range interest of fostering a peaceful and secure global political order so that regional actors can deliver the basic 'political goods' in terms of the internal security and safety of the common people in the face of overwhelming threats from non-state actors such as Lashkar-e-Taiba and al-Qaeda.

The lack of conceptual clarity in the nuances of geostrategics on the part of South Asian government leaders, including a small coterie of strategic analysts boasting of their expertise and analytical incisiveness, further complicates the contents and contours of military and nuclear doctrines. Without an in-depth assessment of their pros and cons from a long-term perspective, advocates of these doctrines have failed to understand and appreciate how geopsychology functions in the South Asian region.

Moreover, it is self-explanatory that no sincere effort has been made in the right direction to change the old mindsets of the political class in concert with the changing character of international relations.[4] It is necessary to flesh out the inbred geopsychological orientation of political communities, which have been nurtured in a long historical process of mutual suspicion and hatred. Steadily, people of India and Pakistan have been psychologically conditioned, to look at one another through the prism of an enemy image.[5]

The chapter argues how new challenges, stemming from the unintended negative fallout of post-Cold War geopolitics, have sought an upper hand in South Asia, the Gulf, and the Middle East. Given the focus on South Asia, this chapter will address the new security and strategic concerns of South Asian states—in particular, those of India and Pakistan.

The South Asian geopolitical environment has tended to assume an uncertain and directionless form for more than a decade in three major fields: strategic planning, security, and ethnopolitics. Though each one of them has its own distinctive nature and form, it tends to overlap the others. In the strategic domain, Pakistan has claimed for the first time that it has attained strategic parity vis-à-vis India by its timely response to India's nuclear tests. Ostensibly, nuclear reprisals by Pakistan have not only lent Islamabad a greater degree of psychological security vis-à-vis New Delhi, but have also emboldened it to employ nuclear weapons as a convenient instrument of political blackmail to resolve, for instance, the protracted Kashmir issue. At times, the contrived fear of nuclear exchange between India and Pakistan also tends to heighten a profound tension among members of the international community.

The geopolitical fallout of the nuclearization of South Asia, in political and strategic terms, is clearly visible in several ways.[6] First, the United States, having acknowledged India and Pakistan as de facto nuclear-weapons states, has begun treating them seriously. Further, the United States' leverage over Pakistan has waned since Pakistan's emergence as a nuclear power; and further, Pakistan's opposition to CTBT has also undermined the United States' diplomatic leverage.[7] This is reinforced by the fact that US appeals to Pakistan to permanently end cross-border terrorism in Jammu and Kashmir has not cut much ice with Pakistani government leaders—both military and civilian.

Second, Pakistan's tone has changed in its dealings with India. It may be recalled that one of the senior members of the Sharif cabinet told the BBC in his interview following the nuclear-weapons tests carried out by Pakistan that India must now 'come to its senses'. In effect, it was a clear message to Indian policy makers that Pakistan was now fully capable of meeting any Indian challenge to its national security. In other words, it would no longer tolerate 'Indian hegemony' in the region. Pakistani rulers even went a step farther, telling the United States that they would neither roll back their nuclear programme nor cease modernizing their defence programme unless India stopped expanding both its nuclear and conventional military modernization programme. What worries the United States is not the possession of nuclear weapons by Pakistan, but that these weapons might fall into the hands of militant and *jihadi* groups. The United States still suspects the transfer of weapon technology by Islamabad to 'autocratic' and 'irresponsible regimes' in volatile regions, as evidenced by the recent disclosure of the Pakistani nuclear scientist A. Q. Khan's overt hand in illegally transferring nuclear technology and components to, for instance, Iran and North Korea.[8]

Third, there is a lurking fear that there might be a nuclear exchange between India and Pakistan.

Fourth, South Asian states such as Nepal, Sri Lanka, and Bangladesh are gripped with a sense of fear that the Indo-Pakistan nuclear rivalry may prove disastrous for the entire region.

Finally, India's defence and security concerns in the altered milieu in and around the region have induced the New Delhi government to modernize the country's defence systems faster.

Moreover, geopolitical contest for power and influence between India and Pakistan has sharpened, following the May 1998 tests. As a result of attaining strategic parity vis-à-vis India, Pakistan has embarked upon a new policy of widening its political and strategic space in the outside world. General Musharraf made hectic diplomatic efforts to deepen his country's geopolitical and economic links with Central Asia, the Middle East, the Gulf, and Southeast Asia. His visits to China, Southeast Asian countries, and the Gulf were intended not only to legitimize his military rule in Pakistan but also to seek these regions' moral and diplomatic succour on the Kashmir issue. Like his predecessors, General Musharraf endeavoured his best to convince the world community that the Kashmir issue was the root cause of estrangement between Islamabad and New Delhi. Also, the current leadership in Islamabad has been urging the United States to mediate over the Kashmir dispute. But the Obama administration has refused to oblige them, asking India and Pakistan to resolve it bilaterally through peaceful dialogue. New Delhi views Islamabad's efforts to rope in the United States as part of Pakistan's political game plan to put pressure on India to resolve the Kashmir dispute by determining the wishes of the Kashmiri people while at the same time blaming India for the continuing political impasse.

Insecurity Syndrome

South Asia has become more insecure and unstable with the end of nuclear ambiguity marked by the nuclear weapon tests carried out by India and Pakistan in May 1998. So long as they managed to maintain nuclear ambiguity, New Delhi and Islamabad were able to sustain the bilateral political dialogue. It may be recalled that the foreign secretaries of both the countries held intensive discussions in 1997 to work out various confidence-building measures to defuse the regional crisis. For the first time, both the countries agreed to a composite dialogue that comprised eight issues, including peace and security in South Asia, and the Kashmir problem. The 1997 diplomatic dialogue was a major breakthrough in Indo-Pakistan relations. The dialogue picked up momentum when high-level official talks took place in New Delhi in November 1998. Multiple dialogues took place between New Delhi and Islamabad at the secretary level on defence, water resources, economic and commercial issues and included comparatively less contentious issues such as the Siachen Glacier, the Tulbul project, and Sir Creek Island. There was satisfactory progress on several issues, and more importantly, on the Siachen and Tulbul issues.

Indo-Pakistan relations registered some degree of improvement when Prime Minister A. B. Vajpayee undertook the historic Lahore bus journey in February 1999, which resulted in the signing of the Lahore Declaration with his counterpart Nawaz Sharif. Both leaders committed themselves to resolving outstanding problems through peaceful dialogue. Also, they underscored the need to 'forget and forgive' the past and move forward with a new vision and approach to foster friendly ties, essential for the economic development and welfare of the people of both countries. Unfortunately, the Lahore spirit was given a burial when General Musharraf summoned the courage to launch an unprovoked aggression in the Kargil sector of Indian territory in May–June 1999. That was a premeditated act of open violation of the Line of Control (LoC), as agreed upon by both the parties under the 1972 Shimla Accord.[9] The Kargil misadventure dealt a stunning blow to the ongoing process of normalization in their relationship. Vajpayee described the Kargil aggression by Pakistan 'as a burial of the bus-diplomacy'.

The Kargil conflict unambiguously proved beyond a shadow of a doubt that decision-making power on defence and security matters rested with Pakistan's military elites. It became further evident from a bloodless coup engineered by General Musharraf when he dislodged the democratically elected government of Nawaz Sharif in October 1999. With the installation of a military regime in Pakistan, relations between New Delhi and Islamabad reached their lowest ebb. Both countries became madly engaged in possibly the worst kind of Cold War, accusing each other of the persisting political deadlock. India's consistent stance has been that a true peace in South Asia cannot take place unless Islamabad ends cross-border terrorism permanently, and destroys the infrastructure of terrorist organisations operating from Pakistani soil. On the other hand, Pakistan has taken up the irreconcilable position that peace in the region is not possible unless the Kashmir problem is resolved first.

Although the possibility of a nuclear exchange between India and Pakistan is a distant one, they need to address the key questions of nuclear-weapons command and control systems, and also the probability of a nuclear accident, and the unauthorized use of weapons of mass destruction. India has already declared a unilateral moratorium on nuclear tests, while Pakistan has stayed away from making a similar announcement. In India, nuclear-command authority rests with the prime minister, a civilian head of government.[10] In the case of Pakistan, it is not yet not clear who exercises nuclear authority. In this murky scenario, India and Pakistan need to undertake concrete measures to reduce the nuclear threat and manage persisting security problems through political dialogue.

It is worth remembering that despite the worst buffets of the Cold War wrangling, the superpowers never stopped talking to each other. Dialogue between New Delhi and Islamabad in the aftermath of the Mumbai attacks in November 2008, on the other hand, froze. It does not augur well for regional peace, stability, and economic development. In this scenario, both sides are required to restart the political process within the framework of the Shimla Accord 1972, and the 1999 Lahore Declaration. If one recalls, President Clinton, during his visit to India in March 2000, reminded his audience, while pointing at Pakistan, that the modern world did not permit boundaries to be redrawn in blood.

Nuclear Deterrence

It is not the intention of this chapter to discuss the theory of nuclear deterrence in detail. It may be pointed out that both India and Pakistan have retained the nuclear-deterrent option as a guarantee of national security from each other's threat.[11] Opinions among strategic experts on the efficacy of nuclear deterrence are, however, divided. According to some supporters of pro-government policies, the retention of nuclear deterrents is absolutely necessary for national security.[12] Independent strategic analysts, on the other hand, question the credibility of nuclear deterrence. In support of their argument they cite the classic case of the Cuban missile crisis, saying that it was not the nuclear deterrents but the statesmanship of Kennedy and Khrushchev that facilitated the avoidance of a nuclear catastrophe. Do India and Pakistan have such statesmen of the stature of Kennedy and Khrushchev? The answer is in the negative.

Basically, nuclear deterrence is structured on a psychological basis.[13] Both India and Pakistan are captives of their narrowly structured perceptions of each other as enemies. These mutually held enemy images tend to become a constant source of tension between New Delhi and Islamabad.

The dilemma facing India and Pakistan is that, though geopolitics has changed at the global level, the geopsychology of the perception of mutual threat remains the same at the regional level. That is why there has been no breakthrough in the continual deadlock over composite dialogue. Enigmatically, sometimes there is a nuclear stand-off—at times a military stand-off—and at present there is a deadlock over the peace dialogue between the two countries. They indulge in a senseless, hysterical debate in which they accuse each other without tangible gains even as they face gargantuan challenges of economic development and welfare.[14]

Perception of the Small States of South Asia

South Asian small and weak states have been gripped by a deep sense of insecurity since India and Pakistan became independent and sovereign nation-states in August 1947. There are three core reasons for it. First, India's giant size and its industrial, economic, and military capabilities in comparison to its small neighbours tend to produce suspicion in their minds about India's intervention in their domestic, external, and security affairs. Their misgivings about India were reinforced by New Delhi's concrete actions, such as its direct role in the dismemberment of Pakistan in December 1971, its conducting a nuclear test in May 1974, its annexation of Sikkim in 1975, and its dispatch of Indian peace-keeping forces to Sri Lanka—although under the Indo-Sri Lankan Accord of July 1987—the airdrop of food and medical aid by the Indian air force in 1987, and its blanket refusal to renew the India–Nepal Trade and Transit Treaty in 1989. These are among a series of events that accentuated fear and insecurity among small states in the region. Second, there is a widely shared perception among South Asian states that India and Pakistan are not only heavily investing their scarce resources in the military build-up but are also advancing their nuclear-missile-building programmes, causing a graver threat to the peace, security, and stability of the region than ever before. Prior to Pakistan's nuclear tests, they identified India as the sole source of nuclear threat to the region.

But with the attainment of Pakistan's strategic parity with India, the small states' perceptions of threat have further deepened for fear of a nuclear exchange between the old rivals. Their sense of insecurity is understandable. Nepal, Sri Lanka, and Bangladesh, for example, were circumspect in their reaction to nuclear tests conducted by India and Pakistan. Girija Prasad Koirala, the then Prime Minister of Nepal, acknowledged that his country was not capable of acting as a 'mediator' between the two nuclear-armed nations. He called upon them, however, to reach an accord on establishing a restrained nuclear regime. Similarly, from the Sri Lankan viewpoint, India and Pakistan could not afford to roll back their nuclear programmes. That was why Colombo's reaction to the nuclear weaponization of the region was cautiously mild. In pragmatic terms, neither Sri Lanka, nor Nepal, nor Bangladesh was psychologically prepared to openly condemn the horrendous consequences of Indian and Pakistan's nuclear-weapons and missile-building programmes, disastrous for peace, development, and stability in South Asia. Third, the question of aid, grants, and contingency assistance looms large in the psyche of these small states because India is still considered an indispensable source of aid and grants for them. Nepal recently received a hundred crore rupees as credit from India to bail it out of economic sluggishness. Bangladesh has occasionally received multimillion dollar aid of one kind or the other from India, especially to meet the recurrent threat of cyclonic disaster in the country. In one particular case in November 2007, India provided aid worth one million dollars for the cyclone in Bangladesh, which killed three thousand and rendered millions of people homeless.

Though India did not provide military aid to Sri Lanka, New Delhi instantly came forward to provide humanitarian assistance in the form of food and medical aid to the internally displaced Tamil civilians in mid-2009 in the aftermath of the civil war there. The Sri Lankan government knew pretty well that without external emergency aid it alone could not tackle such a gargantuan challenge. The above-mentioned factors will continue to remain deeply etched in the psyche of smaller South Asian states.

External dimension

Geopolitics in South Asia took a new turn in the global political order following the May 1998 nuclear tests conducted by India and Pakistan. The United States, in particular, condemned the nuclear tests while expressing the fear that other irresponsible nations in volatile regions might follow suit. As expected, the United States and Japan placed a military and economic embargo on India and Pakistan. The international community also put mounting pressure on India and Pakistan to sign the CTBT without conditions or reservations in order to make the world free of nuclear weapons. Initially, the psychological pressure on both New Delhi and Islamabad was quite intense. Gradually, it subsided. Moreover, the United States reconciled itself to the reality that India and Pakistan were de facto nuclear powers, although it refused to grant them de jure status, as demanded by Indian policy elites.

In reality, the 9/11 tragedy diluted the United States' non-proliferation goal. The United States was obliged to redefine its non-proliferation policy because the Bush administration's priority focused on waging a global war on terror, in which the strategic and military roles of India and Pakistan, especially Pakistan, were indispensable to the United States' mission of eliminating the Taliban, al-Qaeda, and jihadi elements. Pursuant to that mission, the Bush administration lifted some sanctions against India and Pakistan. The administration asked India and Pakistan to exercise nuclear restraint as well as to limit their 'nuclear arsenals'. At the same time, the Bush administration's major concern was to prevent nuclear weapons from falling into the hands of Islamic radical elements operating in Pakistan and Afghanistan.

This apart, in the post-Cold War geopolitics, the Bush administration looked upon China's rising power as a potential challenge to US interests in the Asia-Pacific region. In order to countervail China's growing influence in the region, the Bush administration looked upon India as a balancing force. While keeping the national interest in mind, President Bush not only recognized India as an emerging global player but also demonstrated his keen interest in forging strategic cooperation with India. Thus, the transformation in US policy toward India was aimed at strengthening strategic cooperation between New Delhi and Washington in pursuit of shared interests in areas such as civilian nuclear energy, space, missile defence, trade, and commerce.[15] Also, in the assessment of US policymakers, India could play a pivotal role in preserving and promoting the United States' security, communication, trade, and commercial interests in the waters of the Gulf, the Indian Ocean, and Straits of Malacca. New Delhi also recognized that its security and strategic interests would be better served by cooperating with Washington in the areas of shared objectives.

In contrast, Pakistan's indispensible role in destroying the al-Qaeda terrorist hideouts in Afghanistan obligated the United States to reward Pakistan by committing massive economic and military assistance worth three billion dollars to Pakistan during President Pervez Musharraf's visit to the United States, and also rescheduling funds from international financial institutions such as the World Bank, IMF, and Asian Development Bank. After waiving the sanctions, the Bush administration approved several arms agreements with Pakistan, including exports of helicopters, cargo aircraft, night-vision equipment, radios, and various radar systems. It also paved the way for Pakistan to have greater opportunities to acquire excess US arms by designating Pakistan a major non-NATO ally in June 2004.[16]

In brief, the Bush administration's policy toward South Asia was more focused, clearer, and better goal-oriented, bypassing old ideological shibboleths and moral pretensions or 'ethical egoism'.

Strategic Perspectives of China and Russia

After a lapse of more than ten years since the 1998 nuclear tests, the strategic perspectives of the three great powers—the United States, Russia, and China—have undergone a sea change. For instance, China, which had initially dubbed India's nuclear tests as a projection of its 'hegemonic power', has gradually softened its acerbic tone. High-level political visits on both the sides—for example, the official visits of Prime Minister Vajpayee in 2003, and his Foreign Minister Jaswant Singh's visit to Beijing in 1999—contributed a great deal to dispelling mutual misunderstanding between New Delhi and Beijing. Chinese Premier Zhu Rongji's visit to New Delhi in 2002 helped in expanding trade and economic ties between the two countries, touching fifty-three billion dollars in 2008. Both countries are now engaged in developing a common strategic approach to the establishment of a multipolar structure of the international system to countervail the unipolar movement led by the United States. This was unthinkable during the Cold War period.[17]

On the other hand, China is skeptical about Indo-US cooperation in the defence and strategic fields. It may be recalled that China was keeping a close vigil over the New Vision Paper signed between India and the United States during President Clinton's visit to New Delhi in March 2000. But later on, China clarified that the strategic partnership between New Delhi and Washington would not obstruct in any way the Sino–Indian relationship. From the Indian perspective, China's supply of nuclear and missile technologies to Pakistan is not only a factor of irritation between India and China but also a factor of instability in South Asia. China has not given any assurances to India that it will stop assisting Pakistan in the military and nuclear realm. In realistic terms, China is not going to dilute its strategic partnership with Pakistan at the cost of coming closer to India. In other words, the Pakistan factor will continue to remain a critical variable in Sino–Indian relations despite the end of the Cold War. Nevertheless, what is significant is that in the changing geostrategic scenario following the 9/11 terrorist attacks, China is less likely to extend its support to Pakistan's reiterated demand for self-determination on the Kashmir issue under the UN resolutions. Nor will Beijing express its solidarity with Pakistan's diplomatic and moral support of separatist elements in Jammu and Kashmir, whom Islamabad calls 'freedom fighters'. China cannot afford to support Pakistan directly or indirectly on the question of self-determination because Beijing itself is facing Muslim separatist elements in its Xinxiang province.

The impact of the post-Cold War geopolitics also reflects on Indo-Russian relations. On the one hand, Russia is not keen to play the role of a security manager in South Asian affairs, mainly because of its domestic exigencies as well as its shrunken power base. On the other hand, Russia is committed to developing a close strategic partnership with India and China on the principle of equality.

President Putin realized that a weak, smothered, and shrunken Russia would not be treated on an equal footing by the West. With the NATO bombing of Belgrade in 1999, and the United States-led unilateral military action against Iraq in March 2003, Russia became fully convinced that its strong and enduring strategic ties with China and India were indispensable for reasserting its role in global and regional affairs as well as for the emergence of a multipolar world structure. But at the same time, the Moscow leadership clarified that strategic cooperation among India, China, and Russia was not aimed at forming a military axis against the United States. However, Russia is inherently in favour of constricting the strategic role and potential influence of the United States in the Middle East and Central Asia. The Shanghai Cooperation Organization of six nations, established in June 2001, is aimed at reducing the overarching role of the United States in Central Asia where it has already established its military beachhead. In effect, the United States' deepening strategic presence in Central Asia constitutes a long-term security threat to Russia and China and undermines their economic, energy and trade interests.

Vladimir Putin raised great hopes among his countrymen that Russia would once again carve out its assertive role in world politics. Putin began reviewing the security and strategic doctrines of his predecessor, Boris Yeltsin. At the NPT Review Conference (April–May 2000) held in New York, Russia refused to prohibit transfer of nuclear technology to strategic partners such as India and Iran. It went ahead with setting up a nuclear power plant in Iran even against mounting US pressure on Moscow.

Interestingly, Pakistan also occupies an important place in Russian strategic thinking in the altered geopolitics. Islamabad's geographical proximity to and religious affinity with the Muslim states of Central Asia are of paramount importance in refashioning Russia's policies toward Islamabad. Besides, Pakistan's strategic role is indispensable for peace and stability in Afghanistan. President Musharraf's visit to Moscow in 2003 was interpreted as Russia's overt desire to repair its fractured ties with Islamabad. However, India and Russia have come much closer in the defence sector than ever before. This is reflected in the co-production of high-tech weapons, including BrahMos missiles, by India and Russia. In realistic terms, Russian foreign policy in the post-Yeltsin era has assumed more flexibility and pragmatism in dealing with the outside world.[18]

India and Russia are committed to nurturing a strategic partnership, signed during President Putin's visit to India in October 2000. The Indo-Russian agreement on defence cooperation was signed under which Russia would deliver military hardware worth three billion dollars, including the delivery of 320 T-90 tanks, SU-30 aircraft, the *Admiral Gorshkov* aircraft carrier, and MiG-29 fighter aircraft. Putin's periodical visits to India paved the way for Russian assistance in setting up nuclear power reactors in Tamil Nadu in the southern part of India. During his visit to New Delhi on 25–26 January 2007, India and Russia signed a Memorandum of Intent (MoI) between the Department of Atomic Energy (India) and Federal Atomic Energy Agency (Russia) on the development of cooperation in the construction of additional nuclear power plant units at the Kudankulam (Tamil Nadu) site as well as the Russian design of nuclear power plants at new sites in India.

Furthermore, the two sides endorsed the concept of 'energy security', which envisages an acceptable balance between the security of demand and the security of supply. In view of their corresponding resources, needs, capabilities, and potential, they agreed to further enhance direct dialogue between their oil and gas companies. This is aimed at concluding mutually beneficial commercial agreements for joint work in all segments of oil and gas cooperation in India, Russia, and Third World countries. The arrival of the first shipment of oil to India from Sakhalin-I in early December 2006, as well as the signing of MoU on 25 January 2007 between ONGC (India) and the Rosneft oil company (Russia), setting up two joint working groups—one each for upstream and downstream activities—demonstrate the viability of future India–Russia cooperation in the entire hydrocarbon value chain.[19]

Putin's successor, President Dmitry Medvedev, has been following the footsteps of his political mentor—Putin, now Russia's Premier—so far as concerns Russia's policies toward India in the areas of defence, security, and strategic planning. During his visit to India in December 2008, he gave full assurances that Russia would take urgent steps to set up additional nuclear reactors in Tamil Nadu and deliver the aircraft carrier, *Admiral Gorshkov*, to India by 2012, including the Akula-class nuclear submarine. The Russian supply of military hardware to India, especially nuclear submarines and aircraft carriers, might contribute to strengthening India's naval power to respond to China's increasing naval presence in the Indian Ocean.

A New Geopolitical Swing

Indo-US relations underwent a fundamental transformation after the end of the Cold War. Prior to that, geopolitical and geostrategic differences between India and the United States were conspicuously irreconcilable. During the Cold War period, Indo-US relations were hamstrung by India's non-aligned policy, and the United States' fallacious doctrine of fostering military parity between India and Pakistan. This not only accentuated the arms race in the region, but also it contributed to sharpening the estrangement between New Delhi and Islamabad.[20]

It is a myth that, after the collapse of the Soviet Union, there has been a fundamental change in the United States' policy toward South Asia.[21] There are pessimists who believe that the Clinton team, for instance, was successful in its game plan of extracting maximum commitments from India on issues such as CTBT and Kashmir. But this assessment is far from realistic. In diplomatic negotiations, each country tries to achieve the best it can. No country can afford to ignore the interests of its counterpart.[22] Henry Kissinger once remarked in his address during his private visit to New Delhi that India was capable of playing a major role in global affairs. But he punctuated his remarks with the sarcastic suggestion that India avoid confronting the United States on every global and regional issue. In effect, the United States was ready to cooperate with India to enable it to play its due role in global and regional affairs, but not at the cost of US interests. Indian foreign-policy pundits need to be wary of the US style of conducting diplomacy and foreign relations on its own terms and conditions.

It is also worth mentioning that the United States' proactive diplomacy succeeded in roping India into negotiations. This was evident from the more than dozen rounds of talks between India's Foreign Minister Jaswant Singh, and the US Deputy Secretary of State Strobe Talbott. The underlying motive of US diplomacy was to ensure that India signed the CTBT, and resolved the Kashmir issue through peaceful dialogue. But India did not oblige the US government. India's argument was that, since India was a democracy, it was essential to develop a national consensus on the CTBT issue. Moreover, in the Bush administration's perception, the CTBT and NPT were old instruments of arms control, which had outlived their utility in the face of the possibility that these weapons might fall into the hands of terrorists.

The United States' approach to the Kashmir issue is based on *realpolitik* considerations.[23] The second Clinton Administration, for instance, clarified that the United States had no intention of acting as a mediator on Kashmir. During his visit to New Delhi in March 2000, President Clinton called upon India and Pakistan to resolve the Kashmir issue without third-party intervention. He also told General Musharraf, albeit with a mild chiding, that Pakistan must avoid confronting India, failing which it might have to face horrendous consequences. Clinton gave a clear message to Islamabad that it should not live under the illusion that the United States would intervene in its favour in the case that war broke out between India and Pakistan. It was an important shift in the United States' geopolitical perception of and approach to South Asia, although at the fag end of the Clinton presidency. However, it did try to 'remedy the deficiencies' of the past by attempting a workable roadmap to defuse tension in the region.

With a dramatic change in the strategic environment at the global level, following the tragic events of 11 September, President Bush not only lifted sanctions against India but also demonstrated his keen desire to transform relations with India. In an attempt to do that, the Bush administration publicly recognized India as a 'major global player' and underlined the need for consulting India on global and regional affairs as it did with other major powers such as Britain, France, China, and Japan. India also responded positively to the administration's overtures. This became manifest in India's endorsement of the United States' missile-defence programme, even against the wishes of Russia and China with whom India's relations were on an upswing. This apart, India and the United States signed a non-extradition pact in 2002 under which they would not hand over their citizens to the International Criminal Court for trial on charges of crimes against humanity.

A 'new page' in their military ties was opened when joint exercises were conducted by Indian and US commandos in Ladakh, Kashmir in September 2003 for the first time in their post-Cold War relations. These developments reinforced the mutual strategic necessity of cooperation between India and the United States.

The Obama administration is also carrying forward the legacy of its predecessor so far as nuclear deals, military and security cooperation, and strategic partnerships between India and the United states are concerned. Nevertheless, some change in its policy on nuclear non-proliferation is imminent. Combating nuclear proliferation remains a high priority for the Obama administration.

Secretary of State Hillary Clinton has revived the Clinton administration's old approach to non-proliferation as was evident from the pressure put on India and Pakistan to sign the NPT and CTBT. 'Ahead of next year's review conference on the Nuclear Non-Proliferation Treaty (NPT), President Barack Obama on Thursday successfully piloted a resolution in the UN Security Council, calling upon all countries outside the treaty, such as India, to join as 'non-nuclear weapons states.'[24] The resolution was spurned by India. New Delhi's reaction was that it would not comply with non-proliferation obligations to which it has not provided its sovereign consent. Additionally, it noted that India was a nuclear-weapon state and that there was no question of it joining the NPT as a non-nuclear-weapon state.[25] This situation is likely to create irritants between India and the United States, reminiscent of the first Clinton administration.

It will, however, depend on how the United States treats India—as an equal or a subordinate partner. The Congress-led UPA government of Prime Minister Manmohan Singh made it unambiguously clear that India, unlike the NDA regime under Vajpayee, would not play second fiddle to the United States. Also, it stressed that although India would continue its military and security cooperation with the United States, New Delhi's military relationship with Washington would be decided on a case-by-case basis.

The UPA government does not favour US unilateralism.[26] It may be pointed out here that even Pakistan, to which the United States assigned non-NATO major ally status in 2004, had summoned the courage to spurn the US appeal to send Pakistani troops to Iraq. It shows how a perceptual change has come about in the thinking of the ruling classes of South Asia in post-9/11 geopolitics. This kind of strategic defiance on the part of a junior partner was unthinkable in the Cold War politics.

The Obama administration is equally committed to assigning greater importance to South Asia—especially Pakistan—and Afghanistan. The administration has trebled its military and economic assistance to Pakistan as a reward to Islamabad for delivering strategic, military and intelligence services to US and allied forces that are fighting against the Taliban and al-Qaeda. Further, the Obama administration has turned a blind eye to Pakistan's expanding nuclear-weapons programme as well as its diversion of US funds to the military build-up against India. As a senator, Obama was an arch critic of Pakistan for misusing US funds for offensive purposes. As president, he is much subdued in his dealings with Pakistan. Perhaps he has realized the potency of the functional geopsychology of Pakistani civilian and military elites. Pakistan has been reiterating that it is ready to extend unshakable support to the US war on global terror, provided that its credentials as a responsible nuclear power are not doubted by the United States. Islamabad has further demanded that the United States respect the sensibilities of the Pakistani government over the deaths of civilians in drone attacks, which, in Islamabad's perception, have emboldened, toughened, and strengthened the morale of militant groups.

Conclusion

The fractured geopsychology of India and Pakistan has not only contributed to ruining their fragile economies but has also created a deep social chasm between the people of the two countries. There is a broad consensus among people in both countries—except ruling sections and hard-core religious conservatives—that India and Pakistan must end mutual rivalry, hatred, and animosity. People on both sides are urging their leaders to enter into political dialogue with a positive mindset to end the morbid geopsychology of permanently treating one another as enemies. This lends support to our hypothesis that the political psychology of the leadership is mainly responsible for creating an artificial divide between the two countries. The real dilemma that is likely to continue to grip the two countries is how to overcome a narrowly structured geopsychology in which outmanoeuvring the other by any means is deeply entrenched in each country's national psyche. As a result of this, India and Pakistan have been unable to address the genuine sensibilities of their small neighbours and have never thought of addressing the legitimate security and strategic concerns of other partners in the South Asian Association for Regional Cooperation (SAARC). On the contrary, they have divided the region in a typical fashion by behaving and acting as arrogant and irresponsible regional actors. To restart the bilateral dialogue, geopolitics needs to be informed by geopsychology. More significantly, the critical issues bearing upon regional geopsychology need to be addressed by public- policy makers, strategic analysts, and academia to facilitate connectivity with the geopolitics of mutual interdependence in the light of the emerging global political and economic order and regionalism.[24]

3

INDIA'S NUCLEAR POLICY

India's nuclear policy has traversed a tortuous path from the Nehru era to the present Congress-led United Progressive Alliance (UPA) government under the leadership of Manmohan Singh. It hardly needs to be stressed that India's nuclear policy during the Nehru era (1947–64) was chiefly driven and dictated by Nehru's soaring idealism. While projecting himself as a peace anchorite, Prime Minister Jawaharlal Nehru time and again emphasized that the country's nuclear policy fundamentally hinged on the principle of nuclear non-proliferation and world disarmament. In his policy utterances, Nehru had made it clear that India would stay away from developing nuclear technology for military purposes. However, his principal nuclear mentor, Homi J. Bhabha, a leading scientist, tried to persuade him that the country's national security demanded that India, while pursuing the objective of nuclear technology for development proposes, should develop its nuclear-weapons capability in order to meet any potential threat emanating from India's hostile neighbours, Pakistan and China. Instead of heeding Bhabha's advice, Nehru rejected his security argument because he essentially believed that security threats from India's neighbours could be addressed by employing a proactive diplomacy of dialogue and negotiation. He was later proved wrong when China waged an unprovoked aggression against India in October 1962. Nehru himself acknowledged that China had betrayed his trust in the Panchsheel (Five Principles of Peaceful Co-Existence) Accord India had signed with China in 1954.[1]

Nehru's vision of a nuclear-weapons-free world for establishing international peace and security exhorted him to design India's nuclear policy for peaceful purposes, geared to economic development. He emphasized that nuclear technology was indispensable for India to attain self-reliance in the energy sector, although he was fully conscious of the fact that the United States and the Soviet Union were not enthusiastic about dismantling their huge nuclear arsenals in favour of building a stable and peaceful world order. Despite that irreversible fact, Nehru continued his efforts to achieve the lofty goal of a global non-proliferation regime, as evidenced by his proposal of a comprehensive test-ban treaty in 1954.[2]

After his demise in May 1964, the Indian policy elite were forced to review India's 'nuclear celibacy' in the face of the deteriorating security environment in India's neighbourhood. For instance, China conducted its first nuclear explosion, named 'Device 596', on 16 October 1964. There was a major shift in India's nuclear policy in the post-Nehru era, characterized as a 'guarded' nuclear ambiguity (1966–97)—a reversal of the Nehruvian vision of 'atoms for peace'.[3]

Homi J. Bhabha, the founder and head of the Department of Atomic Energy, urged the United States in 1965 to give India a nuclear device or just the blueprint for one to help it catch up with China's nuclear development. But his plans came to naught.[4]

However, Indira Gandhi, known as a practitioner of power politics, took the momentous decision of exploding a nuclear device in May 1974, although she described it as a 'peaceful nuclear explosion'. India maintained a posture of nuclear ambiguity until 1997. But the NDA government, led by Atal Bihari Vajpayee, re-evaluated India's nuclear policy for a host of reasons including the BJP's political compulsions to strengthen its fragile political position among coalition partners in the government. It ultimately authorized scientists to undertake Operation Shakti-98 (Power-98) to make India a nuclear-weapons state while carrying out five nuclear-weapons tests at the Pokhran site in Jaisalmer, western Rajasthan in May 1998. The world community was shocked by the Indian tests and condemned them.

In order to convince the world of New Delhi's motivation behind these tests, the NDA government brought forth the first ever nuclear doctrine with wider ramifications for India's national security as well as for arms control and global non-proliferation efforts.

Against this backdrop, this chapter examines and rigorously evaluates various phases in the evolution of India's nuclear policy since the early 1940s in order to understand the correlations behind the occasional shifts in India's nuclear policy. It is an incontestable fact that India's first nuclear explosion in May 1974 introduced the new factor of a nuclear-arms race in South Asia, prompting Pakistan to develop its nuclear programme. Further, Pakistan was provoked into responding to India's five nuclear tests by immediately carrying out six nuclear weapon tests. This has fundamentally altered the security and strategic environment in South Asia. In view of the changing security contours, this chapter will also focus on India's nuclear doctrine from a broader perspective to explain whether India can be a stabilizing factor of regional and global peace and security.

The Nehru Era

As mentioned earlier, India's policy of 'atoms for peace' has traversed through the most tempestuous path since it was conceived in the early 1940s. It is tempestuous in the sense that India was faced with making a fundamental decision whether the 'atoms for peace' policy should be reversed in the face of the security threat posed by Pakistan and China's incremental, sophisticated, nuclear and missile-building programmes. As a moralist, Nehru publicly declared on numerous occasions that India's nuclear programme was exclusively devoted to peaceful and constructive uses, although there were voices of dissent from the mainstream opposition. In fact, Nehru commanded such a tremendous moral and political authority in the country and even great respect from his arch-political critics that he could afford to rule the roost on nuclear and security issues.[5] Such deference virtually muted the thunderous voices of pro-nuclear weapons lobbyists in parliament and outside it.

When President Harry S. Truman ordered the dropping of bombs on the Japanese cities of Hiroshima and Nagasaki in a bid to end the Second World War, more than 95 percent of the men, women, children, and non-combatants in those cities were killed. Those horrifying human killings made a deep psychological impact on front-ranking leaders such as Mahatma Gandhi and Jawaharlal Nehru. The latter was convinced that dark forces, either of a chauvinistic ideology or of a nuclear-based military technology, should find no place in any civilized society. Mahatma Gandhi, an apostle of peace and non-violence, was deeply shocked over the employment of atom bombs as an instrument of US foreign policy. Further, at Gandhi's initiative, India not only lent full support to the Washington declaration of November 1945 but also came forward with a comprehensive proposal to ban the use of nuclear technology for devastating purposes. Again, India actively supported the 1946 Acheson–Lilienthal report that emphasized the immediate need for devising an effective mechanism for the international control of nuclear weapons.

Outlining the thrust of the nuclear energy programme in the Constituent Assembly on 4 April 1948, Nehru said:

> Atomic energy is a vast source of power that is coming to the world...if we are to remain abreast in the world as a nation what keeps ahead of things, we must develop this atomic energy quite apart from wars indeed, I think, we must develop it for the purpose of using it for peaceful purposes.[6]

Thus, a passion for peace exhorted both Gandhi and Nehru to condemn the nuclear programme intended for military purposes. Their anti-nuclear-weapons position was reflected in the country's foreign policy as well. Trusted lieutenants, scientists, and technologists worked hard to articulate their views on the thrust of India's nuclear policy. Undoubtedly, Nehru and Bhabha had a shared vision of making India self-reliant in the energy field by embarking on a nuclear-energy programme for two main reasons. First, India's conventional sources of energy were neither sufficient nor cost-effective in fulfiling the incremental energy requirements of the country's rapid industrial development. Second, India's southern and western regions possessed abundant sources of fissionable material that, if fully exploited and harnessed for energy purposes, would be much cheaper.

Institutional Infrastructure

Nehru and Bhabha took the initiative to build up an institutional infrastructure to realize their vision of the nuclear-energy programme, which was launched in March 1944. As mentioned earlier, the prime concern of Nehru and Bhabha was to build up the country's economic sinews as it confronted appalling poverty, disease, and deprivation. In order to make the country self-sufficient in energy, Bhabha approached the Tata Trust for financial assistance to set up an Institute of Fundamental Research in Physics and Mathematics. The Tata Trust's positive response resulted in the setting up of the institute in June 1945. According to Indian government sources, the underlying reasons to develop nuclear energy were:

i. to develop a source of inexpensive energy;
ii. to provide energy in any part of the country capable of developing energy resources such as hydro-electricity powered by fossil fuels; and
iii. along with hydroelectric and thermal power stations, to maximize the economy of the grids. (Nuclear power stations operate most effectively as base-load stations.)[7]

Homi Jehangir Bhabha, who conceptualized the Indian nuclear programme, utilized the country's infrastructural components to fulfil the power requirements of agriculture and industry. Bhabha wanted to develop a sophisticated nuclear-energy programme to give the country a place of pride among nuclear powers. That is why he was motivated to set up nuclear research facilities on a massive scale. As mentioned earlier, he first approached the Dorabji Tata Trust to assist in establishing a basic research institution in the country. The Tata Institute of Fundamental Research was established in December 1945 and was mainly entrusted with the task of promoting fundamental research in physics and mathematics. In fact, Bhabha's singular aim was to fully develop nuclear energy without heavily relying upon external sources to fulfil the country's energy needs. He therefore proposed a three-tier power programme, indispensable for the development of atomic energy for useful purposes. The programme included:

i. building of heavy-water moderated reactors, which could produce power as well as plutonium needed to start the breeders;
ii. utilizing the plutonium produced from first-stage reactors in the fast breeders. This stage will continue until suitable thorium-uranium-233 reactors became available; and
iii. to run II type breeders on a thorium feed to produce uranium-233 and run the second type of breeders on the thorium-uranium-233 cycle.[8]

The Atomic Energy Act was enacted in April 1948, and subsequently the Atomic Energy Commission was set up in August 1948 to promote research in nuclear energy. Clearly, Nehru never intended to develop nuclear energy for military purposes but to improve the material conditions of the populace. While reacting to the opening of the country's first nuclear reactor, Apsara, at Trombay in January 1957, Nehru categorically declined to use atomic energy 'for evil purposes'.[9] A similar tone was reflected in his speech delivered before the Lok Sabha (lower house of parliament) on 24 July 1957. Nehru said:

> We are not interested in and we will not make these bombs, even if we have the capacity to do so and that in no event will we use atomic energy for those most destructive purposes. I hope that will be the policy of all future governments whosoever is in charge.[10]

From the above statement, two important conclusions can be drawn. First, Nehru rejected outright the idea of making nuclear weapons, even if India attained that capacity. Second, Nehru had bound all future governments to refrain from employing nuclear energy for destructive purposes. Even China's 1962 aggression against India did not provoke him into reversing his nuclear stance. That was indeed a litmus test for India's policymakers who restrained themselves from openly supporting a nuclear-weapons-building programme. Nehru's successor, Lal Bahadur Shastri (1964–66), also dispelled the misgivings of the opposition that there might be a major shift in his policy in favour of India's making nuclear bombs in response to China's explosion of its first nuclear device in October 1964. Shastri was saddened by the misuse of nuclear energy for destructive purposes and maintained that India would not 'enter this race for nuclear armaments'.[11]

The Indira Gandhi Era

India's nuclear policy under Indira Gandhi was driven by a host of intertwined factors: regional geopolitics, defence, and development. The persisting Cold War contest between the superpowers in South Asia, the anti-India military nexus between Pakistan and China, growing strategic understanding between Washington and Beijing, and occasional irritants in the India–China relationship left a profound impact on Indira Gandhi's mental make-up, compelling her to reappraise the country's nuclear policy based on a hard-boiled realism. Moreover, her own worldview, cast in the mould of India's independence movement against British imperialism and a discriminatory and an iniquitous contemporary international order, reinforced her perception that 'distributive justice' was a pipedream so long as Third World nations continued to depend on rich industrialized nations for their aid and technology in energy generation.

Indira Gandhi was fully convinced that it was imperative to make India self-reliant in defence and development. How could it be achieved? For that, she looked upon nuclear technology as a catalyst for national security and economic transformation. To strengthen the country's defence sinews, combined internal and external inputs were to be fully utilized. While sensing the perception of threat in and around the region, she embarked upon a dual-track nuclear policy to keep India's nuclear-weapon option open. That was a fundamental departure from India's self-proclaimed single-track policy of the peaceful application of nuclear technology. That policy rested solely with Indira Gandhi; none could influence or reverse it.

Moreover, by instinct and temperament, Indira Gandhi was an uncompromising politician: she never retracted a decision once she had decided to do what was best for national interests as well as for her own political interests and ambitions. Yet, much as she was self-centric, egoistic, and at times an unbridled arrogant ruler, she was a 'superb political strategist' and adept in the art of statecraft, which basically impelled her to never compromise on the country's core national interests.[12] It was manifest in her single-minded devotion to achieve her goal of self-reliance in defence and nuclear power. In fact, her decision to carry out the first nuclear explosion on 18 May 1974 was an integral component of that psyche. Quite significantly, her psyche was reinforced by her past political experiences, which convinced her that the political machinations of Western powers, especially those of the United States, were aimed at preventing India from emerging as an autonomous centre of power in the region and beyond it. Keeping the geopolitical reality in mind, she went ahead with forging closer defence and strategic ties with the Soviet Union, which shared India's security and strategic concerns. Undoubtedly, the Soviet Union accounted for 70 per cent of India's military hardware. The increasing military cooperation between India and the Soviet Union caused some consternation among US policymakers that India was heavily pro-Soviet, which in their perception diluted India's non-aligned character. That criticism was justifiable to some extent. But India's own security exigencies as well as US military assistance to Pakistan on a massive scale left no other option for her than to develop and strengthen security and strategic ties with the Soviet Union.[13]

In order to demonstrate India's power and technological prowess, Indira Gandhi decided to carry out a nuclear explosion in 1974, which she described as 'peaceful'.[14] Many Indian analysts shared a common perception that the 1974 detonation represented more of a 'demonstrative value' than a challenge to the primacy or predominance of China in the nuclear field. On the other hand, some opinion-making sections believed that Indira Gandhi was destined to make India a nuclear-weapons power so that India could command great admiration and respect from major powers. Perhaps that assessment was based on Indira Gandhi's domineering personality, her penchant for power and her insatiable desire as a 'cold-blooded practitioner' of power politics to make India a strong and self-reliant nation in the defence field.

By whatever yardstick one may evaluate India's nuclear policy during her regime, she essentially believed that the raison d'être of the country's real strength and self-confidence lay in its superior military and technological prowess. Though, in principle, opposed to the arms race and the stockpiling of nuclear weapons, Indira Gandhi was acutely scornful of the monopoly enjoyed by a handful of nuclear-weapons states. In her keynote address at the inaugural session of the seventh conference of Heads of State or Government of Non-aligned Countries in New Delhi on 7 March 1983, she emphatically said:

> Our plans for a better life for each of our peoples depend on world peace and the reversal of the arms race. Only general and complete disarmament can provide credible security. Negotiations confined to a closed circle of nuclear weapon powers have made little progress. We are non-nuclear states, who want nuclear energy used only for peace. But we too have a right to live and be heard.[15]

The basic thrust of India's nuclear policy under Indira Gandhi's regime was aimed at developing nuclear energy not only for development and peaceful purposes but also for addressing the country's security concerns and perceptions of threat vis-à-vis India's hostile neighbours. At the same time, she was psychologically attuned to achieving India's nuclear status among select members of the nuclear club. That urge was deeply etched in her mental make-up, for she essentially believed that so long as nuclear imbalance continued, it might be an arduous task to halt nuclear proliferation. It was clearly reflected in the speech she delivered at the United Nations in New York on 14 October 1968:

> The problems of insecurity cannot be solved by imposing arbitrary restrictions on those who do not possess nuclear weapons, without any corresponding steps to deal with the basic problem of limiting the stockpiles in the hands of a few powers. How can the urge to acquire nuclear status be controlled so long as this imbalance persists?[16]

From her above statement, one might draw the broad conclusion that India's nuclear motivation hinged on achieving the twin objectives of nuclear status in the comity of nations and national security.

It will not be an exaggeration to say that if Jawaharlal Nehru laid the foundation of India's nuclear policy for energy and peaceful purposes, Indira Gandhi was the principal architect of a nuclear-ambiguity doctrine, keeping the nuclear option open for the country's defence and security. Though the opposition eulogized Indira Gandhi's authorization of a nuclear detonation in May 1974, Secretary of State Henry Kissinger described the detonation as a 'catastrophe' and an 'incentive' to many countries emulating India, while Congressman Long called the detonation a 'crime'. These were unwarranted overreactions.[17]

Indira Gandhi found no justifiable reasons for the United States' condemnation of India's nuclear policy. She often reiterated that India was fully committed to global disarmament and was an ardent advocate of a nuclear-weapons-free world. She especially underlined that India had consistently been an avid supporter of UN resolutions on global disarmament. At the Committee on Disarmament held in Geneva in 1983, she said that

> [India]consistently tried to keep the focus of negotiations on the most urgent measures in the field of nuclear disarmament, through active involvement in the work of ad hoc working groups on nuclear test ban, on the one hand, and by demanding the establishment of ad hoc working groups on prevention of nuclear war and nuclear disarmament, on the other ... It has been the constant endeavour of India to ensure that the Committee on Disarmament does not detract from the most crucial issues before it, namely, prevention of nuclear war and the cessation and removal of the nuclear arms race.[18]

Also, at the first committee of the UN General Assembly's thirty-eighth session, India again tabled a resolution on the prohibition of nuclear weapons and a 'freeze' on nuclear weapons. The purpose behind this exercise was to reaffirm the importance of these immediate measures, the adoption of which would considerably minimize the threat of a nuclear war.[19] Of the sixty-two resolutions, India co-sponsored ten and voted in favour of forty-three, while abstaining on seventeen and exercising a negative vote on two, which in India's view were of peripheral value or a dilatory nature.

At the twenty-seventh regular session of the International Atomic Energy Agency Conference held in Vienna in October 1983, Raja Ramanna, leader of the Indian delegation, supported major resolutions adopted by the conference to bring South Africa's nuclear establishment under IAEA's safeguards.[20] That, however, did not prevent him from reaffirming the Indian position of not signing the NPT and not accepting IAEA's full scope of safeguards. That policy, however, lacked resilience and maturity of leadership on India's part because it adopted obdurate postures without logically convincing the world community at large.

Dual Track Policy

India's dual-track policy of pursuing its nuclear programme for peaceful uses while simultaneously retaining the right to keep its nuclear option open was essentially rooted in the exigencies of that time. Indira Gandhi spurned outright the idea of foreclosing the nuclear option, based on her assessment that in an iniquitous global schema, perpetually dependent on dominant powers, the country's core values of sovereignty and autonomy must not be compromised to mollify specific powers. It was certainly irksome to Western powers, especially to the United States, which continued to put mounting pressure on India to accept the IAEA safeguards in exchange for nuclear fuel for the Tarapur power plant. India rejected the offer, for it basically went against national pride and its international standing. The Soviet Union, though an ardent advocate of the NPT, refrained from condemning India. Instead, Moscow encouraged New Delhi to attain self-reliance in the realm of nuclear energy.

The US Department of Atomic Energy (DAE), in its annual report (1980–81), accused India of reprocessing the spent fuel from nuclear reactors to extract plutonium for weapons development. It might be remembered that the United States had suspended the supply of low-enriched uranium for India's Tarapur plant under its Nuclear Non-Proliferation Act (NNPA) 1978. India argued that the Act could not be invoked retrospectively. The postponement of the nuclear shipment under the Act considerably affected the power-generating capacity of the plant. However, the United States agreed to give India a three-year grace period under which the supply of nuclear fuel was resumed on the moral assurance of Prime Minister Morarji Desai that India would never make nuclear weapons.

The position further improved when Indira Gandhi paid an official visit to the United States in July–August 1982. The Reagan administration committed itself to making alternative arrangements for the supply of nuclear fuel after the end of the grace period (1978–81) by reaching an understanding with France. Thus, under the tripartite agreement among India, the United States, and France, the latter agreed to continue with the supply of nuclear fuel in accordance with the original Indo-US nuclear deal of 1963. That arrangement finally ended the nuclear-fuel controversy generated because of the NNPA 1978. Thus, with termination of the 1963 agreement and the subsequent French obligation to supply fuel for the Tarapur plant, the US pressure on India to accept IAEA safeguards was considerably weakened.

Given India's bitter experience over the nuclear-fuel issue when the United States stopped the supply of uranium by invoking its Non-Proliferation Act, Indira Gandhi made concerted efforts to achieve India's self-reliance in the energy realm without compromising its known stance on IAEA safeguards. She encouraged research and development in the nuclear field so that India could keep abreast of the latest developments and be in the vanguard of scientific progress.[21] She approved an outlay of Rs 1051.04 crores in the Sixth Five Year Plan for three main sectors: research and development, industry and minerals, and power. An outlay of Rs 248.98 crores for research and development, 352.06 crores for industry and minerals and 450.00 crores for power was approved.[22] These figures show that the power sector was given greater weight than the other two sectors. In the research and development sector, which came under the Bhabha Atomic Research Centre, the construction of the thermal research reactor (Dhruva) was undertaken. In the industry and minerals sector, heavy-water plants were set up at Baroda, Tuticorin, Kota, and Talcher. Other heavy-water plants included Thal (Maharashtra) and Manuguru (Andhra Pradesh).[23] The Thal heavy-water project is based on the mono thermal process. The financial sanction for the project was issued in 1982 at an estimated cost of Rs 187.65 crores. It has the capacity of 110 MT per annum. The Manuguru project, with the capacity of 185 MT/year, had an estimated cost of Rs 421.60 crores. Further, the work of mining and processing uranium was carried out by Uranium Corporation of India Limited. In the Sixth Plan period, the corporation started new mines at Bhatin, Narwapahar, and Turamdih.[24]

To achieve self-reliance, Indian scientists and engineers successfully set up an indigenously built third nuclear power station at Madras. The first one (at Tarapur) was designed and constructed by a US firm, and the second one, in Rajasthan with Canadian assistance. According to the Performance Budget of the department for the year 1984–85:

> All major components are being indigenously manufactured and recourse to import is only for some special items. While Tarapur Atomic Power Station was set up as a twin key project, the foreign exchange component has been gradually brought down to 55 per cent and 40 per cent in the case of Rajasthan Atomic Power Station units I and II respectively and to about 10 per cent in the case of Madras Atomic Power Station. In

> case of Narora and Tarapur Atomic Power…the import content has been further brought down to less than 10 per cent.[25]

Tarapur Atomic Power Station, with a capacity of 2,210 MWe, attained criticality in October 1969. The Rajasthan Atomic Power Station, with two heavy-water pressurized reactors of 220 MWe, started operating with one reactor in 1973 and with two reactors in 1982. The Tarapur research reactor (Dhruva), located at Trombay in Bombay, was approved in 1975 with the original cost of Rs 49.88 crores raised to Rs 76.29 crores during 1984–85. That was intended to 'provide engineering facilities to test proto-type fuel elements for power reactors at appropriate flux levels to further the scope of research in physics, chemistry, activation analysis and biology and to enlarge the isotope facilities'[26]

Indira Gandhi's nuclear contribution lay in harnessing atomic energy for development purposes, and in linking science and technology to improve people's living standards. With a sound nuclear infrastructure, backed up by necessary inputs, India attained the stage of designing, building, and operating nuclear reactors indigenously. Indian nuclear scientists and engineers proved their competence in handling and disposing nuclear waste products, and in making nuclear technology safe.

While assessing Indira Gandhi's nuclear policy, it is clear that she was the principal architect of India's development as a self-confident nuclear state. But she also whetted Pakistan's appetite to attain nuclear-weapons capability, even through clandestine means. Z. A. Bhutto, the real brain behind Pakistan's nuclear programme, had an opportunity to read the political mind and motivations of Indira Gandhi during his last diplomatic encounter with Indira Gandhi at the Shimla Summit in July 1972. Bhutto's perception of Indira Gandhi as a single-minded politician, committed to embarking on a nuclear-weapons path, aroused national pride in him, leading him to think that if Pakistan were to survive, it must attain nuclear-weapons capability by any means. This explains how the psychocultural factor within the geopsychology paradigm functioned in the nuclear decision process.

The Rajiv Gandhi Era

As a young leader of India, Rajiv Gandhi, though a fresh entrant to politics, had a penchant for fast scientific and economic modernization. He articulated the role of science and technology as a driving force in India's modernization and economic development. He nurtured scientific research and development to build a sound scientific and technological infrastructure. His commitment to the peaceful application of nuclear technology was evident from his encouragement of the development of new nuclear power reactors in the country and his earmarking of liberal funds for nuclear-energy development programmes.

Without fundamentally deviating from his mother's defence and nuclear policies, however, he was not prejudiced against the West which, in his perception, was a source of scientific and technological input essential for India's modernization. His spirit of accommodation and cooperation with both superpowers, without tilting one way or another, won him admiration in the United States and the Soviet Union. His perception of peaceful coexistence as an effective instrument of conflict resolution, and his vision of a nuclear-free, non-violent world was taken as a yardstick.

Rajiv Gandhi adopted a high-profile, foreign-policy approach to fundamental issues of nuclear non-proliferation, global disarmament, and integrative economic world order in close cooperation with the superpowers. In collaboration with the Soviet Union, Rajiv Gandhi called for a nuclear-free world. During President Mikhail Gorbachev's visit to New Delhi, Gandhi and Gorbachev signed a Joint Declaration of Principles of a Nuclear-Weapon-Free and Non-Violent World on 27 November 1986. Both leaders reaffirmed that non-violence should be the basis of community life. Rajiv Gandhi stated, 'There is only one answer to the menace of nuclear weapons and that is to dismantle all nuclear weapons, terminating the nuclear-arms race on earth and preventing a nuclear-arms race in space.'[27]

During his official visit to the United States in October 1987, Rajiv Gandhi told President Ronald Reagan that India's commitment to total nuclear disarmament was unconditional and unqualified. He reiterated that India would neither build nuclear weapons nor even favour their presence in its neighbourhood. He emphatically said, 'We have no intention of producing nuclear weapons unless constrained to do so.'[28] This statement revealed how India would deal with its neighbours, if forced to protect India's national security. At the same time, Gandhi hit Pakistan hard for not only clandestinely engaging in nuclear-weapons-building but also for securing high-tech weapons from the United States on a massive scale. President Reagan tried to reassure him that weapons supplied to Pakistan would not be used against India. This assurance was scarcely convincing to Gandhi as he reminded President Reagan that such assurances had been given in the past but to no avail because Pakistan had used those weapons against India. Gandhi flatly refused to accept the US proposal to make South Asia a weapons-free zone. He also spurned President Reagan's proposal that India should sign the NPT.

Moreover, he emphasized that India, in principle, did not favour the proposal of a specific nuclear-weapons-free zone as advanced by Pakistan at the United Nations (UN) in 1986. At the third Six Nation Peace Initiative Summit held in Stockholm in January 1988, India strongly supported the idea of the comprehensive test-ban treaty, including the establishment of an integrated multilateral verification system within the UN framework.

Rajiv Gandhi also put forward the Action Plan for a Nuclear-Weapon-Free and Non-Violent World Order at the Third Special Session of the General Assembly on Disarmament in June 1988. The Action Plan contained 'a package of measures that structurally' linked 'the entire range of issues presently on the world's disarmament agenda,' calling upon the international community 'to negotiate a binding commitment in general and complete disarmament—a commitment which should be total and without reservation.'[29] It aimed at achieving the objective of a nuclear-weapons-free world by the year 2010.

The important feature of the Action Plan was that it contained a 'binding commitment' in which all nations, including the nuclear threshold states, would eliminate nuclear weapons. India specifically proposed that a new treaty to replace the NPT must be negotiated immediately. The new treaty would give legal effect to the binding commitment of the entire industrial community to eliminate all nuclear weapons by the year 2010.[30] Even among the non-aligned nations, India maintained that there was a categorical necessity for cessation of the nuclear arms race. Indian Minister of State for External Affairs K. Natwar Singh, while addressing the Conference on Disarmament, highlighted 'India's commitment and contribution to the multilateral disarmament process'.[31] At the UN Conference on Disarmament and Development held in New York in August–September 1987, India was unanimously elected conference chairman. India continued to maintain that in the nuclear age 'the search for unilateral security through nuclear deterrence must be replaced by a search for global security through nuclear disarmament'.[32]

A global approach to the Action Plan constituted the cornerstone of India's nuclear policy during Rajiv Gandhi's regime, which could be summarized as:

i. global disarmament by all nations;
ii. support of peaceful uses of nuclear energy;

iii. opposition to the militarization of outer space;
iv. establishment of an integrated multilateral verification system within the UN;
v. opposition to selective nuclear-weapons-free zones; and
vi. opposition to the discriminatory NPT regime.

India's nuclear policy during Rajiv Gandhi's era did not depart from the dual-track policy adopted by Indira Gandhi. However, his major accomplishment was the signing of an agreement with Pakistan in December 1988, pledging not to attack each other's nuclear installations. That laid a solid foundation for any future bilateral non-proliferation arrangements in South Asia.

If judged in the context of the current global scenario, Rajiv Gandhi's Action Plan is even more relevant today when the threat of nuclear war from diverse sources appears to be more serious than during the Cold War days. His idea of a non-violent, free world order also offers a good base from which to start managing the threat of violence at different levels. But all these noble and brilliant ideas have remained unfulfilled. So long as governing structures and policies remain based on inequity, oppression, and rampant corruption, they will continue to breed violence around our planet. The stark reality is that any good initiative, originating from poor, developing nations, is unlikely to fructify. The power syndrome will continue to inform world order and world disorder.

The Rao Era

Both the era and aura of charisma in Indian politics, dominated by the Nehru family, suddenly came to a halt with the tragic assassination of Rajiv Gandhi in May 1991 during the electioneering campaign. It was by sheer chance that P. V. Narsimha Rao, a veteran Congress leader and acclaimed intellectual and scholar, was chosen as the consensus candidate for the premiership. He won accolades from world leaders for his political maturity and intellectual acumen combined with great patience. During his visit to Washington in May 1994, Rao conveyed to the Clinton administration, Congress, intellectuals, and the media India's firm commitment to the non-proliferation goal as an article of faith. Much to his chagrin, he was quite often regarded by his critics and party colleagues as 'non-assertive', 'indecisive', and 'incapable' of taking any political risk, even in the national interest. No doubt, Rao was at times the captive of his own political scepticism, and a prisoner of his self-image and belief systems, which held him back from taking decisions on crucial security issues—both internal and external—facing his country. He believed in deferring a problem until it was out of hand. That was often resented by his senior party colleagues. Some of them attempted political coups to oust him but did not succeed.

When Narsimha Rao entered office in June 1991, the country was wading through unprecedented economic ordeals. The foreign exchange reserves were fast depleting, and inflation was running into double digits with a mounting budget deficit. It appeared as if the country were on the brink of economic collapse. Given the economic scenario and unstable political situation, external forces, especially the United States, asked India to cap its nuclear, missile, and space programmes and sign the NPT. The first sign of trouble came when the United States sought to blacklist India's Space and Research Organization (ISRO) and Russia's Glascomos Space Agency, asking the latter to terminate the supply of cryogenic rocket motors for India's space programme. Despite these pressure tactics, Narsimha Rao made it abundantly clear to Washington that New Delhi would not negotiate the country's defence and security interests either by signing the NPT or by declaring South Asia a nuclear-weapons-free zone.

Sadly, the Rao government did not take the Indian parliament and people into its confidence when it acquiesced to the US proposal to hold a secret multilateral dialogue known as 5+2+2 (the five permanent members of the Security Council, plus Japan, Germany, India, and Pakistan) on regional nuclear non-proliferation. The secret London talks, held in April 1994, caused much dismay and fear among opposition parties, and several sections of the Indian community regarded the underhand activities of the Rao government with suspicion. Rao, however, tried to dispel misgivings that India would compromise its vital defence and security interests by yielding to US bullying tactics.

Needless to say, the real motivation behind the US pressure tactics was to prevent India from emerging as an autonomous centre of power and a self-reliant nation in the ambit of rocketry and missile technology because the United States believed India would then be among the few advanced nations capable of producing spin-off technologies, which would be much cheaper than theirs. An eminent Indian space scientist, working in satellite communications, observed: 'The US is afraid that once India attains capabilities to launch rockets or fire missiles, the technology will be five to ten times cheaper than theirs.'[33] Another Indian space scientist revealed that India had had to defer the Prithvi missile programme eight years previously during the Rajiv Gandhi regime because of the US intent to applying sanctions against India.[34] But these pressures did not prevent India from developing missile systems.

So far as the restraint factor is concerned, the Indian scientific community was of the view, according to Pushpa M. Bhargava, a genetic scientist, that India had shown greater restraint than the United States in such matters.[35] Also, Raja Ramanna, a former chairman of the Atomic Energy Commission, U. R. Rao, a former chairman of the ISRO, and M. G. K. Menon maintained that India should not yield to US bullying and bluster.

During his weeklong visit to the United States in May 1994, Narsimha Rao conveyed in a message to President Clinton that the US approach to regional denuclearization was misplaced and therefore would not work. He stressed that there was a need to eliminate nuclear weapons universally and not locally. If the United States, he hinted, was interested in undertaking this task, India was ready to cooperate as it had been doing in the matter[36] of banning nuclear tests and stopping the production of fissile material. Rao time and again stressed that international denuclearization was the only way to eliminate all weapons of mass destruction from the planet. He further added that every nation, large or small, rich or poor, being sovereign, possessed an inherent right and responsibility to its people to ensure their security.[37] The nuclear policy of the Rao government broadly contained the following elements:

i. getting rid of the world of weapons of mass destruction by creating a world order based on equity and non-discrimination;
ii. boosting international consensus on banning nuclear-weapon testing;
iii. preventing the production of fissile materials for weapon purposes;
iv. initiating positive and vigorous steps and efforts toward global denuclearization;
v. doing away with the discriminatory character of the NPT;
vi. opposing regional nuclear disarmament;
vii. favouring the use of nuclear and missile technologies for peaceful and constructive purposes; and
viii. advocating a 'nuclear no first use' agreement to outlaw nuclear weapons, and
ix. simultaneously launching multilateral negotiations for nuclear disarmament.[38]

These components were elaborated upon by Prime Minister Rao when he addressed the Joint Session of the US Congress in Washington on 18 May 1994.[39]

The Rao government's support of international denuclearization and its desire to keep India's nuclear option open for security reasons proved convincing to President Clinton to a great extent. In fact, Narsimha Rao was able to convince the Clinton administration that India, being a civilized entity, had never pursued a course of aggression and aggrandizement against any other country throughout the history of humankind. Instead, India's impeccable record of perpetual quest for a non-violent world order should, he stressed, be a matter of pride to all forward-looking civilized nations. He regretted that the West had often ignored that reality, either out of ignorance, or because of the malicious propaganda launched by India's adversaries.

The NDA Government and Indian Nuclear Diplomacy

India's nuclear diplomacy after the Rao government (1991–96) witnessed a momentous alteration. If one recalls, Prime Minister Narsimha Rao called off the tests in December 1995, even though there was broad consensus in the nuclear establishment in favour of conducting nuclear tests. That is why the opposition described him as a 'weak and wavering' prime minister who avoided crucial decisions, especially on defence and nuclear issues. However, in a one-on-one conversation, P. V. Narsimha Rao disclosed to K. Subrahmanyam, a leading strategic analyst, that 'there was no consensus on the test'. There were divisions not only among economists and administrators but also among scientists. Prime Minister Rao said he would conduct the test if he came back to office.[40]

Whatever charges were leveled against Rao, there was continuity in India's policy of nuclear ambiguity throughout the Congress regimes beginning with that of Indira Gandhi. However, with the change of political guard following the national elections of May 1996, the Bharatiya Janata Party (BJP) emerged as the largest party in a coalition government. Atal Bihari Vajpayee assumed the office of prime minister on 16 May 1996 and authorized nuclear-weapons tests. The coalition government did not last for more than twelve days. Vajpayee's little-known successor, H. D Deve Gowda, also preferred to defer the idea of India's going nuclear. Meanwhile, the Conference on Disarmament at Geneva was in session to propose that the CTBT draft be adopted unanimously. India opposed the CTBT coming into force without spelling out a specific timeframe for global nuclear disarmament that was acceptable to all the parties. There was also an Enter-Into-Force (EIF) clause in the CTBT draft, which included India. India's Ambassador Arundhati Ghosh rejected attempts to coerce her country through the EIF provisions of the treaty and conveyed an unmistakable warning that India was prepared to exercise its power to block CD consensus unless the EIF clause was made less specific. She declared, 'India cannot accept any restraints on its capability if other countries remain unwilling to accept the obligation to eliminate their nuclear weapons.'[41] As noted by Rebecca Johnson:

> Ghose's statement was an extraordinary example of diplomatic judo, in which she manipulated fact, perception and threat to destabilize the opposition and create an impression of the inevitability of the outcome. She positioned India for defection, distracting attention from her state's nuclear ambitions by focusing on the failure of nuclear weapons states to disarm or reduce their core reliance on nuclear weapons; she then couched India's familiar linkage arguments in terms of national security, so that New Delhi's justifications for rejecting the CTBT could be cast as a response to threat and the fault of others, principally the P-5.[42]

Indian diplomacy at the CD invited the wrath of the P-5, which dubbed India's stance on CTBT and NPT as nothing but India's inherent ambition to become a nuclear-weapons state. They also reminded Ghosh that Jawaharlal Nehru had given a firm commitment to the world community that India would never make nuclear weapons. But Ghose made her argument very strong by saying that India still clung to an objective of nuclear non-proliferation, but she underlined that the use of an EIF provision as a pressure tactic to make India accede to the CTBT was neither morally acceptable nor politically desirable. At the final deliberation on the CTBT in August 1996, India threatened to block CD consensus if the CTBT draft was linked to an EIF provision. Ultimately, India carried out the threat. Pakistan's Ambassador Munir Akram attacked India for 'hypocrisy', and said:

> Today the mask of the smiling Buddha has been torn off, revealing the face of the goddess of war. The leaders of our neighbour have proclaimed that they will keep their nuclear options open; that they reserve the right to conduct nuclear tests; that they will go ahead with their short—and medium—range missile programmes.[43]

China and Pakistan used the occasion to attack India for creating obstacles in the way of transmitting the NTB committee report to the UN General Assembly. Pakistan vociferously attacked India for using the veto in face of universal support of a nuclear-weapon test-ban treaty and hinted on the CTBT that India had joined Iran on procedural matters. When the CD met in plenary on 22 August 1996, Pakistan, in order to take the credit, proposed that the NTB Committee Report be transmitted to the UN General Assembly. India and Iran raised objections on procedural grounds. India's strategy of objecting to the NTB Committee Report was further thwarted when Australia requested that the CD document, containing the full treaty text and given the number CD/1427, following Belgium's request, be accorded status as a UN document and attached to the resolution proposing its adoption by the General Assembly.[44] Australia's attempt at bypassing the rules of procedure and consensus was criticized by India and other non-aligned countries. But ultimately, Australia's resolution, with 127 co-sponsors, was adopted at the Geneva conference, and finally CTBT was endorsed by 158 votes at the UN General Assembly on 10 September 1996. India, Bhutan, and Libya voted against the treaty, while Cuba, Lebanon, Mauritius, Syria, and Tanzania were absentees. Though Pakistan supported the resolution, it refused to sign the treaty for 'regional security considerations', implying India. Indian Ambassador Ghose lambasted the way the CTBT draft was manipulated and said that the treaty would perpetuate the discriminatory nuclear regime. As such, India would never sign this 'unequal treaty'. India's voice remained muted in the face of the treaty's endorsement by the overwhelming majority.

India's political situation was quite murky. In 1998, the BJP government under the banner of the NDA came into power with Atal Bihari Vajpayee as prime minister, supported by a labyrinth of disparate regional political parties. The government was feeling shaky and looking out for some opportunity or alibi to consolidate its political position in the coalition government. The most convenient and an easily available option before the government was to exercise India's nuclear option marked by ambiguity. In the perception of top BJP leaders, the decision to carry out a nuclear-weapons test would serve manifold purposes. First, it would send a clear-cut message to coalition partners that the leadership under Prime Minister Vajpayee was strong and assertive. Second, its political credit would go to the BJP by projecting the Congress party's indecisiveness and lack of political will to take a bold decision in the interest of national security. It was implied that the BJP might derive political mileage in the future for consolidating its political power base. Third, it would enhance India's power, prestige, and influence in the region and beyond. The above considerations impelled the NDA government under Vajpayee to conduct nuclear weapons tests in May 1998. Several strategic experts, including P. R. Chari, argued that 'security concerns were not cardinal to this decision'.[45]

India's Nuclear Doctrine

The NDA government under the leadership of A. B. Vajpayee was credited with ending India's policy of nuclear ambiguity that had spanned more than three decades. These tests evoked strong condemnation from America, Japan, and the EU members. At that time, the Clinton administration slapped sanctions on India and Pakistan. However, the Vajpayee government tried to convince the United States of the core reason behind India's weapon tests by citing China as a 'potential threat'. At the same time, India reiterated its commitment to global disarmament and nuclear non-proliferation.

In the aftermath of nuclear-weapon tests, the Indian government set up a National Security Advisory Board, consisting of twenty-seven members, which was entrusted with the task of preparing a draft of India's nuclear doctrine. In August 1999, the NSAB came up with the draft of a nuclear doctrine, which was circulated for public debate. In practice, the debate over the draft was monopolized by a coterie of the Delhi-based public intellectuals and political elites. Even the enlightened and most informed Indian citizenry had neither a voice nor a role to play in shaping the draft of the doctrine. That is why the nuclear doctrine is not free from flaws, which have not been properly addressed until today. However, to allay the fear of the world community, the NDA government not only adopted the 'essence' of that draft but also declared the formal nuclear doctrine and command structure proposed by the NSAB, the main features of which are outlined as follows:

i. No first use;
ii. nuclear weapons will not be used against non-nuclear-weapon states;
iii. unilateral moratorium on nuclear tests;
iv. credible minimum nuclear deterrence;
v. commitment to global disarmament.

Jayant Prasad, India's Permanent Representative to the Conference on Disarmament at Geneva, elaborated upon India's nuclear doctrine on 13 February 2007:

> While maintaining a credible minimum nuclear deterrent, India continues to be committed to the goal of a nuclear-weapon-free world, through global, verifiable and non-discriminatory nuclear disarmament. India's responsible nuclear doctrine is based on no-first-use and no-use of nuclear weapons against non-nuclear weapon states. The doctrine also reaffirms India' readiness to join multilateral negotiations for the reduction and elimination of nuclear weapons. India has continued to observe a moratorium on nuclear explosive tests. We are ready to participate in negotiations, in the conference, on a non-discriminatory, multilateral and internationally and effectively verifiable treaty banning the production of fissile material for nuclear weapons or other nuclear explosive devices.[46]

What is important to bear in mind is that India has embarked upon the policy of attaining self-reliance in the nuclear energy field. According to the UPA government's Report to the People, 2004–08, the total installed capacity of the nuclear power plants is set to rise from 4,120 MWe to 6,780 MWe by 2009 and 7,280 MWe by 2010.[47]

India's latest feat in the field of nuclear technology is its construction of an 80 MWe pressurised water reactor at Kalpakkam near Chennai, which 'marks the beginning of indigenous PWR capability', as stated by Atomic Energy Commission Chairman Anil Kakodkar on 1 August 2009. He said the PWR at Kalpakkam was an addition to the nation's family of reactors.[48] The PHWRs use natural uranium as fuel; India's fast breeder reactors (FBRs) are 'globally advanced'; the advanced heavy-water reactor (AHWR) is globally unique, which would use thorium as fuel, and FBRs would use plutonium-uranium oxide fuel.[49] Kakodkar further added that the capacity factor of nuclear reactors would go up to 65 per cent by the end of the financial year (2009–10) and to 70 per cent next year. By now, India possesses 15 PHWRs that use natural uranium as fuel, and two light-water reactors that use enriched uranium as fuel.[50]

Given India's energy needs, the Bush administration praised India's track record as a responsible nuclear state and decided to enter into a civil nuclear cooperation agreement in March 2006 to fulfil India's nuclear-energy needs. Though the agreement evoked sharp criticism from leftist parties in India and anti-nuclear proliferation zealots in the United States, India has been able to seek a clean waiver from the NSG's forty-five member nations, which would enable India to procure nuclear-fuel-related and nuclear-technology-related components. India has already entered into agreements with the members of NSG: Russia, France, and the United States.

While keeping its increasing energy requirements in view, India's aim is to generate 20,000 MWe by 2020 of which half will come from pressurized heavy-water reactors (PHWRs). Atomic Energy Chairman Kakodkar on 5 December 2008 expressed confidence that 1500 MW of nuclear power could be added to the national grid by 2009 as the country was poised to benefit from the civil nuclear cooperation agreement with Russia, France, and the United States.[51] He further elaborated that the country's first fast breeder reactor was under construction and on schedule to be commissioned in 2010–11. He said:

> The nation has a capacity to generate 4,120 MW of nuclear power, but due to the shortage of nuclear fuel most of the units are running a little over half their capacity.[52] India would require 30,000 MW by 2050, according to Anil Kakodkar, Chairman of the Atomic Energy Commission.[53]

Kakodar said, 'Nobody would give the country technology for developing energy from thorium and high-ash coal, which India abounds in, because such technology did not exist elsewhere.'[54] Given this, India needs to develop indigenous technology through research and development efforts so that its vast resources of thorium can be used to fulfil the country's mounting energy requirements.

For the Congress-led UPA government of Manmohan Singh, the Rajiv Action Plan 1988 has remained a principal mantra, guiding India's views and perspectives on global disarmament. In his statement to Parliament on 29 July 2005, Prime Minister Manmohan Singh said, 'Our commitment to work for universal nuclear disarmament, so passionately espoused by Prime Minister Rajiv Gandhi, in the long run will remain our core concern.'[55]

Subsequently, replying to a debate in the Rajya Sabha (Upper House) on 17 August 2006, the Prime Minister reiterated:

> Our commitment toward non-discriminatory global nuclear disarmament remains unwavering, in line with the Rajiv Gandhi Action Plan. There is no dilution on this count. We do not accept proposals put forward from time to time for regional non-proliferation or regional disarmament. Pending nuclear disarmament, there is no question of India joining the NPT as a non-nuclear weapons State, or accepting full-scope safeguards

> as a requirement for nuclear supplies to India, now or in the future.[56]

In a similar tone, India's Minister of External Affairs Pranab Mukherjee, in an interview to *The Hindu*, published on 21 November 2006, stated:

> We are committed to non-proliferation and disarmament. What Rajiv Gandhi said at the special session on disarmament of the United Nations [9 June 1988] is the guiding principle of our foreign policy. He told the world that we would not graduate ourselves from the threshold level—that was our position then, before 1998. We want that those who have nuclear weapons should stop proliferation—vertically, horizontally—reduce stockpiles and have a time-bound action plan [for disarmament]. And that [commitment] stands. In between, of course, we have gone for the [May 1998 nuclear] explosions. There have been developments and that cannot be erased. It has already taken place—but even in that context we are serious and we are engaging ourselves. In this United Nations session, we are going to move a resolution to this effect [for time-bound disarmament] [57]

Further, India's entry into the select group of five countries with the capability of building and operating indigenous nuclear-powered submarines, launched by Prime Minister Singh on 26 July 2009, is another milestone in India's modernization of its defence system. Singh stated that 'India's entry into the exclusive club will create ripples in the region.'[58] Singh further elaborated it was imperative for India to keep pace with 'global advances' while focussing on regional security. At the same time, Prime Minister Singh tried to assuage the fears of India's neighbours when he categorically said:

> We do not have any aggressive designs nor do we seek to threaten anyone. We seek an external environment in our region and beyond that, conducive to our peaceful development and the protection of our value systems. Nevertheless, it is incumbent upon us to take all measures necessary to safeguard our country and keep pace with technological advancements.[59]

But India's double standards on non-proliferation discourse have come under the severe criticism that India does not use a similar yardstick to criticize the NPT for being discriminatory when it comes to its own 'extended neighbourhood'. One scholar, in his perceptive article, observes:

> Here, on the one hand, India has repeatedly argued that the prevailing non-proliferation regime constitutes 'nuclear apartheid' and that it will, therefore, continue to develop a nuclear weapons programme outside the purview of the Non-Proliferation Treaty (NPT), much to the chagrin of the existing nuclear powers. On the other hand, it has made little effort to disguise its concern when countries such as Iran, Syria and North Korea have attempted to contest the discriminatory principles enshrined in the NPT, because it wants to prevent the spread of nuclear weapons in its extended neighbourhood. This apparent 'hypocrisy' has been mistakenly attributed to a desire to curry favour with the US.[60]

Conclusion

Both India and Pakistan, instead of indulging in mock nuclear exchanges, must concentrate on the social and economic problems of their people, and promote the economic development and social welfare of the neglected strata of their societies, including minorities and the hapless ones at the grassroots level. India must refrain from over-reacting to Pakistan's nuclear programme, for India is fully capable of meeting any threat from Pakistan. What is important is that the two countries should find a reasonable, rational, and pragmatic solution to the nuclear problem.

Moreover, it is plain to the entire world that there is a psychology of rivalry between India and Pakistan, further fuelled by extremist elements in both countries. The situation might be even further aggravated because these nuclear-armed countries have neither parallel interests on security and strategic issues nor consensus on the imperative of developing a common regional security architecture.[61]

4

INDIA AND PAKISTAN: ISSUES, OPTIONS, AND FUTURE DIRECTIONS

India and Pakistan are the two major powers in South Asia, sharing a common history, ethnic ties, and common memories. The British legacy of the tragic partition of August 1947 left deep psychological and political scars on both countries; hundreds of thousands of innocent people were brutally killed, and more than ten million people were dislocated as a result of mass migration on both sides. It is a truism that the birth of Pakistan, based on Islamic ideology in contrast to India's embrace of secularism, also produced a deep psychological rift between the two countries. Simultaneously, the India–Pakistan conflict began with a full-scale invasion of Kashmir by Pakistani armed forces in October 1947. Since then, the Kashmir conflict has culminated in perpetual hostility, showing no sign of any political reconciliation between the two countries.

Be that as it may, myths and misperceptions persist on both sides—some artificially contrived and some rooted in the fractured psychology of each country. Instead of viewing mutual security threats through the prism of human security, New Delhi and Islamabad have exaggerated them. Moreover, the deeply entrenched psychological barriers of mutual fear and distrust have further contributed to accentuating tensions between the two capitals, most prominently over Kashmir and cross-border terrorism, but also on peripheral issues such as the demilitarization of the Siachen Glacier and Sir Creek.

To rub salt in the wound, the notorious Cold War geopolitics transformed South Asia into an arena of superpower rivalry to gain a stranglehold over the region. Although India and Pakistan have made numerous attempts to improve their relations, either bilaterally or at the initiative of the United States and the former Soviet Union, right from the beginning of the Cold War period through the end of the Cold War to the onset of composite dialogue in 2004, New Delhi and Islamabad have failed to reconcile their obstinate and archaic approaches to resolving outstanding bilateral disputes. What are the core reasons for India and Pakistan's difficulty in transcending their narrowly structured policy approaches? They can partly be attributed to the perception of threat among Pakistan's military and civilian elites who have used religious and cultural symbols to influence the gullible domestic public in their projection of India as the prime threat to Pakistan's security and survival. They can also be ascribed to New Delhi's obsession with Islamabad, blaming the latter for every subversive activity or internal security problem in India.

This chapter aims to explain and re-evaluate the factors responsible for this never-ending rivalry and persistence of mutual hatred in order to identify conditions that might foster the two countries' long-term interests of regional peace and stability. It is the hypothesis of this chapter that the single most direct threat to the national security, political stability, strategic assets, and societal structures of both countries is the common threat of terror emanating from extremist elements and jihadi groups.

Volumes of literature on Indo-Pakistani relations have been written by leading scholars, strategic analysts, diplomats, and civil and military elites, including top policymakers. My attempt in this chapter will be to primarily focus on the dynamics of linkages between the Kashmir issue and cross-border terrorism in light of the fact that both India and Pakistan are nuclear-armed nations. Furthermore, the 9/11 tragedy has fundamentally altered the strategic tapestry of the region.

As argued elsewhere, expanding geopsychological identities have tended to reshape the nature and intensity of conflictual and cooperative relations between India and Pakistan. Why are India and Pakistan engaged in a frantic nuclear missile-building race? What constitutes the factor of fear and distrust between New Delhi and Islamabad? How is cross-border terrorism linked to the Kashmir problem? The answers to these questions will be taken up in this chapter.

This chapter argues that despite inherent limitations, geopsychology and psychocultural prophylaxis can be extremely useful tools not only for a correct diagnosis of the persisting India–Pakistan hostility but also for advancing pragmatic solutions to the long-standing bilateral issues.

Backdrop

India and Pakistan have been interlocked in mutual rivalry since their independence in August 1947. Both countries have remained perpetual victims of self-delusion as well as of the image of each other as enemies, mainly because of fundamental differences in their political, economic, and cultural outlooks and geopolitical perceptions, goals, and interests. Notably, their approaches to security and strategic planning are at cross-purposes, resulting in the bloody conflicts of 1947–48, 1965, and 1971, and the Kargil conflict of May 1999. The prolonged impasse in the New Delhi–Islamabad relationship may be attributed to a host of factors, which are partly rooted in their geopolitical divergences and sociocultural differences, and partly in the pangs of the partition of British India, based on the two-nation theory.[1]

Undoubtedly, the Kashmir issue has turned out to be a putrefied ulcer, not by accident, as many scholars believed it to be, but by the well-planned and well-calculated designs of narrow-minded chauvinists, if one looks objectively at the historical facts. One needs to locate the genesis of the Kashmir imbroglio in order to find out who fired the first shot in the Kashmir Valley. It is a well-recorded historical fact that because of Maharaja Hari Singh's prolonged indecisiveness on whether to accede to India or Pakistan during the intervening period (15 August–19 October 1947), Pakistan had more than enough time to annex Kashmir through military means. As part of that strategy, the Pakistani army invaded the Kashmir Valley on 20 October 1947, even against the advice of British Field Marshal Sir Claude Auchinleck. Maharaja Hari Singh's forces were unable to withstand the Pakistani army's overwhelming power to defend the state, and he made an urgent appeal to the government of India for military help. However, it was upon his signing of the Instrument of Accession on 26 October 1947, and its quick acceptance by India's Governor General Lord Mountbatten on 27 October 1947, that the State of Jammu and Kashmir became an integral part of India. Meanwhile, Pakistan had already occupied one-third of the Kashmir Valley, known as Pakistan-administered Kashmir (PAK).[2] This is how the Kashmir issue was transformed into a permanent territorial conflict.

Furthermore, India–Pakistan relations have been deeply influenced by the interventionist role of three major extra-regional powers: the United States, the Soviet Union (Russia), and China. During the Cold War period, the United States roped Pakistan into its military alliances, such as SEATO (1954) and CENTO (1955), under its global strategy of containing communism. India had initially spurned the US offer to join these military organizations, arguing that it would bring the Cold War to the doorsteps of South Asia, which, in Nehru's perception, would be tantamount to a loss of freedom and autonomy while conducting relations with the outside world.

The involvement of the United States in the region deepened India–Pakistan rivalry as well as sowing the seeds of geopolitical distance between India and the United States. The latter's approach of using military aid as a weapon tended to militarize the minds and thinking of Pakistani ruling elites, military and civilian. On the one hand, Pakistan's acquisition of modern and sophisticated weapons from the United States emboldened Islamabad in its belief that it could give a befitting response to New Delhi in the event of a conflict or war with India. On the other hand, the United States' attempts at establishing military parity between India and Pakistan stepped up the arms race in the region. Ashok Kapur writes:

> The US, Pakistan, and China preferred a great power-centric approach to India–Pakistan issues which sought to diminish India's diplomatic and military space in the subcontinental and international sphere while building up Pakistan as a challenger. In this respect, the convergent Pakistani, American, and Chinese policies institutionalized the Indo-Pakistani conflict. The common cause was to contain India, widely seen as the potential regional hegemon in the 1950s.[3]

The 1971 Indo-Pakistani War was a shattering blow to Pakistan, resulting in the emergence of Bangladesh as an independent nation with India's full military support. India's direct military role in the dismemberment of Pakistan created a strong vengeance lobby against it in the Pakistani establishment and the negative repercussions spilled over to every realm of the two countries' relationship. Although Indira Gandhi and Z. A. Bhutto signed the historic Shimla Accord in July 1972, binding the two countries to resolve outstanding issues, including Kashmir, through peaceful bilateral negotiations, Pakistan firmed its resolve to develop nuclear weapons to meet any threat from India's overwhelming preponderance in conventional weapons.

At the same time, the Pakistani ISI actively indulged in aiding and abetting militancy in India's northern region as an integral component of state policy to destabilize India because it had presided over the dismemberment of Pakistan. Worse still, Pakistan became further emboldened to fight a proxy war in Kashmir in the late 1980s when it acquired nuclear capability. It shows that Pakistan had started linking the Kashmir issue with cross-border terrorism after attaining the ability to produce nuclear weapons. Pakistan demonstrated its nuclear capability by responding to the nuclear-weapons tests India conducted in May 1998.

As two nuclear-armed states, India and Pakistan realized that they owned the greater responsibility to keep the nukes safe and secure. To extend the hand of friendship with Pakistan, Prime Minister A. B. Vajpayee, a moderate BJP leader, undertook a historic bus journey to Lahore in February 1999. Vajpayee and his Pakistani counterpart, Nawaz Sharif, signed the Lahore Declaration on 21 February 1999. In it they agreed to resolve outstanding disputes through a composite dialogue. Undoubtedly, the Lahore Declaration was a major breakthrough in their relationship, which had been strained since the nuclear-weapons tests of May 1998. India's External Affairs Minister Jaswant Singh, in his *suo moto* statement in parliament on 26 February 1999, said:

> The Prime Minister's bus journey captured the imagination of the people of India, of Pakistan, indeed, of the world. I wish to state here that seldom has a leader embarked on a journey with such support from his people and such goodwill for his success. His arrival at Wagah, with the Indian delegation, to be warmly received by the Pakistan Prime Minister was a defining moment in India–Pakistan relations.[4]

He further stated:

> This declaration is a landmark for the peace and security of the two nations. The two Prime Ministers have in the Lahore Declaration agreed that the two countries will identify efforts to resolve all issues, including the issue of Jammu and Kashmir, through the composite dialogue process; refrain from intervention and interference in each other's internal affairs; combat the menace of terrorism in all its forms and manifestations; protect human rights; take immediate steps to reduce the risk of accidental or unauthorized use of nuclear weapons and discuss security concepts and doctrines with a view to elaborating measures for confidence-building in the nuclear and conventional fields, aimed at prevention of conflict.[5]

On the other hand, General Pervez Musharraf's highly risky offensive against India in Kargil in May 1999, without taking Prime Minister Sharif into his confidence, dampened the spirit of the Lahore Declaration. Nawaz Sharif conceded that he was let down by Musharraf. Further, the Agra Summit between Prime Minister A. B. Vajpayee and President Pervez Musharraf in July 2001 proved abortive because they had taken irreconcilable positions on Kashmir and in the aftermath of the terrorist attack on the Indian parliament in December 2001, the New Delhi–Islamabad relations touched their lowest ebb.

As regards the Kashmir issue, two important developments took place. First, Pakistan claimed strategic parity vis-à-vis India after having successfully conducted six nuclear-weapons tests in response to India's five in May 1998. The tests naturally emboldened Pakistan to deal with India on Kashmir and many other bilateral issues with confidence and self-esteem. Undoubtedly, the nuclear factor has contributed to an enduring rivalry between India and Pakistan.[6] Second, the Pakistan-sponsored low-intensity conflict in the state of Jammu and Kashmir continues to be Pakistan's key policy instrument. Its debilitating impact reflects the irreconcilable approaches adopted by New Delhi and Islamabad in dealing with the Kashmir issue. India, for instance, has linked the resolution of the Kashmir problem to a permanent cessation of cross-border terrorism, while Pakistan insists on resolving the Kashmir issue first before undertaking concrete steps to permanently end militancy in the Kashmir Valley.

As noted, terrorism is a core issue for India. In the Indian perception, Pakistan employed terrorism as an instrument of its state policy to weaken, macerate, and destabilize India. New Delhi has, therefore, consistently asked Pakistani government leaders to sternly deal with the common enemy of terror in the national security interests of both countries. However, Pakistan has advanced the typical argument that it has no control over non-state militant outfits. It is self-evident that Pakistan is becoming a failed state, unable to control its militants who are fearlessly engaged in destabilizing the country.

To resolve this moribund situation, an alternative option for President Asif Ali Zardari and his political lieutenants is to mobilize a mass movement against militancy because it is the common people who are the soft target of these jihadi elements. In effect, Pakistan is jeopardizing its own internal security as well as undermining the state's capacity to deliver goods to the people because of it is failing to meet the menace of militancy which it fostered in the 1980s. Ironically, the problem has taken a more serious turn with the intensification of public ire over the government's overt or covert permission to US forces to violate the country's sovereignty and territorial integrity, as is manifest in the remote-controlled drone attacks on Pakistan's tribal areas. This reflects the anti-US geopsychology that pervades a large section of Pakistani society.

Mumbai Blasts

The composite dialogue that began in 2004 raised optimism in both countries that they might be able to transcend the bitterness of the past in order and move forward to improve bilateral relations in the interest of regional peace and stability. But the 26/11/08 terrorist attacks on Mumbai once again put the peace process on hold. In these well-planned, well-directed, and well-coordinated attacks, 183 people were killed, including 22 foreigners of different nationalities. New Delhi lodged a strong protest with Islamabad, asking the latter to bring the perpetrators of the attacks to justice. President Zardari assured India that Pakistan would punish the perpetrators and cooperate with India and would not allow its territory to be used against India for 'any acts of terror'. However, he rejected India's demand to hand over the suspected terrorists, including the LeT/Jaish-e-Mohammed (JeM) chief, the mastermind behind the attacks.

In order to defuse the tension, which the Mumbai mayhem had provoked between the two nuclear-armed nations, US Secretary of State Condoleezza Rice made a hectic diplomatic visit to India and Pakistan in early December 2008. She met her Indian counterpart, Pranab Mukherjee, and opposition leaders. She advised India to exercise restraint and reassured Indian leaders that she would ask Islamabad to take the toughest action against 'non-state actors' operating from Pakistani soil to threaten India's sovereignty and internal security. Secretary Rice, in her meetings with President Zardari and Prime Minister Syed Yousaf Raza Gilani, made it clear to them that though Pakistan might not have been directly involved in the Mumbai blasts, it was the state's responsibility to punish indigenous militants who were directly involved in the planning and execution of the Mumbai attacks.[7]

It was under constant US pressure that Pakistan, while showing a gesture of solidarity and sympathy with India, put a dreaded militant, Masood Azhar of LeT, under house arrest on 7 December 2008 and also cracked down on some of the top militants operating from PAK. When the United Nations Security Council branded the Pakistan-based Jamat-ud-Dawah as a terrorist group, and its chief, Hafiz Muhammad Saeed, as a terrorist, the Pakistani government placed Saeed under house arrest on 11 December 2008. But India dubbed Pakistan's steps as a 'political gimmick' to demonstrate its sincerity before the world community. Critics argue that Pakistan had undertaken similar measures when the Indian parliament was attacked in December 2001. In this regard, President Asif Ali Zardari wrote in *The New York Times* (as reproduced in *The Hindu*, 10 December 2008):

> The Mumbai attacks were directed not only at India but also at Pakistan's new democratic government and the peace process with India that we have initiated. Supporters of authoritarianism in Pakistan and non-state actors with a vested interest in perpetuating conflict do not want change in Pakistan to take root.[8]

President Zardari conceded that terrorism in his country was a legacy of the Cold War era when Pakistan was an 'ally' of the West. For that, he stressed, Pakistan had to pay a heavy price. He further elaborated that 'Pakistan continues to pay the price: the legacy of dictatorship, the fatigue of fanaticism, the dismemberment of civil society and the destruction of our democratic infrastructure.'[9] Zardari further noted that, as a result of militancy, 'In 2008, nearly 2,000 Pakistanis lost their lives as a result of terrorism' including 1,400 civilians and 60 security personnel ranging in rank from ordinary soldier to three-star general. In 2008, there were more than 600 terrorism-related incidents in Pakistan.'[10]

Zardari appealed to India to act with caution and patience, as a 'mature democracy', and to refrain from making inflammatory statements. Rather, both the countries, Zardari underlined, must work together to track down terrorists so that their nefarious designs to provoke a confrontation between New Delhi and Islamabad could be nipped in the bud.

Prime Minister Manmohan Singh asked Pakistan to ensure that the 'terrorist infrastructure' be dismantled. At the end of the debate in the parliament (Lok Sabha), the prime minister moved a resolution on 11 December 2008, unequivocally condemning the attacks by terrorist elements from Pakistan, which claimed hundreds of lives.[11] The BJP Member of Parliament (MP) Arun Shourie asked the government in the Rajya Sabha (Upper House of Parliament) to go full blast to win the proxy war unleashed by Pakistan. He said the government must recognize that no war could be won with a strategy of permanent defence.[12]

In order to de-escalate tension between India and Pakistan as well as create a congenial environment to help resume the peace dialogue between them, the United States has embarked upon a proactive diplomacy to encourage New Delhi and Islamabad to resume the composite dialogue. There are palpable reasons behind it. First, Washington wants to make sure that India and Pakistan do not go to war, fearing the possibility of a nuclear exchange between them. Second, from the viewpoint of the United States, US security and strategic interests in Afghanistan will be jeopardized if Pakistan shifts its forces from the Afghan border to deploy them against India. In that eventuality, the US war against the Taliban and al-Qaeda elements along the Afghanistan–Pakistan border might suffer a serious setback. In this scenario, White House officials are trying to construct a balanced policy with great caution and prudence to deal with the post-Mumbai terror scenario.

India has also embarked upon a diplomatic offensive to 'encircle' Pakistan by drawing the attention of the world community to Pakistan's complicity in the Mumbai attacks. Home Minister P. Chidambaram has called on the world community to mount pressure on Pakistan to dismantle the terror infrastructure on its soil. In support of this, India has purveyed to the United States 'dossiers' on the involvement of Pakistan-based militants to prove that the Lashkar-e-Taiba was the architect of the Mumbai attacks.

Given the gravity of the situation, the US Assistant Secretary of State Richard Boucher arrived in Islamabad on 5 January 2009 to discuss the entire post-Mumbai scenario with Pakistani leaders. Prime Minister Gilani apprised Boucher of the steps undertaken by Pakistan to punish the perpetrators of the Mumbai attacks. At the same time, Gilani taunted Boucher by mentioning that if the United States had a parallel interest to stop bloodshed, it should prevent Israel from killing innocent Palestinians and thereby assuage the concerns of the Muslim fraternity. This apart, Gilani added that the United States must hand over the five Pakistani nationals who were detained at the Guantanamo Bay. This was Pakistan's well-orchestrated diplomatic tactic to weaken India's case and blame the United States for playing a double role on the terror issue.[13]

In the ongoing US efforts, India's External Affairs Minister Pranab Mukherjee and Assistant Secretary of State Richard Boucher shared a common assessment that the steps undertaken by Pakistan did not eliminate 'the terrorist threat and its government still had to go a long way to fulfil its international obligations'.[14] Boucher agreed with Mukherjee that Pakistan was trying to disown its direct or indirect involvement in the Mumbai attacks, even though New Delhi had furnished a heap of evidence to Islamabad in this regard, including stunning disclosures by Ajmal Amir Kasab, the lone surviving terrorist of the Mumbai attacks.

On the other hand, Prime Minister Gilani sacked his national security advisor, Major General (retired) Mahmud Ali Durrani, for confirming Kasab's Pakistani nationality. It partly shows that there are multiple centres of decision-making in Pakistan's fragile democracy. Interestingly, Gilani telephoned Geo Television to denounce Durrani for bringing a 'bad name' and causing 'embarrassment' to Pakistan.[15] The editorial further commented, 'Those who lead Pakistan today, and the sections of the news media and intelligentsia who are engaged in resurrecting India as the "real enemy", must realize that persisting in denial will bring the country dishonour.'[16] If Pakistan displays transparency, it might help improve its image in the world community, which looks upon Pakistan as a breeding ground of global terror. Interestingly, an Indian political analyst has attributed Pakistan's inability to tackle its home-grown militants to 'the slow transformation of the Pakistani state into an instrument of the jihadist agenda'.[17] Foreign Secretary Shiv Shankar Menon also attributes the 26/11/08 attacks to terror organizers who are ISI clients.[18]

India's Home Minister P. Chidambaram conveyed New Delhi's concerns to the United States during his visit to Washington in September 2009, saying that 'security threats from Pakistan have not lessened'. Rather, there has been an increase in infiltration from Pakistan.[19] He reiterated that Pakistan did not take any concrete action to prosecute the perpetrators of the Mumbai attacks. Chidambaram further elaborated that the mastermind, Hafiz Muhammad Saeed, founder of Lashkar-e-Taiba, was roaming free in Pakistan despite the massive evidence provided by India.[20]

Chaulia and Richter have noted, 'Through his [Zardari] latest comment that "we're fighting for the survival of Pakistan" against fast-spreading Islamic fundamentalism, Zardari has signaled a concurrence with India's point of view that the immediate threat facing the entire subcontinent is jihadi violence.'[21]

One may note that in President George Bush's perception, The United States would be able to crush the Taliban and al-Qaeda elements by cultivating General Musharraf. But that did not happen. Chaulia and Richer write, 'Since the war in Afghanistan in October 2001, the Pentagon-driven foreign policy of the Bush Administration banked on close friendship with the Pakistani army as the guarantee to fulfilling US interests in the war on terrorism.'[22]

Breaking the Ice

Although the dialogue between India and Pakistan has stalled since the Mumbai terrorist attacks, Prime Minister Manmohan Singh met President Asif Ali Zardari during the Shanghai Cooperation Organisation Summit meeting at Yekaterinburg in Russia on 16 June 2009. Their meeting finally ended the 'bilateral logjam'. The two leaders discussed modalities for resuming the composite dialogue process. Singh told Zardari in unequivocal terms that he had 'come with the limited mandate of discussing how Pakistan can deliver on its assurance that its territory would not be used for terrorists attacks on India'.[23] Zardari agreed that the menace of terrorism was the real threat to both India and Pakistan. An important outcome of their meeting was that both leaders agreed to the imperative of resuming the foreign-secretary-level talks. Pursuant to that decision, India's Foreign Secretary Shiv Shankar Menon and his Pakistani counterpart, Salman Bashir, met on 13–14 July 2009 at Sharm-al-Sheikh in Egypt where the 15th Non-aligned Movement (NAM) Summit was held. They discussed modalities to restart the peace talks, frozen since 26/11/08.

Prime Minister Singh and his Pakistani counterpart Syed Yousaf Raza Gilani who met on 16 July 2009 on the sidelines of the NAM Summit also stressed the urgency of resuming the composite dialogue between New Delhi and Islamabad. Both leaders extensively dwelt on the issue of terrorism in light of the Mumbai terrorist attacks. Instead of focusing on the Kashmir problem, India's prime concern was cross-border terrorism. Singh reiterated his demand to bring the perpetrators of the Mumbai attacks to justice. Gilani assured that Pakistan would do 'everything in its power in this regard'.[24] Rama Laxmi, reporting for *The Washington Post*, wrote:

> Until now, New Delhi had insisted that Pakistan take 'concrete and demonstrable' action to prevent cross-border terrorism as a precondition for the resumption of peace talks. However, the joint statement said that action on terror should not be linked to the composite dialogue process and these should not be bracketed and that terrorism is the main threat to both countries.[25]

A joint statement issued at the end of the meeting between Singh and Gilani generated a furore in the Indian parliament and media. Singh, in his statement before the Lok Sabha, tried to assuage the opposition's fear of India's surrendering to Pakistan by disassociating the composite dialogue from the terror issue. The opposition was not convinced by the prime minister's statement. He was, however, anguished over his own party men who criticized him for signing the joint statement in haste. The Congress supremo, Sonia Gandhi, in her effort to exercise damage control, asked Pranab Mukherjee to handle the controversy surrounding the joint statement.

As part of a face-saving device, the UPA government reiterated its rhetorical stance that the government wanted a firm, 'credible', and 'visible' commitment from Pakistan that it would bring the perpetrators of the Mumbai attacks to book. India's External Affairs Minister S. M Krishna, underlined that such a commitment was necessary to move forward the composite dialogue. Krishna did not agree with Pakistan's projection of Kashmir as the key issue between India and Pakistan. He said:

> I do not know whether I would agree with the projection that Kashmir is the key issue. India has its own issue. We are not unwilling to talk to Pakistan on Kashmir. It is part and parcel of the composite dialogue, which has already been agreed upon.[26]

Nuclear Factor

The nuclear factor has added a new dimension to the persisting irritants between India and Pakistan. They are engaged in a nuclear-arms race to modernize, update, and strengthen their nuclear-deterrent capabilities. Nuclear rivalry in the region began with India's first nuclear detonation at Pokhran in the desert of Rajasthan on 18 May 1974. More significantly, Pakistan has realized, after having experienced humiliating defeat at the hands of India in the 1965 and 1971 wars, that nuclear weapons alone are capable of guaranteeing Pakistan's national security against India's preponderant conventional superiority.[27] However, both countries raise the risk of nuclear disaster, given their geopsychological orientation of treating each other as a natural enemy.

Inapplicable to India and Pakistan are Western scholars' theoretical writings on nuclear deterrence, including, for instance, Kenneth Waltz's argument that there is 'zero probability' of a major war among nuclear-weapons states. The main reason is that India and Pakistan, unlike the superpowers, can hardly be counted as responsible nuclear powers, although President George W. Bush treated India as a 'responsible nuclear power'. The question about India's nuclear behaviour will depend on the political credibility of Pakistan and also on the latter's ability to keep the nukes safe from jihadi elements. Although it is not an easy task for terrorist groups to acquire and use these weapons, nobody knows the mind of Pakistan's military and nuclear establishment. The latter may have a close connection with the ISI and jihadi groups as many US strategic analysts believed it has.

If viewed from the interactive geopolitical and geopsychological framework, both India and Pakistan are set to vying for power, prestige, and influence beyond the shores of South Asia. A perceptional shift among Pakistani elites is clearly visible following Islamabad's attainment of nuclear parity with India. Since then the realization has percolated through the psyche of Pakistani policymakers that their country needs to pursue a proactive diplomacy in order to expand its political, economic, and security space vis-à-vis India, its main adversary. President Musharraf used to reiterate that Pakistan's nuclear-power status enhanced the country's image, prestige, and influence among Muslim countries. Such utterances were primarily intended to exploit the Muslim community's psychology that Pakistan was the only Islamic country with nuclear weapons that would act as a potential deterrence against the enemies of the Islamic world. In other words, Pakistani ruling elites are projecting their country's nuclear-deterrence capability as a force to be reckoned with, capable of challenging Indian preponderance, not only in South Asia but also in the 'extended neighbourhood'.

In this complex scenario, India and Pakistan are relentlessly engaged in a kind of psychotic war. Unfortunately, neither country has yet developed a precise plan to deal with nuclear war inadvertently triggered by misperception and miscalculation or desperation, although the Indian government has announced its nuclear-command authority.[28]

The question arises whether nuclear weapons can be treated as reliable deterrents against each country's threats. In this regard, one should not forget that India and Pakistan have divergent views on the question of the deployment of nuclear weapons. Nevertheless, one thing is clear: a so-called 'limited nuclear war', initiated by the either party, is likely to extend into a total war with total victory or total defeat.

'Reciprocal insecurity' might remain a driving force behind the nuclear exchange. Under existing conditions, both India and Pakistan are not fully capable of controlling and managing the deployment of nuclear weapons. If viewed in the context of the emotionally charged political constituencies of India and Pakistan, government leaders might be tempted into taking irrational decisions on the advice of civilian and military hawks. Without exaggeration, nuclear wars do not emerge from a political vacuum.[29]

There can be no better nuclear strategy for India and Pakistan than the strategy of exercising the utmost nuclear restraint in any provocative situation. They need to make sure through a bilateral agreement that nuclear weapons will not be deployed for assured mutual destruction, given their geographical proximity and the pressing socio-economic problems that should be New Delhi and Islamabad's first priorities. The argument that nuclear deterrents guarantee national security may be good in theory but is redundant, given the fractured mental make-up of the ruling classes in both the countries, especially the Pakistani army's continued projection of India as an adversary.

Hurdles

Though Pakistan has recently returned to democratic governance, it is virtually dominated by the 'troika' on all major issues of national importance. In the power structure, the Pakistani army holds the 'ultimate veto' on critical issues such as the nuclear-weapons programme and the modernization of defence forces. Ahmed Rashid, a Pakistani journalist, writes that 'it is still the army and not the civilian government that calls the shot when it comes to policy toward India and Afghanistan.'[30]

The role of army chiefs Aslam Beg and General Musharraf in overthrowing the democratically elected governments of Benazir Bhutto and Nawaz Sharif is well known. As one scholar notes:

> Pakistan is under siege; the nation is reeling under a relentless wave of terror strikes, targeted primarily against security forces, police and government officials. The civilian government of Asif Ali Zardari has lost all credibility, and the military is once again ascendant. The armed forces of Pakistan have historically viewed themselves as guardians of Pakistani identity, and the need to view India as an adversary has been a constant in Pakistan's politics and foreign policy since its inception. Significant sections of the Pakistani military and intelligence services continue to see themselves in a permanent state of conflict with India and have little incentive to moderate their behaviour as a continuing conflict with India is the raison d'être of their pre-eminent position in Pakistani society.
>
> The Indo-Pakistan peace process also hinges on the ability of Pakistan's political establishment to control terrorist groups from wreaking havoc in India. It is doubtful how much control the civilian government in Islamabad can exert, given that various terrorist outfits have vowed to continue their jihad in Kashmir.[31]

That democratic institutions have not yet taken firm root in Pakistan is attributed to the deeply entrenched interests of the military, feudal elements, and the clergy and drug mafia in nexus with the ruling class. There is no possibility of a positive change in the old mindsets of the clerics and the ISI. Although democracy alone cannot be a magic wand for improving Pakistan's relations with India overnight, it can help create better political conditions to bring normalcy to their relationship. Furthermore, political dialogue between New Delhi and Islamabad needs to be resumed to give democracy the chance to act as a broker in reducing the congenital animosity between India and Pakistan. Undoubtedly, democratic governance will offer a wide social and political space to the people, enabling them to exercise a restraining influence over government leaders to reverse decisions that are detrimental, in the public estimation, to economic health, social cohesion, communal harmony, domestic peace, and prosperity.[32]

As mentioned earlier, the Pakistani army determines, conducts, and directs policies on national security and strategic matters. Democratically elected leaders are, simply speaking, the voice of the military elites in whose perception there cannot be peace and stability in South Asia unless the Kashmir issue is first resolved by determining the wishes of the Kashmiri people in accordance with the 1948 UN Security Council resolution. Islamabad has made it clear to New Delhi that Pakistan is neither prepared to give unilateral concessions to India nor will it accept converting the Line of Control (LoC) into an international border as a lasting solution to the Kashmir problem. India has also made its viewpoint known to Pakistan and the international community that it would not accept redrawing the LoC.

The core problem is that both India and Pakistan are sticking to their respective intransigent positions. On the one hand, India reiterates that demilitarization is not a feasible proposition because there has been no let-up in terrorist and militant activities across the LoC. On the other hand, Pakistan insists that the peace process cannot be taken further unless India withdraws its armed forces from the state of Jammu and Kashmir in order to build trust between the two countries. In response to this, the Indian government has assured Pakistan that it is prepared to downsize its military deployment, depending on the level of militancy. It appears that the obdurate stance adopted by New Delhi and Islamabad will make it extremely difficult to find a mutually acceptable solution to the Kashmir problem.

It may be recalled that Prime Minister Manmohan Singh held a two-day, round-table conference in Srinagar in May 2006 to address the problems of the Indian state of Jammu and Kashmir. It was attended by the People's Democratic Party chief, the National Conference president, the Panther Party chief, and various sections of the Kashmiri community, whereas the Hurriyat Conference, led by Mirwaiz Umar Farooq, boycotted it. Singh reiterated his government's stand that he was prepared to talk to militants provided that they abandon militancy. It was decided at the conference to set up five working groups, entrusted with the task of recommending feasible measures to give more autonomy to the state of Jammu and Kashmir within the constitutional framework.

India can do little to promote stability in Pakistan, although it considers stability in Pakistan indispensable for all South Asian countries. Stability is linked to the regime's ability to deliver the goods on law and order, and on education and health. At the same time, Pakistani civilian leaders are trying, through the United States, to put pressure on New Delhi to restart the dialogue. India is reluctant to resume the dialogue unless Pakistan takes concrete action against militant groups, especially the Lashkar-e-Taiba, established with Pakistani funding in the late 1980s to destabilize the state of Jammu and Kashmir. Unless Pakistan undertakes sincere and effective steps against terrorists, there is little hope that peace will be ushered in even though Pakistan is fighting the Taliban in South Waziristan on behalf of the United States, rather than taking similar measures against its own home-grown militants. Moreover, Pakistan's internal stability will depend on the credibility of the civilian government, otherwise the military might return to power. Further, India can take no other option than to resume the dialogue with Pakistan.

Conclusion

Pakistan's nightmarish phobia of India is a fundamental cause of the perpetual hostility between them, and India's Pakistan 'bogey' is a classic case of competitive geopsychology. Both India and Pakistan must wake up to the geopolitical reality that perceptions of mutual threat are things of the past; both countries need to abandon their deeply entrenched predilections and prejudices structured on a competitive psychology to outmanoeuvre the other. If India needs to abandon its hegemonic aspirations, Pakistan also needs to shed its anti-India biases on bilateral and regional issues.

The widely held perception that the Kashmir problem is the root cause of hostility between India and Pakistan is wrong. The Kashmir imbroglio is symptomatic of deeply rooted historical and cultural differences. Even if the Kashmir problem were resolved, India and

Pakistan would remain interlocked in mutual hostility unless their old mindsets and psychocultural prejudices are dissolved.

Moreover, 'psychic influences' on India and Pakistan are likely to accentuate mistrust, fear, hatred, and rivalry between them. Unless the root sources bedeviling their relations are fully addressed, there is not much hope for a durable friendship between the two countries. It is also a well-known fact that their bilateral problems are inextricably linked to their cultural and psychological prejudices toward each other. If historical documents are objectively scanned and analyzed in the context of the persisting tensions, one may find that misperceptions, false images, and mistrust have basically emanated from irrevocable, divergent cultural values and ideological differences, producing fractured mutual perceptions, and 'constrained visions' among the ruling classes in India and Pakistan. The study suggests that in order to heal the psychic malady, a psychic therapy is needed. It is up to public therapists—the common people, enlightened citizenry, media, and voluntary peace activists—to launch a peace offensive in order to bring about a perceptional change in the deeply rooted psyche of mutual hostility. This might help build bridges of mutual understanding between the two countries.[33]

The national interests of both countries demand the ending of their persistent hostility. India's stability is Pakistan's stability and vice versa. It is not in India's interests to see Pakistan become a failed state because its negative fall-out will affect India. Similarly, the bleeding of India by Pakistan's non-state terror actors will have horrendous consequences for Pakistan's internal security as well as for its economic progress and the well-being of the common people. Any attempt by one country to achieve short-term tactical gains against the other will be disastrous for both countries.

Three broad conclusions emerge from this study. First, despite their divergent security and strategic interests in South Asia, India and Pakistan are capable of contributing to the peace and stability of the region. Second, the geopsychology of mutual enmity will be mitigated considerably provided that both countries undertake positive steps toward bilateral and regional economic reconstruction. Third, the peace dialogue must continue with civilian intervention to help resolve outstanding bilateral disputes, including Kashmir.

However, fundamental uncertainties concerning the pace, scale, and direction of mutual interdependence are still looming large over the region. This is likely to produce a state of inertia and inaction among South Asian states in their response to geostrategic and geopsychological realities. South Asian policy elites have been caught in the dilemma of choosing between appropriate responses and euphoric reactions to the discourses on 'the end of ideology', the end of the political game rules, and the beginning of a new strategic thinking. There is no clarity, for instance, in terms of goals and priorities in the composite post-Mumbai dialogue between India and Pakistan.

5

INDIA AND OTHER SOUTH ASIAN COUNTRIES: POLITICAL, SECURITY, AND STRATEGIC DIMENSIONS

India's relations with South Asian countries have undergone a major transformation following the unprecedented political developments in its neighbourhood, which have a profound bearing on India's myriad national interests. Nepal, for instance, has undergone a political metamorphosis with the abolition of 240-year-old monarchy in May 2008: the installation of a coalition government led by the CPN-UML under the leadership of Madhav Kumar Nepal signalled a crucial change, particularly after the dramatic resignation of Prime Minister Pushpa Kamal Dahal following a row over his sacking of the army chief, General Rookmangud Katawal. In view of these developments, India needs to reassess the entire gamut of its relationship with Nepal. It also needs to bear in mind that Madhav Kumar's past pro-China credentials and anti-India rhetoric on the 1950 Treaty of Peace and Friendship were already well known when he was deputy prime minister and foreign minister in the cabinet of Manmohan Adhikari (1994–95).

Regarding Sri Lanka, the end of the ethnic conflict with the decimation of the LTTE, which had strangulated the country for over two decades, brought a new lease of life, the credit for which goes to President Rajpaksa Mahinda, widely seen as a hardliner. What poses an enormous challenge to the government is the gigantic task of rebuilding the nation, and also redressing the legitimate grievances of Sri Lankan Tamils and Muslims. This apart, Mahinda is faced with an uphill task of redefining Colombo's relationship with New Delhi in light of India's blanket refusal to supply military hardware to Sri Lanka at a critical juncture when President Rajpaksa Mahinda was firmly committed to eliminating the LTTE. Moreover, India–Sri Lanka relations are likely to come under a severe strain after China's strategic intrusion into regional security affairs after Sri Lanka procured weapons from China to fight the LTTE.

With regard to Bangladesh, India welcomed the return to power of the Awami League with a landslide victory under the leadership of Sheikh Hasina. She was sworn in as prime minister on 6 January 2009. Prime Minister Manmohan Singh termed the Awami League victory as 'historic' and 'a landmark'. In New Delhi's perception, the Awami League's pro-India stance will not only bolster bilateral ties to a new height but might also facilitate the early resolution of outstanding bilateral issues, notably, the illegal migration of Bangladeshis to India, and the operations against India of terrorists and insurgents from Bangladeshi soil.

Against this background, the chapter will re-evaluate India's relations with Nepal, Bangladesh, and Sri Lanka.

India and Nepal

Indo-Nepalese relations are fundamentally driven by their mutual geopolitical and strategic compulsions. Both history and geography have cast upon the two countries a special obligation to cultivate and maintain friendly and stable ties in order to keep their core national interests intact. Both countries share a 1,750-kilometre border.

The emergence of Communist China in October 1949 and Mao's swift military action to annex Tibet in 1950 compelled New Delhi and Kathmandu to enter into the 1950 Treaty of Peace and Friendship under which they would consult each other on foreign and defence matters. But gradually the Kathmandu leadership began to realize that the treaty undermined the country's sovereignty and autonomy in the realms of defence and external affairs. With a motivation to stay away from India's hegemony, King Birendra proposed that Nepal be declared a 'zone of peace', which in the Indian perception would outlive the relevance of the 1950 Treaty. India was hardly convinced by King Birendra's contention that the 'zone of peace' proposal would help institutionalize peace on the Indian subcontinent. On the contrary, New Delhi felt that Kathmandu was attempting to undermine India's political, security, and strategic role in the region. In the early 1960s,

Nepal's bold policy decision to allow China to link Lhasa with Kathmandu caused the misgiving in India's South Block that Kathmandu was acting against India's security interests because the direct link between Lhasa and Kathmandu constituted a grave threat to India's national security. As a result of divergent perceptions on political and security issues, relations between New Delhi and Kathmandu became bedevilled.[1]

Additionally, the 1965 agreement requires Nepal to purchase arms from India or from others with India's permission only. Ironically again, it was India that stopped the supply of arms during the gravest challenge in Nepal's modern history of combating terrorism and insurgency in 2005, forcing Nepal to buy arms from China and Pakistan.[2]

India-Nepal relations oscillated between high optimism and deep despair after the inauguration of democracy in the early 1990s under Nepal's new constitutional framework. From India's viewpoint, a democratic Nepal with a symbolic constitutional monarchy would serve India's national interests better. But Indian optimism proved euphoric. A Communist government under a new democratic system was installed for the first time in Nepal's history under the leadership of Manmohan Adhikari (1994–95) whose ideological tilt toward China constituted a factor of irritation in the age-old special relationship between India and Nepal. As a result, a major change came about in Nepal's India policy that became manifest in Prime Minister Adhikari's insistence on the imperative of reviewing the 1950 Treaty of Peace and Friendship while arguing that the treaty had lost its relevance in the post-Cold War era. In effect, the treaty's redundant clauses needed to be scrapped altogether. New Delhi was reluctant to alter the essentials of the treaty because, from its viewpoint, tampering with its core principles might prove disastrous to the political, economic, and security interests of both countries. Though Prime Minister P. V. Narsimha Rao assured his Nepalese counterpart, Manmohan Adhikari, that the issue would be taken up at government level,[3] India's nonchalant attitude and ambivalent commitment did not satisfy Adhikari.

The new leftist leadership in Nepal is also trying to hammer out the point that the end of superpower rivalry in South Asia, in addition to a growing *rapprochement* between India and China, make it sensible to review the 1950 Indo-Nepal Treaty in its entirety. It is true that India–China relations are on upswing, as evident from the signing of an agreement on a strategic and cooperative partnership during Chinese Premier Wen Jiabao's visit to New Delhi in April 2005. In addition, since 1993, they have undertaken a series of confidence-building measures (CBMs) on the boundary issue. Security and strategic concerns loom large in

Indian thinking and touch on the question of reviewing the treaty in its entirety. On the other hand, in Kathmandu's assessment, the revision and updating of the 1950 treaty will not only enable Nepal to maintain a distance in its ties with New Delhi and Beijing but also provide a greater degree of freedom and autonomy to conduct its multifaceted relations with the outside world.[4]

Be that as it may, India must also realize that it can no longer keep Nepal a captive of its foreign policy and strategic designs. Rather, New Delhi should respect Kathmandu's sensitivities, and understand the geopsychological perceptions of the people who abhor the frequent intervention of India's foreign-policy establishment in their internal and external affairs. At the same time, Kathmandu should also bear in mind that its geographical location, its demography, topography, natural resources, and political system ensure that Kathmandu's long-term national interests will not be served by cultivating Beijing at the cost of New Delhi. It is also true that the Indian political leadership and the foreign-policy establishment's old mindset of dominance has not yet changed toward Nepal even as the world heads rapidly toward multi-partner interdependence.

Political Change in Nepal

Nepal witnessed a sweeping political change with the coming into power of a Maoist-led government under the leadership of Pushpa Kamal Dahal Prachanda (nickname meaning fierce) in August 2008. It may be recalled that the Maoists secured the largest number of seats in the national elections to the Constituent Assembly in April 2008. In May 2008, the 240-year-old monarchy was dismantled and Nepal was declared a Federal Democratic Republic. India's relationship with the Maoist-led government was initially ambiguous. Gradually, India came to terms with Dahal's government in order to reshape the bilateral ties between New Delhi and Kathmandu.

With a view to redefining the Kathmandu–Delhi relationship, Prime Minister Pushpa Kamal Dahal arrived in India on a five-day official visit beginning on 14 September 2008. He held intensive discussions with Prime Minister Manmohan Singh, mainly focused on reviewing the 1950 treaty, sharing water resources, border security management, and trade and transit arrangements. Prime Minister Singh agreed in principle to review the treaty because Nepal dubbed it an 'unequal document'. According to a statement issued at the end of Dahal's visit on 17 September 2008, India and Nepal have decided to set up a high-level committee of their foreign secretaries to 'review, adjust and update' the 1950 treaty and other agreements 'giving due recognition to the special features of the bilateral relations'.[5] India also agreed to update the fifty-eight-year-old Trade and Transit Treaty.

Prime Minister Singh and Prime Minister Dahal also discussed at length the Kosi River Treaty (1954) and the Mahakali Accord (1996). Dahal assured India that his government favoured attracting Indian industrialists to make an investment in key areas such as hydropower, agriculture, and infrastructure. Both leaders agreed to review the grave security situation arising out of anti-India activities carried out by the ISI on the Nepalese soil.

Meanwhile, a new political development took place with the resignation of Prime Minister Dahl following a row over his sacking of the army chief, Rookmangud Katawal, who refused to enlist former Maoist rebels in the army. President R. B. Yadav rejected Dahal's decision, leaving Dahal no choice other than to resign.

The CPN (UML) nominee Madhav Kumar Nepal was chosen as the new prime minister replacing Dahal. In order to reshape Indo-Nepalese ties, Madhav Kumar visited New Delhi in August 2009. He held wide-ranging discussions on outstanding bilateral issues with Prime Minister Manmohan Singh. They included the 1950 treaty and the utilization of water resources. At the end of his visit on 22 August 2009, he reassured India that Nepalese territory would not be used against India. New Delhi also expressed its firm support to the coalition government's tough new stand against the integration of Maoists combatants in the Nepalese army. Prime Minister Nepal and his advisors concurred with Indian insistence on the need to preserve the professional character of the Nepalese army.[6] Apart from this, India and Nepal signed the revised Treaty of Trade and Agreement of Cooperation to Control Unauthorized Trade, which might contribute to further enhancing bilateral trade. India has also agreed to invest Rs 1,485 crore to strengthen Nepal's rail and road linkages in the Terai region.[7] Under a new Trade Treaty signed on 22 August 2009, New Delhi agreed to allow duty-free access of Nepalese goods to India. At present, bilateral trade stands at $1.9 billion, which is likely to be further increased. Moreover, India is the principal foreign investor in Nepal.

International Border Dispute

The border dispute over some pockets has persisted between India and Nepal for over three decades. Recently, this issue has become one of the major irritants between the two countries. Historically, the dispute dates back to 1882–83 when the surveyor of the Indian government, Captain Turner, suggested that fixed boundaries could be the only solution to the problem. In this respect, both governments had agreed to build permanent border pillars. According to a survey officer, Ram Bahadur Malla, 'both sides agreed at the meeting to construct permanent border pillars in the river area, repair dilapidated pillars, collect data in case of border encroachment and restore the pillars removed earlier.'[8] The border problem is mainly attributed to the shifting of the river Gandak's course toward Indian territories. As a result, border pillars either have submerged or have been uprooted, further causing misunderstanding among the Nepalese people that India is encroaching upon their territory. High-level official talks have already taken place between New Delhi and Kathmandu to resolve the problem arising out of shifting of the Gandak's course, resulting in the erosion of Indian soil, particularly in the villages of Belgawa, Tharhi, and Rampurwa. Furthermore, the Indian government is worried about the incidents of crime and kidnapping because criminal elements seek refuge in the displaced territories.

India–Nepal boundary talks, including discussion of the imperative of improving and upgrading border infrastructure, have registered some progress. According to the *Annual Report 2007-08* of the Ministry of External Affairs:

> Strengthening of border infrastructure along the India-Nepal border was high on Government's priority. Several new projects launched in consultation with the Government of Nepal to improve and upgrade border infrastructure, development of integrated check-posts and road and rail connectivity between the two sides of the border made further progress. Once implemented, these projects would not only facilitate trade and transit but would also contribute to efficient management of the border.[9]

A joint working group is also intensively engaged in resolving the border dispute. After years of painstaking surveys, deliberations, and extensions, the JTC (Joint Technical Level Boundary Committee) was successful in delineating 98 per cent of the border on strip maps, which were signed by experts from both countries in December 2007. Now, the Indian government is awaiting the Nepalese government's consent to formalize the strip maps. Once these maps are formalized, demarcation of the boundary on the ground would start by checking and reinstalling border pillars. This would solve all the problems along the border except in two disputed pockets, Kalapani and Susta, which can only be resolved through a political dialogue.[10]

Prime Minister Madhav Kumar, during his visit to India in August 2009, also assured New Delhi that his government would make serious efforts to resolve the boundary dispute amicably. However, each side entertains reservations on the question of who extracts the better deal. Also, it is an uphill task to arrive at a mutually acceptable agreement on maps and field surveys and the documentary evidence that each country submits to substantiate its claim. These problems deserve the utmost attention of both sides to resolve them in a friendly manner. More importantly, open borders between India and Nepal should not be allowed to be misused by each side lest they provide sanctuary to militants, insurgents, and smugglers, which might have an adverse effect on their national security interests.

Other bilateral issues, such as the distribution of water resources, the Trade and Transit Treaty, the work-permit system, cross-border smuggling, and the Ganges as an international boundary, have had a cumulative impact on Indo–Nepalese security and strategic relations. If one recalls, the Communist Party of Nepal (UML) launched an anti-India tirade on the Tanakpur project, a 120 MW project located at Banbassa on the Mahakali, claiming that Nepal sold itself out to India. But the facts are otherwise: the project was planned and developed on the consensus that it would be completed after the transfer of 4093.88 acres of Nepali land for the transfer of an equal amount of Indian land to Nepal. The new Tanakpur barrage, though not located on the land, was ceded to India. Of its total 1000-cusecs capacity, it diverts 150 cusecs of water to Nepal, giving away 20 million units of energy free of charge.[11]

Trade and Transit Treaty

India–Nepal relations reached their lowest ebb when the Rajiv Gandhi government took the unprecedented decision not to renew the Trade and Transit Treaty in March 1989 unless Nepal agreed to address India's security, economic, and trade concerns. That ill-thought-out decision caused the severest hardship to the people of Nepal who were dependent on essential goods from India, including petroleum products, food, and agricultural items. After the defeat of the Congress Party under the leadership of Rajiv Gandhi in the national elections, a new coalition government, led by V. P. Singh, tried to infuse a new spirit into the New Delhi–Kathmandu relationship. 'Special security relations' were re-established during Prime Minister K. P. Bhattarai's visit to India in

June 1990. Bhattarai conceded that irritants to the Trade and Transit Treaty had adversely affected the bilateral security relationship. When Nepalese Prime Minister G. P. Koirala visited India in December 1991, he underlined the need for retrieving the special ties between the two countries by dispelling the lingering suspicions they had harboured against each other. His visit not only resulted in the signing of two separate trade and transit treaties (earlier it was a single trade and transit treaty) but also paved the way for restructuring the fractured bilateral ties on a firm basis. The Transit Treaty is renewed every seven years, and the Trade Treaty, every five years.

The Trade Treaty, revised in 1996, was a 'turning point' that enabled Nepal to expand its industrial base and to attract Indian investment. Although Nepal has a large trade deficit with India, New Delhi's readiness to revise the trade treaty is likely to open up new avenues for enhancing bilateral trade. As mentioned earlier, the revised Trade Treaty and Agreement on Cooperation to Control Unauthorized Trade will not only facilitate greater access to Nepalese goods in India but will also enable Nepal to forge new ties with Indian exporters, which will encourage Kathmandu to further open up its internal market to the outside world.

Despite these signs of optimism, the new Nepalese government will need to address India's concerns over the ISI's expanding network in Nepal. Both India and Nepal need to evolve long-term planning and strategy to effectively offset overt or covert militant and insurgent activities and ensure that the borders remain calm and peaceful. The Indian government has repeatedly alleged that the ISI established its robust network in Nepal in order to pursue its anti-India activities. This claim is a cause of tension in the security relationship between New Delhi and Kathmandu. There is also a possibility that the ISI, having consolidated its strategic presence in Nepal, might extend its network to another Himalayan state, Bhutan, with which India shares a 699-kilometre border.

India-Bangladesh Relations

India–Bangladesh relations are characterized by common historical experiences of British colonialism, close historical and cultural linkages, and geographical proximity. India shares a land border of 4,096 kilometres, and a maritime border of 180 kilometres with Bangladesh, which is a landlocked country, bound by India on three sides: north, east, and west. This virtually makes Bangladesh dependent on India for exploitation and utilization of water resources as well as for uninhibited access to the Bay of Bengal for communication with and transportation to the outside world. Also, India and Bangladesh are co-states in the Ganges and the Brahmaputra river basins, which inevitably make them mutually dependent.

It is an undeniable historic fact that India played a key role in the establishment of Bangladesh as an independent sovereign nation in December 1971 and provided shelter to ten million Bangladeshi refugees. India lost nearly twenty thousand soldiers in its efforts to help Bangladesh seek independence from Pakistan. Sheikh Mujibur Rahman, the founding father of Bangladesh, paid rich tributes to Indian soldiers for their supreme sacrifices and expressed his deepest gratitude to India for extending its unconditional military, material, and moral succour to the liberation of Bangladesh.

India–Bangladesh relations began on a positive note with the historic state visit of Prime Minister Indira Gandhi to Bangladesh in March 1972. Prime Minister Sheikh Mujibur Rahman gave her a rousing reception in Dhaka. He again acknowledged his country's indebtedness to India's heroic role in Bangladesh's freedom struggle. Both leaders signed the Treaty of Friendship, Cooperation and Peace on 19 March 1972, for a period of twenty-five years, declaring to maintain fraternal and good-neighbourly relations and transform their border into one of eternal peace and friendship. In a joint declaration issued on 19 March 1972, both leaders agreed to set up a permanent Joint River Commission to ensure the 'equitable sharing' of water resources. Pursuant to it, the Commission was established in November 1972.

The flowering relations between New Delhi and Dhaka did not last long. Hard-line nationalists and conservative Muslims in Bangladesh accused Sheikh Mujib of tilting toward India and disapproved of his declaring Bangladesh a secular and socialist state, which, in their perception, was a rejection of Islamic ideology. After the assassination of Sheikh Mujib Rahman on 15 August 1975, a series of coups and counter-coups took place in Bangladesh. In this murky situation, India–Bangladesh ties turned sour with General Ziaur Rahman's coming into power through a military coup staged in November 1975. He soon reversed Sheikh Mujib's state policy of secularism and socialism, and made Islamic ideology the basis of the state. Tensions started brewing up between the two countries for a host of reasons, which included a continual anti-India tirade, Dhaka's closer strategic and security ties with Islamabad and Beijing, Bangladeshi illegal migration, and border skirmishes.

After the assassination of President Ziaur Rahman in May 1981, following yet another military coup engineered by General H. M. Irshad in March 1982, a new turn took place in the Dhaka–New Delhi relationship with the signing of the Agreement on Inland Water Transit in 1984 for the development and maintenance of inland waterways. Nevertheless, a host of outstanding, unresolved bilateral issues came to the fore. These included the repatriation of Bangladeshi Chakama refugees, the Teen Bigha corridor, and the sharing of Ganges water on the Farakka Barrage.

The Chakma refugees, hailing from Chittagong Hill Tracts in the southern part of Bangladesh, fled to India's northeastern sector in the late 1980s and early 1990s, following their persecution and the confiscation of their landed property by dominant Bengali Muslims. The influx of the Chakma refugees caused a severe financial burden on the exchequers of India's central and state governments. The problem further intensified when the Chakma refugees were found forging close ties with Indian insurgents in the states of Assam, Tripura, Manipur, and Nagaland. Over a protracted period of negotiations between the Bangladesh government and the refugee leaders, the problem was resolved in February 1997 with a twenty-point economic package for the resettlement of fifty thousand Chakma refugees.

Another bilateral issue that rocked the New Delhi–Dhaka relationship pertained to the transfer of the Tin Bigha Corridor, a 178×85-metres piece of land in the Cooch Behar District in the state of West Bengal, to facilitate the connection of the Angarpota and Dahagram enclaves to their mainland. This issue was resolved in June 1992 with the transfer of a 'corridor to Bangladesh on a perpetual lease' in accordance with the 1972 and 1984 agreements between New Delhi and Dhaka. On the sovereignty question, the Indian Supreme Court maintained that leasing the Tin Bigha to Bangladesh did not amount to a dilution of India's sovereignty. The Court was emphatic in its judgement, stating that no right to administer the Tin Bigha had been granted to Bangladesh, nor had it been given the right to construct buildings or fortifications therein.

The Ganges Water Issue

A more complex issue that remained a constant source of friction between Bangladesh and India was over the distribution of the Ganges water.The controversy initially arose over India's construction of the Farakka Barrage near Monohorpur in 1975 to protect the Calcutta port from silting during the lean season. An interim agreement was signed in 1977 between the two governments on the sharing of Farakka water to enable Bangladesh to utilize a maximum quantity of water except during the dry season. A Memorandum of Understanding (MoU) was signed between India and Bangladesh to work out modalities of 'reasonable and equitable' utilization of the Ganges waters. However, the Bangladesh government quite often accused India of blocking the Ganges water. According to the *Banglapedia*:

> The efforts at negotiation broke down in September 1976, and Bangladesh decided to internationalize the issue. It was first raised at the Islamic Foreign Ministers' Conference in Istanbul in May 1976, and then at the summit of Non-Aligned Movement (NAM) in Colombo in August of the same year. Bangladesh's decision to raise the issue at the 31st Session of the UN General Assembly in 1976, led to a flurry of diplomatic activities. At the request of Senegal, Australia, and Sri Lanka, the Political Committee of UN General Assembly urged upon India and Bangladesh to settle the issue amicably. At the initiative of Syria, Egypt, Sri Lanka, Algeria, and Guyana, both India and Bangladesh agreed to sit at Dhaka for talks. But negotiations produced no positive results.[12]

The New Delhi–Dhaka relationship received a further setback when Prime Minister Begum Khalida Zia sought to internationalize the issue by raising it at the UN in October 1995. She lambasted the Indian government for the unilateral withdrawal of the Ganges water, causing chronic problems of desertification, environmental degradation, and unemployment in Bangladesh. The Indian government dismissed these charges as a complete canard. However, with a change of political regime in Bangladesh, the issue was resolved when Bangladeshi Prime Minister Sheikh Hasina and her Indian counterpart, H. D. Deve Gowda, signed a thirty-year Treaty on Sharing of the Ganges Waters in New Delhi on 12 December 1996.

The treaty was a major breakthrough in the hitherto ruptured ties between the two countries. Further, the secretaries of the water resources of both countries met in New Delhi in August 2007 to discuss the pending issues in water resources sector. In addition, a separate technical-level meeting, headed by members of the India–Bangladesh Joint Rivers Commission, was held in Dhaka on 25–27 September 2007 to discuss the modalities of sharing the Teesta River water. Both governments discussed pragmatic measures to be taken to ensure the equitable sharing of the Ganges water at the Thirty-Sixth Joint Committee meeting held in Dhaka on 26–29 May 2007.[13] However, 'Dhaka's biggest grouse is that while there is a water-sharing accord with regard to the Ganges, similar accords are also needed for the remaining 53 rivers.'[14]

Misuse of Bangladesh Territory Against India

India-Bangladesh relations have been adversely affected by the anti-India activities of the ISI on Bangladeshi soil in conjunction with Indian insurgent groups such as ULFA and NSCN, causing internal security problems for India. To deal with it, India and Bangladesh held a series of bilateral dialogues at the high-official level. In April 2003, Indian Foreign Secretary Kanwal Sibal went to Dhaka to meet his Bangladeshi counterpart, Shamsher Mobin Chowdhury, to discuss outstanding bilateral issues, especially that of Indian insurgents operating from Bangladesh. In addition, the home secretaries of the two governments met in Dhaka in September 2004. They discussed a wide range of bilateral issues concerning the national security of each country, including cross-border insurgency, illegal immigration, drug trafficking, and smuggling. The Indian home secretary especially drew the attention of his Bangladeshi counterpart to the massive unabated illegal immigration from Bangladesh into India. It is unofficially estimated that twenty million Bangladeshis are living illegally in different parts of India. Also, India has sought extradition of ULFA General Secretary Anup Chetia who fled to Dhaka in 1997. Though he was sentenced for illegal entry into Bangladesh and was released after completing his jail term, Dhaka has refused to hand him over because there is no extradition treaty between the two countries.

Instead of handing over Chetia to India, anti-India forces in Bangladesh are alleged by some sections in New Delhi to be actively trying for his political asylum. At the consultative talks held in New Delhi in June 2005 between India's Foreign Secretary Shyam Saran and his Bangladeshi counterpart, Hemayet Uddin, both secretaries focussed on the imperative of the peaceful management of the borders and the prevention of illegal Bangladeshi immigrants from sneaking into India. During his visit to Dhaka in August 2006, Foreign Secretary Sharan met Prime Minister Begum Khaliada Zia and apprised her of New Delhi's sensitivities to the presence of ISI-sponsored camps in Bangladesh that train Indian insurgents. Prime Minister Zia flatly denied the charge, despite India's submission of massive evidence of anti-India activities carried out by insurgents in the region northeast of Bangladesh. India has even handed over to Bangladesh a list of more than 170 insurgent camps inside Bangladesh and has provided sufficient evidence in the form of maps and exact locations of these camps. Nevertheless, no concrete action has been taken on the list by the Bangladeshi government. Indian intelligence agencies claim that the ISI and various militant organizations based in

Pakistan have changed their modus operandi and are now using Bangladesh as a transit point for pushing terrorists into India.[15]

This apart, India's border-security force submitted a list of 195 camps, run from Bangladeshi territory, to the Bangladesh Rifles (BDR) in August 2004, which the latter denied. On the other hand, Bangladesh also gave a list of 39 anti-Bangladesh camps, allegedly active on Indian soil.[16] Amid the battle of charges and countercharges, India continued to reiterate its serious concern at the activities of Indian Insurgent Groups (IIGs) in Bangladesh. At the eighth home-secretary-level talks held in New Delhi on 2–3 August 2007, India pointed out incidents of terrorism in India with clear links to the Bangladesh-based HuJI and JMB. India also underscored the need for sustained action by Bangladesh against elements indulging in cross-border terrorism. Both countries agreed to designate nodal points for the continuous and regular sharing of real-time and actionable information in the area of mutual security concerns.[17] According to the *Bangladesh Assessment* 2008:

> It is useful to recall that HuJI-B, involved in a number of recent terrorist incidents in India, has deep linkages with terrorist organizations based in Pakistan, including al-Qaeda, which constitutes a significant international terrorist threat, and figures in the US State Department's list of 'other terrorist groups'. Towards the end of 2007, however, the interim government appeared to have initiated some action against this group as well. On October 28–29, nine suspected HuJI-B militants were arrested from Narsingdi, Jhenidah, Magura, Khulna and Dhaka along with 60 kilograms of explosives, 16 grenades, rifles, handguns, various kinds of equipment and ammunition. Whether the arrest was a result of the interim government's deliberate attempt at pursuing the outfit, or a mere accident, however, remained unclear, and it is notable that the regime is yet to act with a firmness comparable to that shown in the case of the JMB-JMJB, against the HUJI-B leadership.[18]

India's Home Minister, P. Chidambaram, while voicing his concern about the growing anti-India activities emanating from Bangladesh, stated in the parliament on 15 December 2008 that Bangladesh must stop anti-India insurgency groups from using its territory. He cautioned that the sheltering of insurgents might recoil on Dhaka. In particular, he cited the Harkat-ul-Jihad-al-Islami (HuJI) and said that Bangladesh was duty-bound to control its activities, particularly as there was enough intelligence input to suggest that the HuJI had links with banned outfits such as the United Liberation Front of Assom and the National Democratic Front of Boroland.[19] Chidambaram identified five issues that needed to be addressed urgently to deal with terrorism in the northeast: illegal immigration from Bangladesh, tardy progress of border fencing, lack of development of the region for a variety of reasons, a perception of pervasive corruption, and tardy implementation of the National Identity Card Programme.[20]

Border Security Management

In order to prevent infiltration, narcotics and weapons smuggling, and insurgent activities from across the border, India launched, more than a decade ago, a massive project of erecting fencing along its 4,096-kilometre border with Bangladesh. The border is being fenced in Assam, Meghalaya, Mizoram, Tripura, and West Bengal. It is a gigantic task, filled with attendant problems of a varied nature, including the displacement of the people and their immovable properties, and more prominently, the problem of an alignment for topographical reasons. At the same time, the Bangladeshi government has charged India with violating a 1975 agreement under which no defensive structures would be raised within 150 yards of the zero line.

Exchange of fire between the BSF and BDR has become a regular feature, causing tension between two countries. Their relations were considerably strained in April 2001, following the BDR's unprovoked firing on Indian security forces in the border village of Pyrdiwah in India's northeastern state of Meghalaya. The BDR claimed that the village belonged to Bangladesh and had been illegally occupied by India during the 1971 Indo-Pakistan war. The BDR occupied the village and killed sixteen BSF men. These border clashes led to accusations and counter-accusations on both sides. The Indian government lodged a strong protest with the Dhaka government. Pursuant to an intensive diplomatic exercise on both sides, the tense situation was de-escalated. The Bangladeshi prime minister agreed to maintain the status quo ante following which the BDR withdrew from Pyrdiwah, and Indian BSF personnel pulled out of the Boriabari area in retaliation for the BDR's occupation of Pyrdiwah village. Sheikh Hasina realized the danger of the escalation of tension in Indo-Bangladeshi relations.

The Dhaka government promised to investigate the causes of the border clashes in which the BSF suffered heavy casualties while the BDR lost two of its personnel. The bodies of BSF personnel were found decomposed and mutilated when they were returned by the

BDR. The entire episode is believed to be the handywork of forces hostile to good-neighbourly relations between India and Bangladesh. Some Indian strategic analysts clearly see behind it the dirty game of the Pakistani ISI,[21] which is already active in Bangladesh, where it encourages and supports insurgent activities in the northeastern part of India.

Following the armed clashes between the BSF and the Bangladesh Rifles (BDR), the BSF director, General Ranjit Sekhar Mooshahary, visited border areas in the northeastern states in May 2005 to take stock of the situation. The BDR objected to fencing in more than a hundred places along the border with Tripura, arguing that India had erected them within 150 yards of the border, violating the 1975 Indo-Bangladeshi border guidelines.[22] But India clarified that in most places the fencing had been erected more than 150 yards from the zero line. Both governments are in touch with each other to resolve the contested claims.

The border issue also came up in the discussion with Bangladeshi Foreign Minister M. Morshed Khan during Indian External Affairs Minister Natwar Singh's visit to Dhaka in August 2005. While acknowledging that there existed 'some differences' in the interpretation of the 1975 border guidelines, both sides agreed to maintain peaceful borders free from illegal movements, a step necessary to prevent huge revenue losses on both sides.[23]

According to India's BSF officials, Dhaka initially put up stiff resistance to fencing in seventy-five places along the international border in the Northeast, but has recently allowed the work to continue in forty-six places. Official sources said that the BSF drew the attention of Union Home Minister P. Chidambaram to a large-scale influx from across the border during a top security meeting held in Guwahati on 2 January 2009. The BSF pointed out that only 91 kilometres of the border have been fenced and work is still in progress on 129 kilometres of the 577-kilometre Bangladeshi border in Assam and Meghalaya, a portion seen as the most infiltration-prone.[24]

It may be mentioned here that in Phase I of the Indo-Bangladeshi fencing project, started in 1989, fencing was completed in an 854-kilometre area against the approved target of 857 kilometres. Phase II involved 2,429 kilometres of the total 4,096-kilometre-long border. Currently, Phase III is in progress in Assam's Dhubri district. Around 364 kilometres of the fencing that was constructed as part of Phase I of the project has been replaced as parts of the old fencing become outdated and damaged.[25] About 861 kilometres of fencing constructed under Phase I will be replaced by 31 March 2010. Chidambaram has conceded that the Centre was not satisfied with the progress of the fencing on the India–Bangladesh border and would take steps to speed up the project. While the Centre had decided to floodlight the entire fenced border, only a stretch of 277 kilometres has been completed so far as part of a pilot project.[26]

Economic and Trade Cooperation

India and Bangladesh have a common interest and objective to boost closer economic and trade cooperation between them. The first trade agreement was signed in March 1972. Since then they have signed over a dozen MoUs for expanding bilateral trade and economic cooperation.

India–Bangladesh economic ties have grown by 145 per cent in the last five years from about $1 billion in 2001–02 to $2.55 billion in 2006–07. India mooted the idea of a bilateral free-trade agreement (FTA) in 2002, and a draft proposal was sent to Bangladesh, though Dhaka has not yet decided on it despite two rounds of talks in 2003 and 2004.[27]

Although trade has been rapidly growing, Dhaka's major grouse is its massive trade deficit with India. India's exports to Bangladesh in 2002–03 stood at $1,250 million. Its imports were at a meagre $84 million. The trade deficit against Bangladesh widened from $867 million in 1999–2000 to $1,166 million.[28] Bangladesh's trade deficit with India in fiscal years 2001–02 to 2007–08 was US $12,278.26 million. According to Bangladeshi Commerce Minister Muhammad Faruq Khan, the country's trade deficit with India was $968.71 million in 2001–02; $1,274.18 million in 2002-03; $1,513.23 million in 2003–04; $1,881.59 million in 2004–05; $1,626.04 million in 2005–06; $1,979.59 million in 2006–07; and $3,034.92 million in 2007–08.[29]

He informed the House on 7 July 2009 of steps undertaken by the government to reduce the trade deficit with India:

> The government has undertaken different steps to reduce the trade deficit with India. The measures include initiatives to export more duty-free commodities to India under the South Asia Free Trade Arrangement, formation of joint-secretary-level Joint Working Group on Trade for removal of non-tariff barrier, steps for development of physical infrastructure of land customs stations and road infrastructure to expand land trade between the two countries.[30]

Moreover, Bangladesh's exports to India are estimated to touch the mark of $1 billion by the end of 2011. Also, Bangladesh does not find much advantage in entering into a free-trade agreement (FTA) with India. Rather, it prefers a broad-based liberalization of long-term economic benefits to the country.

On the energy front, India can explore avenues for energy cooperation with Bangladesh, which is rich in natural-gas resources. Petroleum and Natural Gas Minister Mani Shankar Aiyar met his Bangladeshi counterpart A. K. M. Mosharraf Hossain in Yangon in Myanmar on 12–13 January 2005 to attend the tripartite conference called by the Myanmar government to discuss cooperation in developing regional energy resources and infrastructure. Hossain raised the following issues on bilateral cooperation between the two countries with his Indian counterpart, Mani Shankar Aiyer.

i. Transmission of hydro-electricity from Nepal and Bhutan to Bangladesh through Indian territory;
ii. Corridor for supply of commodities between Nepal, Bhutan, and Bangladesh through Indian territory; and
iii. To take necessary measures to reduce trade imbalance between the two countries.[31]

Aiyer reassured his Bangladeshi counterpart that India would examine his government's proposals. Regarding Bangladesh's concern at rectifying the balance of trade, he acknowledged that there was an inescapable need to expand bilateral trade between the two countries in order to narrow the trade gap.

Indian External Affairs Minister K. Natwar Singh's visit to Bangladesh in August 2005 was an attempt at reshaping the 'common destiny' for the better.[32] Leaders of both countries agreed that there was a great potential for expanding two-way trade and investment in education, science, and technology. Singh also expressed India's interest in holding talks on the Myanmar–India gas pipeline passing through Bangladesh as part of India's energy security project. But the Dhaka government demanded, in exchange, a land route to Myanmar through Indian territory as one of the conditions to concretize the gas pipeline proposal. India is reluctant to accept that demand mainly due to the China factor.

According to a report of *India News Online* of 8 August 2005, Bangladesh toned down its pre-conditions on the gas pipeline. Earlier, Bangladesh had put forward three conditions for providing a transit facility through India to facilitate transmission of hydro-electricity from Nepal and Bhutan to Bangladesh, a corridor through India for trade between Bangladesh and Nepal/Bhutan, and measures to reduce the

$2 billion trade imbalance between Bangladesh and India. Though there was no official statement from Bangladesh regarding which condition was to be dropped, sources in the Indian Petroleum Ministry hinted at the possibility of the most contentious issue, relating to trade imbalance, being removed from the pre-conditions.[33] But imposing conditionality might have a negative fallout on energy cooperation between India and Bangladesh.

Although serious differences continue to persist regarding various issues, India and Bangladesh have an enormous opportunity to work together in the economic and trade fields as well as to harness natural resources to their mutual benefit. Bangladesh and India can boost both the value and volume of trade through border trade, eco-tourism, and the aviation business, as suggested by a high-powered Indian business delegation visiting Bangladesh in July 2009. They urged the government of Bangladesh to increase connectivity between the two countries to enhance bilateral and regional trade. Also, Bangladesh Commerce Minister Muhammad Faruk Khan asked the Indian side to remove non-tariff barriers from Bangladesh exports so that the trade gap could be narrowed.[34]

In addition, both countries need to sort out through mutual consultation the problem of the demarcation of the maritime boundary so that their respective economic interests can be protected by judiciously sharing the products and resources of the area. Furthermore, they need to realize the inevitability of geostrategic interdependence in order to promote their respective national interests.

Indo-Sri Lankan Relations

Indo-Sri Lankan relations are rooted in their shared history, cultural commonality, and geographical proximity. Strategically, Sri Lanka occupies an important place in the security of India and South Asia. Sri Lanka, an island state, is situated in the south of the Indian Ocean. Its distance from the southeastern coast of India is twenty-two miles. Sri Lanka's Trincomalee Harbour has always remained a central focus of major powers. The harbour during the Cold War period was considered by the extra-regional powers to be strategically indispensable to carrying out signals intelligence, as evident from the SIGNIT facility established by the United States and the Soviet Union. According to a former Indian diplomat, the governments of the United States and United Kingdom were serious about bringing their warships into Colombo, Trincomalee, and the Gulf.[35]

Indo-Sri Lankan relations have witnessed vicissitudes on myriad issues, notably on the 1983 ethnic conflict, following the discriminatory policies practised by the Sinhalese ruling elites against Sri Lankan Tamils of Indian origin, constituting 18 per cent of the ethnic composition. In the ethnic clashes, thousands of civilians were killed. Minority groups lost confidence in the post-colonial political culture of the 'majoritarian autarchy' in Sri Lanka. As such, the 'Tamil frustration' started deepening in the unitary structure of the state.

Gradually, the ethnic violence against the Tamils created a permanent cultural wedge between Tamils and Sinhalese and gave rise to militancy. Velupillai Prabhakaran launched the Tamil movement by setting up the Liberation Tigers of Tamil Eelam (LTTE) in 1976. The LTTE's one-point demand was for a separate state in the northeastern region of Sri Lanka where Tamils were in an overwhelming majority. The Sri Lankan government rejected its demand outright. When the internal security situation took a turn for the worst, Sri Lankan President Junius Richard Jayawardene urged India to come to his rescue, although India's mediatory role in peace talks between the Sri Lankan government and Tamil militants had failed in 1985. However, after intensive deliberations between New Delhi and Colombo, Prime Minister Rajiv Gandhi and President Jayawardene signed the Indo-Sri Lankan Accord on 29 July 1987. Under Indian pressure, Prabhakaran endorsed the accord and agreed to lay down arms and accept the devolution of power on a provincial basis.[36] Also, as part of the peace-building process, the Sri Lankan government gave assent to the sixteenth amendment to the constitution under which the Tamil language was assigned the status of an official language.

Under the Indo-Sri Lankan Accord, Rajiv Gandhi ordered Indian peace-keeping forces (IPKF) to help maintain law and order in the country, especially in the troubled region of the northeastern provinces of Sri Lanka. But the political situation in Colombo took a new turn with the election of Rana Singhe Premdasa as president in the December 1988 national elections. As he had promised during the election campaign, he asked the Indian government to withdraw its forces, which in his perception constituted a violation of Sri Lankan sovereignty. He also threatened not to participate in the SAARC summits unless India withdrew its forces. Under these circumstances, India was forced to withdraw the IPKF in March 1990, which facilitated the easing of tension between New Delhi and Colombo. However, the IPKF had failed in its strategic mission in which thousands of Indian soldiers lost their lives. That was a great failure of Indian diplomacy; it had not learned appropriate lessons from the abysmal failure of the United

States' intervention in Vietnam, and of the Soviet Union's intervention in Afghanistan.

After the assassination of former Prime Minister Rajiv Gandhi by the LTTE in May 1991 in retaliation for IPKF 'atrocities' perpetrated on the Tamils, India embarked on a cautious policy of non-interference in Sri Lanka's internal affairs. Prime Minister P. V. Narsimha Rao categorically stated that the ethnic problem was Sri Lanka's internal matter and India would not do anything that might cause unnecessary tension in Indo-Sri Lankan relations. Successive governments in New Delhi virtually followed that policy of non-interference in Sri Lanka's internal matters.

With President Chandrika Kumaratunga's coming to power in 1994, a sense of optimism prevailed in the country about an early end to the civil war. She offered a peace package to the LTTE, which included granting greater political autonomy to Tamils within the country's constitutional framework. But the LTTE supremo, V. Prabhakaran, spurned the offer, reiterating his demand for a separate homeland for Sri Lankan Tamils. It set back the efforts to end the ethnic conflict.

The situation in Sri Lanka took an unprecedented turn in May 2000 when more than twenty-five thousand Sri Lankan troops were trapped in the Jaffna peninsula where the LTTE was strategically in a better position to capture them. Given the gravity of the security situation, the Sri Lankan government appealed to India for immediate help to evacuate their trapped soldiers. But the NDA government led by Prime Minister A. B. Vajpayee flatly refused to militarily intervene in view of India's bitter experience of the IPKF's miserable failure. India's Foreign Minister Jaswant Singh went to Colombo in June 2000 on a diplomatic mission to take stock of the situation there. He held wide-ranging discussions with Sri Lankan President Chandrika Kumartunga, her foreign minister, and other prominent political leaders. Singh conveyed Prime Minister Vajpayee's message to Kumartunga that although India was in favour of resolving the conflict through political dialogue with the LTTE's supremo, V. Prabhakaran, New Delhi would not supply military hardware to Colombo. Not surprisingly, India's refusal to provide military assistance to Sri Lanka facilitated China's strategic presence in the region. China readily agreed to supply weapons to Sri Lanka, which naturally eroded India's strategic and diplomatic role and limited its options in facilitating the resolution of the ethnic conflict in Sri Lanka.

The Indian strategic community charged the NDA government with adopting a myopic stance toward Sri Lanka under political pressure from Tamilnadu's AIDMK government—one of the key allies of the

NDA—to appease that country. The exigencies of the coalition government forced Prime Minister Vajpayee not to consider India's long-term national interests concerning defence and security relations with Sri Lanka. Moreover, India's reluctance to play a proactive diplomatic role in diffusing the ethnic crisis in Sri Lanka after the IPKF's strategic failure was shortsighted. India exposed to the outside world the fact that it was incompetent to manage even regional affairs while, at the same time, entertaining the ambition to play a much larger role in global affairs. That criticism was fair and justifiable.

India's stoic silence over the continuing ethnic crisis facilitated the role of Norway as a mediator, resulting in a ceasefire agreement between the Sri Lankan government and the LTTE in February 2002. Both parties agreed to abstain from 'offensive military operations'. Pursuant to the agreement, peace talks were held in Thailand and Japan, arousing some hope for a political settlement of the long-standing ethnic conflict. After six rounds of talks, the LTTE suspended its participation in the peace dialogue. Meanwhile, the European Union's decision to place the LTTE on its list of terrorist organizations was intended to prevent Norway from playing the role of mediator. As reported by the *Sunday Times*:

> After President Mahinda Rajapaksa was elected to office, he resumed the peace process with two rounds of peace talks in Geneva in February and April 2006. However, the third round of talks which was scheduled to be in the Norwegian capital, Oslo, from June 8–9, never took place even though both delegations arrived there for the talks. The LTTE delegation refused to attend the talks, saying the delegation was under-represented.[37]

President Rajpaksa was convinced, contrary to the perceptions of his predecessors, that the ethnic conflict could not be resolved through a peace dialogue with the LTTE. As a hard conservative and pragmatic leader, he devised the strategy of weakening the LTTE through both military and political means.

His visits to New Delhi in December 2005, April 2007 (SAARC Summit) and October 2007 (*Hindustan Times* Leadership Summit), provided him several opportunities to interact with Indian political leaders, including Prime Minister Manmohan Singh, and to learn their views on ending the ethnic conflict. They made it clear to Rajpaksa that India was not in favour of a military solution to the conflict. 'India expressed its conviction that there is no military solution to the ethnic problem in Sri Lanka and the only way out is a negotiated, political settlement acceptable to all communities in Sri Lanka.'[38]

Realistically enough, Rajpaksa did not heed the Indian advice. He deployed armed forces to crush the backbone of the LTTE in order to clear the northeastern province of the LTTE's influence. Having achieved initial successes, Rajpaksa was emboldened to wipe out the LTTE quickly. In his message to the LTTE, he asked Prabhakaran to surrender and lay down arms to pave the way for facilitating the democratic process so that the hardships of Tamil civilians could be mitigated. Regarding the Tamil question in Sri Lanka, Rajpaksa said, 'there are no military solutions to political questions.'[39] In light of the Sri Lankan forces' successful operations against the LTTE, he re-emphasized the point that the solution had to be given to the Tamil people, not to the LTTE. He said, 'What is the use of giving a solution to terrorists? They are not giving up terrorism.'[40]

The Indian government kept a close vigil on the developments taking place in Sri Lanka. Tamil Nadu's Chief Minister M. Karunanidhi put pressure on the UPA government to ask the Sri Lankan government to exercise the utmost restraint on the use of force against Sri Lankan Tamils who were facing enormous problems with the introduction of the registration system for Tamils. The registration was made compulsory for those Tamils who were from the northeastern areas and had migrated to other parts of Sri Lanka. India's National Security Advisor M. K. Narayanan called Sri Lanka's deputy high commissioner in New Delhi in October 2008 to convey New Delhi's serious concern about the plight of Tamils living in Sri Lanka.

Jehan Perera notes that the Sri Lankan government's military victory at Thoppigala and the recapture of the east had given a 'temporary respite' to the government but stressed that 'the best hope of ... achieving the basis for a political solution today is for the Sri Lankan polity, including civil society, to seek the re-invigoration of the All Party Conference process aimed at generating the framework of a lasting political solution.'[41]

Sri Lankan forces ultimately succeeded in their military campaign, launched after August 2006, by destroying the assets and capabilities of the LTTE cadre with the killing of its supremo, Velupillai Prabhakaran, and his top lieutenants on 18 May 2009. President Rajpaksa confirmed the death of Prabhakaran, while sharing the news on the telephone with India's External Affairs Minister Pranab Mukherjee.[42]

The LTTE was the ultimate loser in a civil war lasting over two decades, although it was in a better bargaining position at the time of the 2002 ceasefire agreement when it was militarily strong and politically assertive. That past is over now. In the post-conflict scenario, the Sri Lankan government needs to provide a healing touch to the Tamils by granting them equal rights so that they can live with dignity. An editorial in *The Hindu* noted:

> Now in the post-Prabhakaran era, he [President Rajpaksa] needs to address two big tasks: rehabilitation of hundreds of thousands of Tamils who have been through a prolonged nightmare, and crafting an enduring political solution based on far-going devolution of power to the Tamils in their areas of historical habitation.[43]

New Delhi is also concerned about the welfare of nearly 300,000 displaced civilians. National Security Advisor M. K. Narayanan and Foreign Secretary Shiv Shankar Menon arrived in Colombo and met Sri Lankan authorities, including President Rajpaksa, on 21 May 2009 to exchange views on many and varied issues, especially the humanitarian crisis following the end of the war with the LTTE cadre. 'India and Sri Lanka are on the same wavelength over the need for an early political package to address the legitimate aspirations of Tamils and other minorities in the island state.'[44] Rajpaksa in his address to the nation on 19 May 2009 stated:

> At this victorious moment, it is necessary for us to state with great responsibility that we do not accept a military solution as the final solution … the responsibility that we accept after freeing the Tamil people from the LTTE is a responsibility that no government in the history of Sri Lanka has accepted.[45]

Rajpaksa categorically stated that the solution to the problems of the Tamils and other minority sections could not be an 'imported one', rather than an 'indigenous one'. In addition to Rs 25 crore offered by the Tamil Nadu government, New Delhi offered the Tamils a rehabilitation package of Rs 500 crore for war-displaced people, in addition to Prime Minister Manmohan Singh's relief package of Rs 100 crore. Further, India also reiterated that the root causes of the conflict should be addressed so that 'all communities in Sri Lanka, including the Tamils, could now feel at home and lead lives of dignity of their own free will'.[46]

Simultaneously, the Indian government ought to persuade the Sri Lankan government to adopt a cooperative rather than 'confrontational' approach to deal with the post-war situation in Sri Lanka. A major challenge facing Rajpaksa is the economic reconstruction of the hitherto war-ravaged northeastern provinces as well as the nation-building task of power-sharing and winning the hearts of the 'estranged Tamils'. As one political analyst has noted, 'Any meaningful political concessions to the Tamils and Muslim people by President Rajpaksa would not be viewed with suspicion. He is therefore in a position to introduce it without risk of a Sinhala backlash.'[47]

Conclusion

Given the fragile nature of sub-regional cooperation, India will have to anticipate and evaluate not only its wider implications for regional stability but will also have to reassess how solidly Nepal and Bangladesh will stand by India, perhaps depending on internal political conditions in Kathmandu and Dhaka. Whatever compulsions each country might have, they need to be adequately addressed within the parameters of their inevitable mutual geostrategic, geoeconomic, and geocultural interests.

Furthermore, Dhaka's failure to contain the growing rise of Islamic radicalism in Bangladesh could prove disastrous not only for Bangladesh but also for other South Asian states in general, and for India in particular. In addition, effective measures must be adopted at the regional level to curb the activities of insurgents through a cooperative security mechanism. Moreover, India has a greater responsibility to chart out the path of political reconciliation and positive engagement with smaller states of the region in order to reverse its widely held image among them as a 'regional hegemon'.

6

INDIA, THE UNITED STATES, AND SOUTH ASIA: EMERGING TRENDS AND STRATEGIC CHALLENGES

There have been persisting myths as well as deeply entrenched flawed notions about US policy toward South Asia. Until the end of the Cold War era the vast majority of South Asian scholars subscribed to the view that South Asia was a 'low priority' in US foreign policy. This view was based on an assessment that the region did not offer much incentive in terms of natural resources, diplomatic leverage, and economic and trade potential. Rather, it was considered a huge liability for the United States, given the congenital animosity between India and Pakistan. On the other hand, the proponents of realism argued that South Asia was geopolitically indispensable to the United States in order to maintain the balance of power in the region between India and Pakistan, the United States' Cold War military ally.

Without exaggeration, the triangular relationship among the United States, the Soviet Union, and China was a major factor in shaping the political, security, and strategic landscape of the South Asian region. India and China were at loggerheads with each other after the 1962 Sino-Indian War, prompting the formation of the China–Pakistan strategic axis against India. On the other hand, New Delhi's tilt toward Moscow, resulting in the 1971 Indo-Soviet Treaty of Peace, Friendship and Cooperation soured India's relations with the United States. Furthermore, the Soviet military invasion of Afghanistan in December 1979 obligated the United States to assign Pakistan the status of a frontline state, which enabled it to extract the maximum possible military assistance from United States. That not only disturbed the regional balance of power but also indirectly contributed to Islamabad's attainment of nuclear-weapons capability.

This chapter examines the waxing importance of South Asia for the United States in the post-9/11 security and strategic environment. It is argued that on the one hand, the tragic terrorist attacks on United States enhanced the strategic value of Pakistan in the United States' war on global terror. On the other hand, India's emergence as a rising global power is seen by the United States as an indispensable counterweight to China. The chapter also discusses problematic issues and disturbing trends in United States–South Asia equations.

Background

The United States' South Asia policy, right from the Cold War through the end of the Cold War to the post 9/11 world order, has been punctuated by its oscillating security and strategic concerns in the region. The Cold War psychology of the two superpowers fundamentally contributed to polarizing and militarizing South Asia in order to realize their respective political, security, and strategic interests and objectives. For example, by incorporating Pakistan into its military alliance system through SEATO and CENTO, the United States sought to create a balance of power structure in South Asia. In this respect, writes Howard B. Schaffer:

> The Eisenhower administration's decision in 1954 to welcome Pakistan into the US-led Western security system ushered in a new phase in American perceptions of its South Asian interests. The region, or at least Pakistan, now became important to US containment strategy. Initially, Washington saw Pakistan as part of a shield of northern-tier powers that would help the United States and Western allies safeguard 'Free World' interests in the Near East. But it soon perceived the country's security and well-being as important to US interests for their own sake.[1]

Contrary to the United States' assessment, its interests were ill served by drawing Pakistan into its strategic fold. First, US arms policy, tilting in favour of Pakistan, not only contributed to a perpetual hostility between India and Pakistan but also created occasional irritants between the two great democracies: New Delhi and Washington. Second, instead of containing the influence of Communist China in South Asia through its alliance systems, the United States' purblind policy brought Pakistan closer to China after the two countries entered into a border agreement in March 1963.

Viewed in hindsight, the United States' South Asia policy was not based on a long-term approach. Its short-sighted policy alienated Third World countries, mainly India, a founding member of the Non-Aligned Movement. However, there was a perceptible shift in the Kennedy administration's (1961–63) South Asia policy. Contrary to past stereotypes, the administration looked upon India's pivotal role as a leading non-aligned nation in building a peaceful world order. Further, Kennedy wanted to project a democratic India as a model of economic development with US assistance in order to refurbish the United States' image among developing nations. Third, to put it simply, Kennedy did not subscribe to his predecessors' assessment that India's non-aligned policy was responsible for creating ruptures in the New Delhi–Washington relationship. Instead, he believed that a non-aligned India was a major force for stability in the international system. Fourth, a major policy shift was reflected in the Kennedy administration's strategic postures toward India and Pakistan on the Kashmir issue and the 1962 Sino-Indian War. In the latter case, Kennedy argued that India needed US military assistance to protect India's borders against Communist China, which, in Kennedy's view, was a potential threat to the security and stability of South Asia.[2]

On the other hand, the Nixon administration's South Asia policy was heavily tilted toward Pakistan, which brought the New Delhi–Washington relationship to its lowest ebb, especially in the wake of the 1971 India–Pakistan war. The administration's indifference to the genocide perpetrated by the Pakistani military regime on the people of East Pakistan was a serious strategic and political blunder. Moreover, the dispatching of the Seventh Fleet to the Bay of Bengal proved ineffectual because the United States could not prevent the dismemberment of Pakistan in the December 1971 war. Further, the Nixon administration's 'misapplication of global strategy' in South Asia forced India to encourage Soviet influence in South Asia.[3] After the resignation of President Nixon over the Watergate scandal, Secretary of State Henry A. Kissinger, schooled in the politics of realism, recognized India as a 'pre-eminent power' in the region following India's first nuclear test conducted in May 1974. During his official trip to India in October 1974, he publicly recognized India's non-aligned policy for the first time and emphasized that the United States was desirous of cultivating friendly ties with New Delhi.

With a major transformation in South Asia's strategic environment following Soviet military intervention in Afghanistan in December 1979, the Reagan administration committed massive military assistance to Pakistan, a package worth $3.2 billion. This aid revived former grievances between India and the United States on the one hand and escalated tension between India and Pakistan on the other.

The Soviet invasion of Afghanistan proved a blessing in disguise for Pakistan. Islamabad diverted US financial aid to the development of a nuclear-weapons programme, though officially the Reagan administration continued to harp on its policy of nuclear non-proliferation. If dispassionately analyzed, the United States' arms aid, touching four billion dollars in 1986, not only contributed to the emergence of Pakistan as a nuclear-weapons state but also laid the foundation for breeding militancy and facilitated the rise of the Taliban as a global ideological phenomenon in the wake of Washington's efforts to combat Soviet intervention in Afghanistan.[4]

As mentioned before, the Reagan administration glossed over its non-proliferation goal in South Asia, knowing full well that Pakistan had a clandestine nuclear programme. So long as Soviet troops remained in Afghanistan, the administration did not slap sanctions on Pakistan under the Symington Amendment Act (1976) and the Glenn Amendment (1977). The Bush administration (1989–93), however, invoked the Pressler Amendment (1985) against Pakistan in October 1990 after the withdrawal of Soviet troops from Afghanistan in February 1989. The point to be underscored is this: the United States' double standards regarding its non-proliferation goal further hardened India's stance on the NPT. Though the Clinton administration (1993–2001) demonstrated its commitment to the non-proliferation goal by imposing sanctions on India and Pakistan after they conducted nuclear-weapons tests in May 1998, the administration amended its policy, asking India to sign the CTBT without freezing its nuclear-weapons programme.

The Bush Administration (2001–09)

The Bush (junior) administration brought about a fundamental transformation in US policy in South Asia by attaching greater importance to India than to Pakistan where its relationship was primarily confined to the military and strategic realm. In reality, the Bush administration looked upon India not only as a stabilizing factor in Asia but also as a force in shaping the new global balance of power. President Bush expressed the administration's intention to make India a 'major world power', although much to the chagrin of Pakistan, the United States' strategic ally. The policy shift might be attributed to two core factors. First, President Bush realized that India, ignored by his predecessors, could be a balancing factor in an emerging Asian order in which a rising China, in the administration's perception, posed a potential threat to US interests. Moreover, President Bush also realized that India did not constitute even a distant threat to the United States' security and strategic interests in the Asia–Pacific region. In his assessment, India, unlike China, was a self-satisfied power, which did not constitute a threat to the United States' global economic and technological supremacy. Second, given India's track record in nuclear non-proliferation, President Bush crafted a new nuclear-policy approach while dealing with India and Pakistan separately.[5]

Bush set aside a widely held assumption that India and Pakistan, being nuclear-armed states, posed a grave threat to international peace and security. Rather, he believed that nukes falling into the hands of non-state actors posed a bona fide threat to global and regional security. Furthermore, a huge shift was clearly visible in Bush's policy following the tragic events of 11 September 2001 that brought about a radical transformation in the global security and strategic environment.

Therefore, in his bid to transform US relations with India as a 'major global player', President Bush underlined the imperative of treating India—where global and regional issues were concerned—on a par with other major players such as Japan, China, and the European powers. No doubt, India and United States are coming closer with their rapidly expanding military cooperation. A new page in their relationship opened with the undertaking of joint military exercises by Indian and US commandos in Ladakh (Kashmir). These developments reinforce India and the United States' mutual strategic goals.[6]

The strategic relationship between New Delhi and Washington, if viewed in larger political, economic, military, defence, and security contexts, is based on shared expectations in realizing their respective national interests. The United States expects India to cooperate in promoting regional stability, strengthening the non-proliferation regime, reviving the peace dialogue with Pakistan, and increasing US entrepreneurs' access to Indian markets. On the other hand, India's desire to build 'deeper relations' with the United States is impelled by Indian expectations that the United States will extend full diplomatic support to India's candidacy for a permanent seat on the Security Council and use its influence over Pakistan to permanently end cross-border terrorism.

Despite shared security and strategic interests, the strategic partnership between India and the United States might face tough challenges from the lingering scepticism and narrowly structured perceptions of public policy makers and bureaucrats in both countries. On the question of arms-control measures, for example, the US bureaucracy's perception is that India is part of the problem rather than part of the solution in controlling the proliferation of weapons of mass destruction. Consequently, it sometimes causes hiccups in the New Delhi–Washington relationship.

On the other hand, government leaders and bureaucratic elites in India have a deeply entrenched perception that the United States has not done enough to help permanently end cross-border terrorism in Jammu and Kashmir in accordance with political assurances given to New Delhi, especially in the aftermath of the terrorist attacks on the Indian parliament in December 2001 and the Mumbai blasts in November 2008. Also, there is the widely held belief about the United States in the Indian community that it abandons its friends and allies once its objectives are fulfilled.[7] In this scenario of conflicting perceptions, a fundamental question to be addressed by policymakers in each country is how to develop mutual faith and trust.

The United States' Non-Proliferation Policy in South Asia

India's first underground nuclear explosion, conducted on 18 May 1974, triggered worldwide condemnation, led by the United States. US policy makers looked upon India's nuclear blast as a flagrant violation of the non-proliferation treaty (NPT).

The United States was at loggerheads with India because New Delhi had flatly refused to sign the NPT, arguing that the treaty was discriminatory and basically defective in nature. The White House strategic analysts were not convinced by the Indian argument. It may be mentioned that in order to halt the horizontal nuclear proliferation, the United States' federal government had enacted a series of legislative acts, such as the Symington Amendment (1976), the Glenn Amendment (1977), and the Pressler Amendment (1985).

In addition, nuclear-related technology exports to India were suspended under the 1978 Nuclear Non-Proliferation Act (NNPA), and the 1954 Atomic Energy Act because New Delhi had refused to place its nuclear facilities under the International Atomic Energy Agency's system of safeguards. On the other hand, Pakistan was subjected to sanctions under the Symington and Pressler Amendments, restricting economic and military aid to the country. Pakistan's woes were further magnified following additional US sanctions on it in light of Islamabad's clandestine import of China's medium-range missiles. Though the administration gradually lifted most non-military sanctions on bilateral and multilateral economic aid to India, sanctions on the transfer of nuclear fuel and reactors to India continued until the Section 123 agreement (of the US Atomic Energy Act of 1954) on civil nuclear cooperation with the United States was operationalised.

It might be recalled that President Bill Clinton imposed sanctions against India under the Glenn Amendment in May 1998 when India broke its self-imposed twenty-four-year moratorium on carrying out nuclear-weapon tests. Clinton invoked similar sanctions against Pakistan when it responded to India's tests by conducting six nuclear-weapons tests on 28 May and 30 May 1998 in order to demonstrate its nuclear prowess.

However, in the aftermath of the terrorist attacks on the United States on 11 September 2001, President Bush, while exercising his waiver authority, lifted all nuclear-related sanctions against India and Pakistan, arguing that 'certain sanctions' were not in the United States's national security interests. The rationale behind the presidential waiver was to elicit the strategic cooperation of Pakistan and India in the administration's declared policy of global war on terror. Pakistan agreed to provide intelligence and logistical support to the United States. *The New York Times* noted, 'In another show of support, Senator Joseph R. Biden Jr., Chairman of the Foreign Relations Committee, who had opposed the waiving of the sanctions against Pakistan, changed his mind after Pakistan said it would support the antiterrorist campaign.'[8] No doubt, in the aftermath of 9/11, the core threat to US homeland security principally emanated from terrorists. That is why President Bush quite often reiterated that possession of nuclear weapons by state actors constituted no existential threat to the United States. Rather, he was more concerned about what measures were to be undertaken to prevent weapons of mass destruction from falling into the hands of terrorist groups.

The India–United States Nuclear Deal

After signing the Henry J. Hyde United States–India Peaceful Atomic Energy Cooperation Act in December 2006, President George W. Bush said, 'The deal will help keep America safe by paving the way for India to join the global efforts to stop the spread of nuclear weapons.'[9] Bush elaborated that the nuclear deal would not only help meet India's energy requirements, the latter being the fifth largest consumer of the world's energy, but would also enable both countries to meet the security challenges of the twenty-first century. Indian Prime Minister Manmohan Singh hailed the deal as a 'landmark agreement' for ensuring global energy security as well as meeting the challenge of climate change. On 10 October 2008, India's External Affairs Minister Pranab Mukherjee and US Secretary of State Condoleezza Rice signed the 123 agreement that formally operationalised the 'path-breaking' bilateral nuclear deal. The agreement reflects the convergence of fundamental interests of both countries.[10] Mukherjee, booming with optimism, said that the 123 agreement would enable India to connect with the rest of the world in civil nuclear energy.

A long and heated controversy in both countries surrounded the India–United States nuclear deal. As regards India, the coalition government's leftist supporters unreasonably raised a hue and cry over the deal, arguing that India had mortgaged its nuclear sovereignty to the United States, thereby stalling the deal for a long time. Similarly, non-proliferation lobbyists in the United States attacked the Bush administration for rewarding India—a non-NPT member—by entering into a civil nuclear cooperation agreement with India. In fact, the India–United States nuclear deal represents a paradigm shift in the foreign policies of both India and the United States. The 45-member Nuclear Supplier Group's recent decision(September 2008) to grant a waiver to India has been described as a 'milestone'.

The United States described the granting of waiver to India by the Nuclear Suppliers Group as a 'landmark decision' for strengthening the non-proliferation regime and tackling the global challenge of clean energy. The waiver not only ended India's nuclear apartheid, which had lasted over three decades, but also enabled it to begin nuclear commerce with the international community. The perspective of M. K. Narayanan, a former national security advisor, was contrary to that of Indian Foreign Minister Pranab Mukherjee who said that India would not carry out nuclear-weapons tests in the future. Narayanan, however, clarified: 'We hope that we never have to conduct a nuclear test. But if the necessity arises we will conduct a test and we are prepared to do that. We have never compromised on our strategic interest.'[11]

This apart, the defence and security relationship between New Delhi and Washington introduced a new factor in South Asia, which, in the perception of the Indian strategic community, was a major departure in the United States' policy toward India. Since the beginning of the Malabar exercise series in 1992, India–United States defence cooperation has been rapidly expanding. It was further boosted with the signing of the New Framework for the United States–India Defence Relationship in June 2005. The agreement identified common interests and established an ambitious ten-year programme of shared objectives. In 2006, both countries created the India–United States Framework for Maritime Security Cooperation. Both countries pledged to jointly protect the free flow of commerce and to counter threats that could undermine maritime security. This includes piracy and armed robbery at sea; threats to the safety of ships, crew, and property; transnational organized crimes in all dimensions; illicit trafficking in weapons of mass destruction; and environmental degradation and natural disaster.[12]

Further, the Bush administration, in a bid to establish a military sales relationship with India, took a momentous decision to transfer an amphibious transport ship to India, and in 2008, India purchased a billion dollars' worth of transport aircraft from the United States.[13] This relationship caused a flutter in the power corridors of Islamabad, which could not stomach the fast-expanding defence and strategic cooperation between New Delhi and Washington. Pakistani military elites, in order to offset the ever-deepening India–United States military and security engagement, decided to turn to China for nuclear and military hardware. China has also positively responded to step up naval and military cooperation with Islamabad, as is evident from its construction of Pakistan's Gwadar Port with an estimated cost of $1.16 billion, of which China has contributed about $198 million for the first phase—almost four times the amount Pakistan has forked out for this phase—which includes construction of three multi-purpose ship berths. China has invested another $200 million toward building a highway connecting Gwadar Port with Pakistan's largest city, Karachi, which is also a port on the Arabian Sea.[14]

Not only this, China is engaged in conducting military activities in PAK, intending to encircle India in its northern region of Kashmir, which might have grave defence and security ramifications for India. Both New Delhi and Washington are closely keeping track of the evolving Pakistan–China strategic nexus and are striving to develop a counter-strategy based on their shared objectives and interests to offset the negative implications of the Islamabad–Beijing strategic understanding.

The Obama Administration

The Obama administration's South Asia policy is focused on Afghanistan and Pakistan to root out the Taliban and al-Qaeda. For this, Pakistan will remain indispensable to the United States' security strategy in South, Southwest, and Central Asia. The administration has further clarified that it will follow through its predecessor's policy of deepening defence and strategic cooperation with India. President Obama has assured India that civilian nuclear cooperation between the two countries will not be hampered. Both President Obama and his Secretary of State Hillary Clinton have reiterated that Washington's relationship with New Delhi is an integral component of the US policy of building a secure, stable, and peaceful global order.

However, the incontrovertible logic of some US public opinion makers is that India should not be rewarded by treating it as an exception on the question of the transfer of nuclear energy, dual-use technology, and military hardware, even though it has consistently refused to sign the NPT and CTBT. Undoubtedly, the nuclear-proliferation zealots have been striving hard to stymie the implementation of the 123 agreement of October 2008. On the eve of Hillary Clinton's visit to India in July 2009, *The New York Times*, in its editorial column, asked the Obama administration to adopt a tough stand against India on the nuclear issue as well as on its much-hyped non-aligned policy. At the same time, the editorial recommended that the administration address Pakistan's 'genuine security fears' and do something to help resolve the Kashmir dispute:

> One of our many concerns about the nuclear deal was that it would make it easier for India to expand its arsenal—and drive Pakistan to produce more of its own weapons. With access to global fuel markets, India can use its limited domestic uranium stocks for weapons. President Obama and Secretary Clinton both endorsed the deal. Now they have a responsibility to do what President George W. Bush never did: push India to stop producing more weapons fuel rather than waiting for a multinational treaty to be negotiated. That would make it easier to press Pakistan to do the same. Both India and Pakistan claim that they want only a 'minimal credible' nuclear deterrent—but who knows what that means?[15]

The editorial further commented that the Obama administration should ask India to abandon its pretentious non-aligned policy. It further wrote:

> India wants to be seen as a major world power. For that to happen, it will have to drop its pretensions to nonalignment and stake out strong and constructive positions. President Obama and Hilary Clinton say they consider India a vital partner

> in building a stable world. Now they have to encourage India to behave like one.[16]

Sumit Ganguly, who teaches at Indiana University in Bloomington, in his rejoinder to the above editorial's unwarranted moral preaching to the United States and India, wrote:

> Most importantly, despite the *Times'* jejune harangue that India was engaged in an arms race with Pakistan, the secretary and her entourage found ways to reach an agreement with India on the vexed issue of end-user agreements on weapons sales. Now two major American aerospace firms, Lockheed Martin and Boeing, which have both been vying for the largest, single Indian defence contract involving some 126 multi-role combat aircraft, will be able to compete without any hindrance.[17]

The editorial board of the *Christian Science Monitor*, writing in the context of Secretary Clinton's visit to New Delhi, has taunted that India, like other emerging powers, is still 'shy' of being an 'American ally' for fear of US interference in India's relations with its neighbours. It observed:

> And while India enjoys new US attention, it remains vigilant against any American meddling in its touchy ties with Pakistan, especially over the issues of Kashmir and Afghanistan. India is rightly worried that Pakistan's recent attempts to crack down on terrorists will extend only to those militants not interested in attacking India. Memories are still raw over last year's massive killings in Mumbai (Bombay) by a group of Pakistani gunmen.[18]

India's concerns about the Mumbai terror attack were fully noted by Hillary Clinton during her five-day visit to India in July 2009. She told Pakistan in unambiguous terms that it must dismantle 'terror outfits' such as Lashkar-e-Taiba. At the same time, she said that the administration was satisfied with Pakistan's efforts toward cracking down on the perpetrators of the Mumbai terrorist attacks. She said on 18 July 2009 in Mumbai, 'Much greater effort and commitment to combat terrorism has been seen at the government level.'[19] Secretary of State Clinton's views did not satisfy India. Her above remarks were interpreted by the Indian strategic community as an attempt to mollify Pakistan in order to galvanize its power elites to fight the Taliban and al-Qaeda militants and jihadis with greater vigour and force. On bilateral issues, including

Kashmir, between India and Pakistan, Clinton categorically stated that the United States was not involved in promoting any particular position.[20]

On the question of finalizing the 'arrangements and procedures' regarding the reprocessing of the spent fuel from US reactors, both India and the United States have yet to arrive at a final decision. India has asked for a one-year deadline until 21 July 2010 to reach an understanding on this issue. However, India's scepticism is rooted in its bitter experience over the Tarapur Atomic Power Station when the Carter administration stopped supplying uranium by invoking the 1978 Nuclear Non-Proliferation Act, although the United States was under a legal obligation to supply uranium for a period of thirty years from August 1963. Furthermore, India's consternation has been reinforced by President Barack Obama's move at the G-8 Summit, held in L'Aquila, Italy in July 2009, to make its leaders agree to prohibit the sale of enrichment and reprocessing (ENR) items to India despite the clear waiver India had received from the 45-member Nuclear Suppliers Group in September 2008.[21]

India's Atomic Energy Chairman Anil Kakodkar had cautioned the UPA government in advance that such a move was afoot, which, he said, was a 'breach of trust' and contrary to the 'spirit' of India's bilateral agreement with the United States.[22] The proposed conditions for enrichment and reprocessing (ENR) transfers include NPT adherence. 'The US also went on record last October (2008) to say getting NPT conditionality at the NSG was its top priority.'[23] Kakodkar sounded the UPA government about the United States' attempt at linking the ENR to NPT. He repeatedly argued that the ENR was a critical issue so far as India's national image and pride was concerned because India was being targeted for not signing the treaty. The United States-sponsored G-8 resolution, banning the export of enrichment and reprocessing materials and technology to India, was viewed as a return to policies designed to cap India's nuclear programme.[24]

Moreover, this situation might create irritants in the New Delhi–Washington relationship and might further accentuate mistrust between them. In fact, President Obama's move on the ENR issue reveals that his administration was more concerned with its agenda of non-proliferation than with ignoring India's open defiance of the United States' appeal to sign the NPT. In effect, it is tantamount to a reversal of President Bush's nuclear policy. As mentioned earlier, President Bush had declared the NPT 'irrelevant' in the wake of 9/11, arguing that the real threat emanated from non-state actors who might get hold of nuclear weapons.

The other three non-signatories to NPT—Pakistan, Israel and North Korea—have already been banned from acquiring any nuclear material or technology. But Kakodkar insisted that the NSG waiver was more important for India. Also, India needs to be sure that the waiver is not diluted by taking concerted action. In April 2009, President Obama laid out his vision of a world free of nuclear weapons and reaffirmed his commitment to strengthening the NPT. He sent a clear message to countries such as India that they should place their civilian and non-civilian nuclear facilities under the IAEA's system of safeguards. On 24 September 2009, President Obama chaired a special session of the UN Security Council, supporting the revitalizing of nuclear disarmament and non-proliferation. A draft resolution, put forth by the United States, was unanimously adopted by the fifteen-member council. The resolution called for strengthening the NPT regime and enhancing measures to prevent the illicit transfer of nuclear-weapons materials to terrorist groups.[25]

The resolution clearly intends that all states outside the NPT, including India, must sign it. This clearly amounts to the reversal of the India–United States Civil Nuclear Cooperation Agreement, signed during the Bush administration and under which India agreed to place its civilian nuclear reactors in the IAEA's system of safeguards.

During Secretary of State Clinton's visit to New Delhi in July 2009, three high-tech agreements were signed between India and the United States on 20 July 2009. These agreements are: the End-User Pact (for greater defence cooperation), the Technology Safeguards Agreement (TSA) in the space sector, and the Science and Technology Cooperation Agreement. This apart, India has approved two sites for setting up United States-made nuclear power stations.[26]

During her meeting with Prime Minister Manmohan Singh, Clinton expressed her desire to deepen the India–United States strategic partnership. She acknowledged that India and the United States entertained 'different perspectives' on certain global and regional issues, which needed to be sorted out through dialogue. The most contentious issue looming large between the two countries was Iran's nuclear programme. Both Clinton and Singh agreed that Iran's nuclear-weapons programme was a threat to global security.

As regards India-United States defence cooperation, a recent controversy arose around the conclusion of the India-United States End-Use Monitoring Agreement (EUMA), which was finalized during Hillary Clinton's visit:

> It involves US government inspectors continuously monitoring all high-tech weapons and advanced electronic systems and equipments across a broad front imported by India from the US to ensure that they are used by the Indian defence services and the Department of Atomic Energy and the Department of Space only for the purpose—'end use'—for which they are imported.[27]

Though Prime Minister Singh defended the agreement, arguing that it was in India's national security interests, the mainstream opposition, the Indian scientific community, and the media expressed serious reservations over EUMA's long-term implications for India's national security. Their objections to EUMA mainly hinged on the question of why the United States insisted on the end-use restriction under EUMA while in the past no other countries had done so when they transferred high-tech defence equipment to India. Russia, for example, never asked India to enter into such an agreement on the question of supplying Sukhoi-30 MKI supersonic fighter bombers and visual-range air-to-air missiles and assisted in building and designing India's nuclear-powered submarine, INS *Arihant*, which was dedicated to the nation in July 2009.[28] In this respect, Ashok Parthasarathi, a former science advisor to the late Prime Minister Indira Gandhi, writes:

> It is important to also note that all the three defence service chiefs have vehemently and repeatedly, verbally and in writing, individually and collectively conveyed to New Delhi at the highest levels their strong and total opposition to India entering into EUMA with the US because of its serious national security-comprising character. But the Cabinet Committee on Security chaired by the Prime Minister brushed aside these acute concerns and went ahead and approved EUMA.[29]This shows the puerile culture of the Indian breed of political class as well as the intellectual nervousness of bureaucratic elites while dealing with asymmetric power.

Primacy of Pakistan

In the post 9/11 security scenario, US policy toward South Asia was focused on Pakistan, a frontline strategic ally in fighting the global war on terror. President Bush's quick decision to attack Afghanistan in October 2001 was based on his strategic calculation that the United States would be able to defeat al-Qaeda with President Musharraf's undiluted military, intelligence, and logistical support to US forces fighting in Afghanistan. He had pinned his entire hopes on Musharraf, but the latter failed to deliver the expected result, mainly attributed to Musharraf's incoherent and half-hearted approach to deal with the Taliban and jihadists. Musharraf might have had his own exigencies, fearing to go beyond a particular point to break the close nexus between the Taliban and Pakistan's ISI.

It may be recalled that Senator Joseph Biden (now the vice-president) asked the administration to triple its non-military assistance to Pakistan from $500 million a year to $1.5 billion, and to provide a 'democracy dividend' of an additional $1 billion a year.[30] That would, in Biden's perception, enable Pakistan to stabilize itself economically and politically to fight the Taliban more vigorously. In this regard, the United States has already spent more than $11 billion on aid to Pakistan in the hope that the Musharraf-led government would be able to crush the Taliban and al-Qaeda elements operating from Afghanistan and Pakistan. But US hopes were dashed.

With the onset of the Obama administration in January 2009, new hopes were raised that the administration's fresh approach toward Afghanistan and Pakistan might be able to defeat the Taliban and al-Qaeda. Toward that goal, the Obama administration embarked upon the policy of extending economic assistance to Afghanistan and Pakistan to enable them to fight on multiple fronts: the Taliban, indigenous militant and jihadi groups, the ever-deepening political and economic turmoil, and the worsening internal security situation. In the Obama administration's assessment, Pakistan's failure to 'take action against the extremists could endanger its partnership with the United States as well as American strategy in neighbouring Afghanistan.'[31] As reported by De Young:

> Defence Secretary Robert M. Gates publicly expressed frustration over the reports that Taliban forces were getting stronger and pointed out that America needed appropriate actions to deal with them. He stated that Pakistan's stability was central to US efforts in neighbouring Afghanistan. Gates further added that Pakistan was also 'central' to the United States' future partnership with the government in Islamabad.[32]

But a critical problem facing the Obama administration is how to break the ISI's direct links with the Taliban. As reported by Mark Mazzetti and Eric Schmitt in *The New York Times*, 'there was an irrefutable proof of a direct nexus between the Taliban and Pakistan's

ISI, filtered through electronic surveillance and trusted informants.'[32] They further added:

> American officials have complained for more than a year about the ISI's support to groups like the Taliban. But the new details reveal that the spy agency is aiding a broader array of militant networks with more diverse types of support than was previously known—even months after Pakistani officials said that the days of the ISI's playing a 'double game' had ended.[33]

It is now time for serious introspection on the part of the Obama administration to ascertain whether dispatching additional US forces to Afghanistan will prove effective to win the war on Taliban-centric terror in that country as well as in tribal areas of the northwest Pakistan: the Swat Valley and Peshawar. 'But the inability, or unwillingness, of the embattled civilian government, led by President Asif Ali Zardari, to break the ties that bind the ISI to the militants illustrates the complexities of a region of shifting alliances. Obama administration officials admit that they are struggling to understand these allegiances as they try to forge a strategy to quell violence in Afghanistan, which has intensified because of a resurgent Taliban.'[34] *The Economist* commented:

> The Taliban insurgency goes from strength to strength, aided immeasurably by the support and sanctuary the insurgents enjoy across the border in Pakistan, and by the chronic weakness of that country's own feuding and shambolic government. It was entirely honest of Mr. Obama to admit in a recent interview that America was 'not winning' in Afghanistan, and right for him to order a strategic review from a former CIA official, Bruce Reidel, to avoid the danger of drift.[35]

Richard Holbrooke, Special Representative for Afghanistan and Pakistan, argued that development and military assistance to Pakistan would be instrumental in dismantling the Taliban sanctuaries in the west as well as in deterring the Taliban advances toward Islamabad. As a component of the Obama administration's strategy, India has been asked to exercise maximum restraint while dealing with Pakistan on the cross-border terrorism issue so that Islamabad could be spared to effectively deal with the extremist forces.

At the trilateral summit held in Washington on 5–7 May 2009, President Obama unequivocally told Pakistani President Asif Ali Zardari and Afghan President Hamid Karzai to take the toughest collective action against the Taliban, which has challenged the legitimacy of state's authority as well as its political capacity by establishing physical control over the Swat Valley—a danger signal to the survival of Pakistan as an independent and sovereign nation. President Obama criticized both presidents for their flawed approach to dealing with the Taliban, although he praised their support of US priorities in the region.[36]

Richard Holbrooke also underscored the need to strengthen Pakistan's democratic institutions and not pick political favourites. He blamed the Bush administration for committing an egregious blunder by backing Pakistan's former strongman, General Pervez Musharraf, despite wide-ranging opposition to his rule.[37]

The Obama administration has come to realize that unless the Taliban is totally eliminated through the employment of a solid multilayered strategy, war in Afghanistan is 'unwinnable'. US and NATO military troops have been unable to prevent the resurgence of the Taliban, not only in Afghanistan but also in Pakistan, as is manifest from the Taliban's imposition of Sharia law (Islamic law) in Pakistan's northwestern Swat Valley. The law was signed off by President Zardari after it was passed by Pakistan's National Assembly in April 2009 in order to avoid a direct confrontation between the Taliban and Islamabad. But the Obama administration described it as a 'dangerous step' to appease the Taliban, which in the administration's perception, weakens the United States' resolve to fight the Taliban to the finish. Declan Walsh, writing from Islamabad for *The Guardian*, writes:

> Pakistan's Western allies worry that the new law represents a surrender to the forces they are fighting across the border in Afghanistan, where President Barack Obama has approved the deployment of an extra 21,000 American troops. Hours earlier in Islamabad, the government welcomed former US presidential candidate Senator John Kerry, who has tabled a bill in congress that would boost non-military aid to Pakistan to $1.5 billion a year.[38]

In realistic terms, the Taliban, in collaboration with Lashkar and Jaish-e-Mohammed, has managed to spread its tentacles from Pakistan's northwest tribal areas to Lahore. The terrorist attack on Lahore's police training centre on 30 March 2009 resulted in the loss of thirty-seven military and armed personnel, sending shock waves through Pakistan. Also, India needs to be on hyper alert because Lahore is fewer than ten kilometres away from India's Wagah border. As such, terrorists operating from Pakistani soil can easily enter Indian territory. Following the terrorist attacks on Lahore, President Zardari publicly acknowledged that the threat to Pakistan's security was not an external but an internal one.[39] Pakistan is reported to have eighty-seven terrorist camps across the country: thirty-seven in the northeastern region and fifty in Pakistan-administered Kashmir.[40]

Recurrent terrorist attacks on Pakistan have further eroded the morale of European and US forces in Afghanistan. They are convinced that it is infeasible to remain there indefinitely. The alternative of an exit strategy is not easy; to allow the Taliban to roost the rule both in Afghanistan and Pakistan is fraught with greater danger. Its negative fallout might be on Iraq where the United States has been struggling hard to bring normality back into the country. *The Economist* comments:

> al-Qaeda has now been driven into Pakistan, but it would return re-energized the moment the insurgents regained power, which they could well do if NATO fled before building an Afghan government and army capable, like Iraq's, of standing on its own feet.[41]

US Aid to Pakistan

Military aid has been a principal instrument of the United States' policy toward Pakistan since the Cold War era to fulfil its long- and short-term goals and interests. The only change that one can witness in the case of Pakistan is the latter's strategic defiance of the United States after Islamabad's attainment of nuclear-weapons capability. No doubt, Pakistan's nuclear-weapons status has marginalized the United States' political leverage over it. Pakistani military and political elites have proved their political skill and diplomatic finesse in extracting the maximum benefit from the United States with a minimum of strategic investment. This is amply borne out by the fact that Pakistan has managed to receive more than ten billion dollars in aid since the beginning of the United States' global war on terror in the aftermath of 9/11. According to the Washington-based think tank, Centre for Strategic and International Studies, Pakistan has, since 9/11, channelled a significant portion of US aid into arming itself for confrontation with India instead of conducting a war on terror.[42] Frederick Barton, a senior advisor at the

Centre for Strategic and International Studies (CSIS) in Washington, DC said:

> It appears that the Pakistan military is continuing to arm more for its confrontation with India than it is for the war on terror because these weapons really don't have that much application for the kinds of low-grade persistent Taliban fighters and al-Qaeda fighters that you find in the Northwest part of Pakistan.[43]

As reported in the *Indian Express*, 'Pakistan has used a substantial amount of military aid from the US meant to fight terrorism to build up its army with modern weapons and equipment for a conventional warfare against India, Pentagon documents have revealed.'[44]

The Pentagon documents also revealed that a major post-9/11 US defence supply to Pakistan under FMF had nothing to do with its fight against terrorism. While the Taliban and al-Qaeda gained ground in the tribal areas of Pakistan bordering Afghanistan, Islamabad bought eight P-3C Orion maritime patrol aircraft and their refurbishment, worth $474 million. It also placed orders for 5,250 TOW anti-armour missiles worth $186 million. Of these, 2,007 have already been delivered and the rest are in the process of being supplied.[45]

According to the Pentagon report, Pakistan diverted US funds for improving and upgrading its defence during 2002 and 2009 to blunt 'India's edge' in conventional weapon systems. As reported in the *Times of India*:

> Pakistan's big-ticket conventional military buys include 18 new F-16 C/D Block 50/52 combat aircraft (valued at $1.43 billion; none delivered yet), F-16 armaments including 500 AMRAAM air-to-air missiles; 1,450 2,000-pound bombs; 500 JDAM tail kits for gravity bombs and 1,600 enhanced paveway laser-guided kits, also used for gravity bombs ($629 million); 100 Harpoon anti-ship missiles ($298 million); 500 Sidewinder air-to-air missiles ($95 million) and six Phalanx close-in naval guns ($80 million).
>
> Pentagon concluded $4.89 billion worth foreign military sales (FMS) agreements with Pakistan between 2002 and 2008, although the bulk includes the F-16 sales. The US gave $1.9 billion foreign military financing with what it calls a 'base programme' of $300 million a year from 2005-2009. It is this that has been used to buy US military equipment.[46]

Stephen P. Cohen, a Senior Fellow at the Brookings Institution, Washington, in his testimony on 10 June 2008 to the United States' Senate Committee on Homeland Security and Government Affairs, stated:

> We have poured many billion of dollars into Pakistan, but as in the past, we have not done good job of linking aid, loans, and grants to specific policy goals. We should stovepipe our aid, linking it to performance on these areas we judge to be most important. In addition, the aid process must be far more transparent.[47]

Cohen further continued:

> Finally, we should marginally increase our engagement in India-Pakistan relations. The Pakistan army still regards India as its main threat, and nuclear weapons as its main defence. We need to address their chief incentive to acquire more and bigger nuclear weapons.[48]

Michael Krepon, co-founder of the Henry L. Stimson Centre in Washington, DC, is of the view that though Congress is authorized to attach strings to the aid that the United States provides to Pakistan, the aid conditionality might prove counterproductive in the long term. He observes:

> Members of Congress have every right to attach conditions to foreign assistance legislation, given the prior track record of US aid that has done little to check Pakistan's decline. But insisting on conditions that are unlikely to yield benefits while trampling on Pakistani sensibilities is an odd way to make this partnership more functional. Take, for example, the House Foreign Affairs Committee's insistence that US officials gain access to A. Q. Khan, who is the father of the uranium enrichment programs in Pakistan, Iran, and perhaps North Korea. A. Q. Khan has great difficulty telling the truth. What, exactly, do Members of Congress intend to achieve by making access to him a condition for US assistance?[49]

In brief, despite supplying massive military aid to Pakistan, the United States has failed to achieve its strategic goals in Afghanistan and Pakistan. The United States' 'short-term counter-terrorism objectives' without unequivocally defining its long-term specific objectives in the present Afghanistan-Pakistan security scenario have not delivered the desired goods. Moreover, theoretical conditions attached to the aid are meaningless unless some 'credible mechanism is put in place to make sure that the aid is being judiciously utilized by Pakistan'.[50]

Another major difficulty is that a mushroom growth of think tanks in the United States makes it extremely difficult for the administration to choose the most feasible policy recommendation in the national interest because every think tank looks at a problem from its own specific angle, giving, at times, recommendations that contradict those of its institutional counterparts. This situation arises mainly because of the fact that think tanks lack an in-depth grasp of the geopsychology of the ruling class. As a result, their superficial knowledge about regional political and psychological dynamics makes it difficult for them to judge the real motivation of the ruling elite who are adept in the art of lying and twisting things as and when the situation so demands. For example, the Pakistani ruling elite—civil and military—are better negotiators compared to India and the United States. No doubt, Pakistani political leaders and diplomats are capable of constructing policy approaches in accordance with the situational exigency. Thus, the geopsychological dimension of the United States–Pakistan relationship needs a careful review by US public policy makers. They need to bear in mind that Pakistani leaders, diplomats, and top military brass are capable of outsmarting their counterparts in the United States and India.

Given the highly fluid political situation in a decrepit Pakistan, US aid cannot be guaranteed to control the advances of the Taliban unless there is a strong political will to fight the Taliban to the finish. Further, democratic reforms alone in Pakistan are not a panacea in the face of an overwhelming existential threat from the Taliban and indigenous militant groups. Indeed, Pakistan needs to focus on resolving its immediate problems on the domestic front such as internal security, appalling poverty, and intrareligious conflicts. What is critically important is that the United States and India need to address the geopsychological impulses of Pakistan's top military brass and political leaders who at this critical juncture are confronted with unprecedented political turmoil and deepening internal social unrest. This requires a patient introspection on the part of think-tank pundits dealing with South Asia.

It is equally important that unless there is a reorientation of the Pakistani military mindset, US efforts to promote peace and stability in South Asia and Afghanistan will remain a pipedream. Also, it is neither feasible nor desirable for the United States to pursue proactive diplomacy to promote a permanent settlement of the Kashmir problem. It should be left to India and Pakistan's leadership who are capable of finding a mutually acceptable solution. If the past is any guide, US policymakers, including President Kennedy, made it absolutely clear that they were unable to resolve the problem either through US mediation or diplomatic channels because Kashmir was a highly emotionally charged issue. At best, the United States can encourage India and Pakistan to resolve the problem through bilateral dialogue.

President Obama's policy toward Pakistan appears to be fundamentally flawed. First, he is taking public pronouncements of the Pakistani military and ruling political leaders at face value that the existential threat to Pakistan is more from the Taliban and local Jihadi elements than from India. In his misplaced judgement, Pakistan's India-centric perceptions of threat have shifted to the Taliban and militant groups. Second, there is no concrete evidence to justify President Obama's clean chit to Islamabad that nukes in Pakistan are in safe hands. In effect, President Obama appears to be fully convinced that there is no cause for worry that nuclear weapons might fall into the hands of jihadi or radical Islamists. Although it might sound comforting to Islamabad, the civilian democratic government was slightly unhappy about President Obama's high praise for the military's ability to keep its nuclear arsenal safe from militants.[51]

President Obama further elaborated:

> I am gravely concerned about the situation in Pakistan, not because I think that they're immediately going to be overrun and the Taliban would take over in Pakistan. I'm more concerned that the civilian government there right now is very fragile and don't seem to have the capacity to deliver basic services.[52]

Given the above statement, Obama underlined the urgent need to deliver education, healthcare, quick justice, and other essentials to the people.

Prime Minister Yousaf Raza Gilani, however, asserted that the elected government was not 'fragile' as described by President Obama, and that it was functioning effectively.[53] In his strong rejoinder, Gilani stated that the United States was responsible for the 'weakening of democratic institutions' in Pakistan by supporting the military regime of President Musharraf for nine years. At the same time, President Zardari has been trying to convince the Obama administration that his government is not only in a position to arrest the advancing 'wave of Talibanisation' but is also capable of delivering basic services to its people.

Be that as it may, the Obama administration is committed to channeling massive economic and military assistance to Pakistan to bail it out as a pragmatic measure. The administration's assessment is that the civilian government is capable of fighting the extremist elements on its soil more vigorously, provided that Pakistan's economic and social conditions improve. Perhaps President Obama is familiar with Pakistan's tactical and diplomatic moves to extract as much economic and military aid as possible from the United States, as President Pervez Musharraf had secured during his regime. Not surprisingly, Musharraf's reiterated assurances to the United States that he would exterminate with full force the menace of militancy ultimately proved an illusion.

Moin Ansari writes:

> Field Marshall Ayub Khan, General Zia and General Musharraf even after receiving copious support from the US in the end did not support American policy. Ayub Khan threw the Yanks out of Badabare and created bridges with China. General Zia double crossed the CIA and continued making the bomb. General Musharraf refused to assist the CIA in bombing Iran.[54]

As noted, there is a litmus test for the Obama administration's South Asia policy to ensure whether a new democratic government under Zardari-Gilani leadership would be able to control internal extremist elements by pursuing a well-intentioned and well-integrated policy in concert with the army and ISI.

The United States' Security Concerns

The Obama administration is worried about the deteriorating security situation in a nuclear-armed Pakistan that, as Secretary of State Hillary Clinton told the House Foreign Affairs Committee, 'poses a mortal threat to the security and safety of our [United States] country and the world'.[55] Hillary Clinton further elaborated that Pakistani nuclear scientist A. Q. Khan was the 'world's greatest proliferator. The damage that he's done around the world has been incalculable.'[56] To deal with the situation arising out of Khan's network, she underscored the need for dismantling his strong network to ensure the security of the United States and the world. Without mincing words, Hillary Clinton, while recalling the Swat Peace Accord signed between Taliban insurgents and the Pakistani government, cautioned that ceding more territory to the Taliban posed an 'existential threat' to Pakistan.

The Obama administration has expressed its grave apprehension that Pakistan poses a 'mortal threat' to the United States and the world in the wake of rapid Taliban advances and has bluntly told Islamabad it was 'abdicating' power to the militia and extremists by agreeing to Islamic laws in parts of the country.[57] Thus, the clear-cut message from the Obama administration is that Pakistan is a most difficult country to be seriously dealt with. In his article titled 'Obama Strategy Deepens Commitment to Afghanistan, Pakistan,' Spencer Ackerman, a Washington-based journalist, has given a frank assessment about the administration's strategy of improving and strengthening 'governance and economic development' in Afghanistan so that the Afghan people can be insulated from the threat of Afghan militia and insurgents. He writes:

> Significantly, Obama identified the source of the al-Qaeda problem as emanating from Pakistan, where for years, US intelligence assessments have judged that the jihadist organization has constituted a safe haven in tribal areas largely out of the control of the Pakistani government. Obama offered a wide-ranging package of economic and diplomatic support for the government of Asif Ali Zardari to help Zardari confront militants, some of which are linked to al-Qaeda and many of whom strike US and Afghan forces across the porous border with Afghanistan, who have made advances in taking territory away from Pakistani forces in recent months. Richard Holbrooke, the special envoy for Afghanistan and Pakistan, said the Pakistanis had given the administration a 'red line' against the deployment of US troops in Pakistan, although the new strategy devotes an unspecified number of troops to train Pakistan's special operators and the Frontier Corps soldiers whom Zardari relies on to conduct counterinsurgency operations in the tribal areas.[58]

Vice-President Joe Biden also advocates a more 'focussed counter-terrorism mission' in order to save US resources and troops:

> Though the President plans to endorse the concepts of counterinsurgency as a means to fight the Taliban, it will not be the primary objective of US and NATO troops. US policy also focuses on improving the legitimacy of Afghan government

> institutions by endorsing anti-corruption drives, by devoting US resources to counternarcotics missions, and by providing basic goods and services to Afghans outside Kabul.[59]

Michael Krepon in his testimony on 12 June 2008 before the Senate Committee on Homeland Security and Governmental Affairs stated:

> What, then, can the United States do to help Pakistan improve its nuclear safety and security? There is very great suspicion in Pakistan about US intentions. Mistrust grows with every press report or idle comment about US contingency plans to 'seize' or otherwise take action against Pakistan's nuclear assets in the event of an imminent breakdown of governmental authority or a prospective rise of Islamist extremists into leadership positions. Such speculation reinforces the natural instinct of Pakistani military authorities to keep US officials at a safe distance from their crown jewels. This, in turn, limits the amount and kind of security assistance that the Pakistani authorities are willing to accept.[60]

He further testified:

> The United States can also help promote nuclear safety and security on the Subcontinent by acting as a crisis manager if and when Pakistan and India again go eyeball to eyeball. Crisis avoidance and peace making are far, far better than crisis management. Regrettably, Washington has focused very little on ways to promote a Kashmir settlement and reconciliation between India and Pakistan.[61]

In this testimony, Krepon stressed that given the power configuration in Pakistan, its nuclear assets are controlled by the military. He testified:

> Current events in Pakistan provide ample grounds for further uncertainty. The country's political leadership is unsettled, especially with respect to relations among Pakistan's President, Prime Minister, and Chief of Army Staff. All three positions have key roles in Pakistan's National Command Authority, which oversees all matters pertaining to nuclear weapons. Control over the nation's nuclear assets will remain in the hands of the military, even if the locus of power shifts away from the President.[62]

Lisa Curtis, a senior research fellow at the Heritage Foundation in Washington, DC, in her testimony on 27 June 2007 before the Subcommittee on the Middle East and South Asia and the Subcommittee on Terrorism, Non-Proliferation, and Trade of the Committee on Foreign Affairs of the House of Representatives, said:

> The potential for the intersection of terrorism and nuclear weapons is arguably the greatest threat to American national, even global, security. As the US seeks to deter the possibility of terrorists gaining access to nuclear weapons, it must consider carefully its policies toward Pakistan. The results of investigations into Pakistani nuclear scientist A. Q. Khan's nuclear black market and proliferation network demonstrate in stark terms the devastating consequences of nuclear proliferation by individuals with access to state-controlled nuclear programmes.[63]

Curtis further stated:

> Preventing Pakistan's nuclear weapons and technology from falling into the hands of terrorists should be a top priority for the US. Revelations about the devastating impact of the A. Q. Khan proliferation network and nuclear black market will prevent Washington from considering a civil nuclear cooperation agreement with Pakistan similar to that being pursued with India. US policy toward Pakistan's nuclear programme should instead focus specifically on nuclear safety and security cooperation and encouraging India-Pakistan dialogue that will improve Pakistan's regional security perceptions.[64]

The above-mentioned testimonies offer some tangible proof that there are lingering doubts about the safety of Pakistan's nuclear weapons. It will patently be in the security interests of the United States to make sure that Pakistani nukes are absolutely safe, even in a worst possible scenario. It is an uphill task for the Obama administration to understand the geopsychological dynamics of the region. President Obama will need to hire innovative and well- informed area specialists who have an impeccable grasp of regional specificities and particularities in terms of the history, culture, psychology, and political dynamics of the region.

Illusion

The Obama administration is perhaps living under an illusion that massive economic and military assistance to Pakistan on certain conditions would deliver the desired goods or services. The administration has decided to send thirty thousand additional US troops to Afghanistan to 'dismantle and defeat' the Taliban and al-Qaeda operating from Pakistan and Afghanistan. At the same time, the Obama administration is also concentrating on enhancing the 'credibility and effectiveness' of civilian governance in Afghanistan to facilitate the withdrawal of US forces in July 2011 as part of the administration's strategy.[65]

Moreover, strategic analysts doubt that the Obama administration's policy of pumping more money into Pakistan would help strengthen civilian institutions in both Pakistan and Afghanistan. In fact, the democratically elected government in Pakistan is virtually a puppet government that could be dislodged by the military with US blessings if the government fails to ensure internal security and deliver on the economic front. Doubtless, domestic political institutions in Pakistan, unlike India, are not sound and strong enough to withstand both internal and external pressures. In this scenario, massive economic and development assistance alone will not prevent the country from sliding into serious turmoil. Friends of Pakistan, including the United States, the EU, China, Japan, and Saudi Arabia, have also offered an additional economic-aid package to help improve Pakistan's chaotic economic conditions. At best, it can provide some temporary relief to Pakistan. But the question arises of how long the aid incentive will be able to protect Pakistan from the continuing threat of Taliban elements and indigenous extremists. Another problem is that of 'Pakistani paranoia' with regard to Pakistan's perception that India poses a threat. Further, the Obama administration has neither a clear-headed policy nor a well-planned and well-integrated strategy 'to disrupt, dismantle and defeat' al-Qaeda in Pakistan and Afghanistan. To that end, Obama has pledged to send an additional four thousand troops to Afghanistan to train Afghan security forces to improve and strengthen the capabilities of the Afghan army and police force.

Conclusion

Be that as it may, the divergence between India and the United States will continue to persist on many bilateral, regional, and international issues. Both countries will find it hard to develop convergent security and strategic interests on all major issues. The Obama administration's shifting priorities and interests also need to be seriously taken into account by New Delhi, although immaturity and imprudence on the part of India's foreign-policy establishment will rule the roost. Because Pakistan is a critical variable in the ongoing war on terror in its tribal areas, the Obama administration should expect India to accommodate Pakistan's internal security problems in order not to exacerbate tension with Islamabad. Furthermore, India's plans 'to spend an estimated $100 billion on defence over the next decade to modernize its Soviet-era arsenal'[66] as well as New Delhi's ongoing efforts to obtain cutting-edge military technology from the United States to upgrade its weapon systems are causing nauseating anxiety to Pakistan.

7

THE RISE OF CHINA: STRATEGIC IMPLICATIONS FOR SOUTH ASIA AND INDIA'S RESPONSES

The geopolitical and security environment in South Asia has undergone an amorphous and ambiguous transformation with China's dramatic ascent to global-power status, attracting a great deal of attention throughout the world. This is attributed to a host of factors, which include China's burgeoning military spending on the modernization of its defence forces; its expanding military, nuclear, and missile capabilities, as manifest from its defence budget pegged at $70.27 billion (March 2009), coupled with its possession of the fastest growing economy in the world; and a phenomenal surge in its foreign trade and investment. Undoubtedly, China's insatiable ambition to play a more assertive role as a global actor stems from its leading roles in, for example, the Shanghai Cooperation Organisation (SCO), the East Asia Summit, ASEAN, and APEC, and also as a mediator in the Six-Party Talks to bring about the denuclearization of the Korean peninsula. Undoubtedly, China has an edge over its principal strategic rivals—India and Japan—in the Asia–Pacific region.

During the past couple of years, China's awesome naval build-up in the Indian Ocean region and its strategic hobnobbing with Myanmar, Sri Lanka, and Pakistan have been seen by New Delhi as Beijing's long-term strategy to encircle India. It is an open secret that China has already established its strategic presence in Myanmar's Coco Islands and in Pakistan, by assisting in the construction of its Gwadar deep-sea port. Further, Beijing's recent arms sales to Sri Lanka in the latter's fight against the LTTE, and its signing of two key development projects worth $350 million with the Sri Lankan government in August 2009, are primarily aimed at gaining an 'access to the port at Hambontota on the island's southern coast'.[1] This apart, China's interest in shoring up ties with the Maoists, and its building of rail links between Lhasa and Kathmandu, including heavy investment in Nepal's development projects, have raised eyebrows in New Delhi. Undeniably, these developments cannot be comforting to India so far as New Delhi's security, strategic, economic, and investment interests are concerned.

This chapter aims to examine China's South Asia policy in order to assess the longer-term implications of the paradigm shift in Beijing's policy in the post-Cold War context. The chapter will also discuss China's perception of threat with a view to making an objective evaluation of behavioural patterns in its dealings with South Asia.

Evolutionary Process and the Dynamics of China's Rise

If viewed from a realistic perspective, the end of the Cold War structure, and the demise of the Soviet Union facilitated the rise of China as a major player in the international system. In *realpolitik* terms, China has been a principal beneficiary of the end of the Cold War geopolitical paradigm. In its emergence as an ascendant power in the altered global political and geoeconomic order, China is motivated to replace Russia. Given this, China's perceptions of the post-Cold War world order have undergone a profound transformation in terms of ideology, policy goals, and approaches. Although China is still an illiberal and undemocratic state, it has embraced the capitalist-based path of free market economy, driven by a pragmatic desire to adjust itself to the hard-boiled realism of global economic, scientific, and technological interdependence. Simultaneously, its high-profile role in South, Southeast, Central, East and Northeast Asia and the Middle East is perceived by the Beijing leadership as compatible with China's growing power in the fields of economic modernization, military-arms sales, technological innovations, and nuclear and missile development. Its expansionist designs are reflected in its exclusive territorial claims to the Spratly and Paracel Islands in the South China Sea, its expanding role in the security and strategic affairs of South and Northeast Asia, and its nuclear-technology transfer to volatile regions such as the Middle East and South Asia.

Over the long term, China aims to constrain US military and strategic influence in the Asia–Pacific region. Schooled in the realism of power politics, coupled with a monolithic political system, China's foreign-policy makers are scarcely driven by constructive and creative goals such as fostering liberal democracy, promoting human rights, and working toward the promotion of world peace and stability. On the contrary, China's motivation and policy goals are driven more by its sheer political ambition to attain superpower status along the lines of the United States in the coming two to three decades or so, although its leaders have disowned such a claim.

Fourth-generation leadership in China views the world through the spectrum of the strategic challenges faced by Beijing in its commanding role as a global actor in the existing power hierarchy. Moreover, a country's deep-seated national psyche does not dramatically alter overnight with a changing global and regional milieu. That is why the motivating factor behind China's firm resolve to emerge as a superpower is grounded in its history and culture of self-pride. In any evaluation of China's worldview, as well as its relations with the outside world, Chinese leaders' perceptions, beliefs, and national images need to be taken into serious account.

Perceptual Prism

If viewed from a historical perspective, the 'Mao-in-command' model of governance dominated China's foreign policy until Mao's death in 1976. During Mao's long authoritarian regime, China's policy remained icon-centric amid unprecedented upheavals in international politics, ranging from Cold War politics to the era of détente. Mao was an uncrowned monarch in both domestic and foreign policy. In effect, Beijing's responses to the international policy system emanated from Mao's personal idiosyncrasies as well as his strong whims. It may not be an exaggeration to say that Mao was very dominant and made almost all of the 'big decisions'.[2] His Cultural Revolution (1966–76) perfectly exemplifies his purge of the bourgeoisie. It not only isolated China from the international community but also contributed to China's economic stagnation and social backwardness.

After Mao's demise in 1976, Chinese foreign policy shifted from a normative framework to pragmatism based on an 'interest-driven policy' under the 'paramount leadership' of Deng Xiaoping.[3] Though Deng was not a political heavyweight compared to Mao, he commanded high respect from the rank and file of the Communist Party apparatus. His open-door policy toward the outside world not only facilitated foreign investment in China but also helped shore up China's arms market in Third World countries. About 80 per cent of Chinese arms sales in the 1980s, valued at more than $15 billion, was transferred to the Middle East, not only to warring Iran and Iraq but also to Egypt, Syria, Libya, and Saudi Arabia.[4]

Deng's vision, based on pragmatism and the hard-boiled realities of the international system, made him realize that unless China opened up its economy to the outside world, it would not only remain isolated from the mainstream of international politics but would also continue to remain an economically poor and backward country.[5]

In his drive for economic modernization, Deng launched a four-point programme in the fields of agriculture, industry, defence, and science and technology in order to transform China into an economically strong, politically robust, and militarily self-reliant country. Repeatedly, Deng endeavoured to convince the world community that China did not subscribe to the policy of confrontation. Instead, he emphasized that it needed peace and tranquility on its borders to speed up the country's economic development. On several occasions, he reiterated that China believed in fostering friendly relations with all countries, based on the five principles of peaceful co-existence.

As an architect of modern China, Deng envisioned China as economically sound, progressive, and self-reliant. At the same time, he embarked on projecting China as a responsible and 'cooperative international actor'. Toward that end, he applied the 'classical concept of realism'.[6] Mel Gurtov and Byong-Moo Hwang agree that the salience of the PRC foreign policy under Deng was based on a realistic assessment of the country's 'national interest, power politics and geopolitcs'.[7]

This apart, 'strategic culture' forms one of the key components of China's worldview. It is based on China's experiences in terms of rebellions and wars it has fought with aliens and the humiliation it suffered at the hands of imperialists. Samuel S. Kim observes, 'If Chinese analyses of their own concepts of military strategy and operations are any indication, Chinese military planners are deeply wedded to the *para bellum* doctrine that preparing for war is still the only way to keep peace.'[8] This view is widely shared by many realists . William T. Tow writes:

> Realists argue that China is a dissatisfied power and will try to project decisive force further afield as its military strength grows—that as a result China will threaten the security of other regional states to an extent that they will be forced to form counter-coalition, or if they do not, they will have no choice but to submit to China's will and ambitions.[9]

China's Notion of the New World Order

In China's perception, the new world order based on a 'set of world regulations', and articulated through Western concepts and parameters, poses a threat to its state sovereignty. In this context, Samuel S. Kim writes, 'Despite twists and turns in Chinese foreign policy over the years, the Westphalian sovereignty-centred notion remains dominant in the Chinese image of world order.'[10]

Several explanations can be offered in this regard. More pertinently, with the widespread international condemnation of the 1989 Tiananmen carnage, Chinese leaders voiced their strident opposition to power politics and the big power hegemony. In China's perception, the motivation of the Western world, especially the United States, is aimed at effecting political reforms in China, and pressurizing it to improve its record on human rights and religious freedom.[11] China considers this a well-calculated move to interfere with its domestic affairs. Though it has reiterated its firm commitment to and cooperation with the United States on issues such as international terrorism and global disarmament, it has made it crystal clear that any outside interference with its domestic policies under the guise of democracy or human rights will not be tolerated. To be more precise, China favours a fair and just multipolar world in which state sovereignty would remain a key component of its foreign policy. In effect, Beijing's policy prescriptions within statist parameters of international order are well suited to China, politically and strategically.

China's Threat Perceptions

China has the world's largest population and a vast land mass with thirty-two thousand kilometres of coastal line and a land border stretching twenty-two thousand kilometres. A complicated geographical environment poses a challenge to the country's sovereignty, security, and territorial integrity.[12] It shares borders with a long list of Asian neighbours. 'Her land frontier stretches from Vietnam, Burma, Nepal, India, Pakistan, Afghanistan in the South, Southwest Asia and Korea, Outer Mongolia to Russian Siberia and Inner Asia in the north and northeast.'[13]

China's threat perceptions have been shaped and articulated by its geographical location on the world map. Geographically proximate states are seen by China as a threat to its national security and territorial integrity. It is pertinent to point out that China's Great Wall was erected with the overriding objective of preventing any nomadic invasion from the North. Undoubtedly, China has been extremely wary of foreign intrusions into and encroachment upon its territories:

> Modern China has experienced two revolutions: one in 1911 with the establishment of the republic and another in 1949 when

> a communist regime came to power in Peking. One of the most important motivations in these revolutions was the recovering of national sovereignty and territorial integrity lost to the imperialist powers in the so-called unequal treaties.[14]

Sun Yat-sen, the founding father of the Chinese Republic, gave a clarion call to carry out an internecine struggle to abrogate the past treaties imposed on China by colonial powers. After his death, Mao Zedong vigorously carried the struggle forward.

The Beijing leadership embarked on an irreversible policy approach in which the 'unequal treaty system' handed down by the imperialists must be 'abrogated, revised and renegotiated'. To achieve this, China adopted a two-pronged diplomacy: a mix of compromise and coercion. As regards Afghanistan, Burma, Nepal, and Pakistan, it chose the path of negotiation, compromise, and reconciliation, resulting in the signing of treaties with them: the 1961 Sino-Nepal Boundary Treaty, the 1963 Afghanistan–China boundary agreement, and the 1960 Burma–China border agreement. China could not settle the boundary disputes with India and the former Soviet Union by bullying them into signing border agreements.

China's Grand Strategy

China's grand strategy has been primarily influenced by a combination of ancient tenets of Chinese statecraft and its modern national-development theory. Further, geopolitics has shaped China's grand strategy toward its neighbours. In fact, the Beijing leadership was faced with the longstanding geopolitical challenge of maintaining control over the heartland of China and major elements of 'Inner Asia'. Moreover, China's major geopolitical concern has been to secure the vast periphery of coastal and land boundaries as well as maritime territory in regions populated by traditional rivals and enemies. These challenges have contributed to shaping China's grand strategy for dealing with the outside world, while aspiring to a favourable domestic and international strategic configuration of power.

It may also be noted that Chinese policymakers, diplomats, and think tanks are engaged in making a 'rigorous study and analysis of how other nations approach international security affairs'[15] with a view to improving their approaches to security, strategic, and development issues. Be that as it may, China is proud of its history, heritage, and culture. Hinton observes:

> Communist China like traditional China believes that it is the repository of unique values and ought to be accepted by all mankind and that this acceptance should create a willingness to acknowledge Chinese political leadership even in remote areas where China's power can not reach, and still more where it can.[16]

The nationalistic fervour among Chinese people is quite deep and strong. It fundamentally emanates from China's sociopsychic structure rooted in its social beliefs, values, and practices. Historically speaking, the Chinese national psyche culminates from the countries past bitter experience with aliens at whose hands the Chinese were ill treated and from suppressed national ego and pride. Edgar Snow writes:

> If, after a nation has been exploited, robbed, opium soaked, plundered, occupied and partitioned by foreign invaders for a century, the people turns upon its persecutors and drives them from the house, along with the society whose weakness permitted the abuses, is it suffering from paranoia?[17]

China has suffered humiliation and insults in the past. Not surprisingly, it has looked negatively upon Western powers as exploiters, divorced from 'moral scruples'.[18]

In view of the above-mentioned perceptions and perspectives of China's policymakers, this chapter will examine China's expanding military and strategic engagement with South Asia.

With reference to India, the Chinese leadership has demonstrated its proclivity for erasing persistent irritants between the two countries over the unresolved boundary question. Prime Minister Rajiv Gandhi's historic visit to China in December 1988 was a watershed in building the new bridge of understanding between New Delhi and Beijing. The net outcome of his visit was the signing of an agreement between the two countries, setting up a joint working group, aimed at defusing tension along the borders. To provide further momentum to the bilateral relationship, Prime Minister Narsimha Rao visited China in September 1993. The two countries signed the Line of Actual Control (LAC) agreement to maintain peace and tranquility on the borders.[19] In November 1996, President Jiang Zemin paid a state visit to New Delhi to boost multifaceted bilateral ties. During his visit, an agreement on Confidence Building Measures on Military Affairs was signed between the two countries.[20] Under the agreement, they decided to downsize their respective armed forces along the line of actual control.[21]

However, it needs to be recalled that India–China relations slipped into reverse gear when India cited China as a 'potential threat', compelling New Delhi to conduct nuclear-weapons tests in May 1998. President Zemin's reaction to the nuclear tests was acerbic, arguing that India's hegemonic ambitions contributed to regional imbalance as well as to the acceleration of tension between New Delhi and Islamabad. Later on, India tried to patch up its ties with Beijing when Prime Minister Vajpayee stated that China did not 'pose a threat to India, nor does India believe that China regards India as a threat'.[22] Thus, India's damage control exercise facilitated the resumption of political dialogue at the highest political level between the two countries.

Prime Minister Vajpayee's visit to China in June 2003 was another milestone in strengthening ties between New Delhi and Beijing, resulting in an agreement to appoint their respective special representatives for an early political settlement of the boundary dispute. This agreement is a unique experiment in undertaking the political exercise at the special-representatives level. They also agreed to reopen border trade, deadlocked since the 1962 war.

With the institutionalization of talks at the special-representatives level, regular meetings have taken place between the two countries to work out modalities for resolving the boundary dispute. As of August 2009, thirteen rounds of talks on the boundary dispute have taken place. In the thirteenth round of talks, held in New Delhi in August 2009, National Security Adviser M. K. Narayanan represented India, while Vice-Foreign Minister Dai Binguo represented China. They discussed the second stage of modalities to resolve the boundary dispute, but the details were not disclosed.

India–China relations reached new heights when both sides agreed to upgrade their ties to the level of the Strategic and Cooperative Partnership for Peace and Prosperity during Chinese Premier Wen Jiabao's visit to New Delhi in 2005. Under the agreement, both the countries decided to undertake joint military exercises. This is evident from 'Hand-in-Hand 2008' joint military exercises undertaken in December 2008 to fight the common threat of terrorism.

In July 2006, both countries agreed on reopening border trade at the Nathu La pass after a gap of more than four decades. It will help boost bilateral trade between the two countries. In November 2006, President Hu Jintao's visit to New Delhi imparted further momentum to the New Delhi–Beijing ties. Jintao emphasized the imperative of expanding bilateral trade because India and China are two of the world's fastest-growing economies. Their increasing bilateral trade is expected to touch sixty billion dollars by the end of 2010.

Despite these positive developments, China's incursion into Tawang, to which it claims legal and historical rights, has caused ripples in Indo-Chinese relations. Further, the Beijing government raised an outcry over Prime Minister Manmohan Singh's visit to Arunachal Pradesh in October 2009, which further accelerated the tension in their relationships. Ma Zhaoxu, China's foreign-ministry spokesman, said in reaction to Singh's visit, 'We demand the Indian side address China's serious and just concerns and not trigger disturbances in the disputed region so as to facilitate the healthy development of China–India relations.'[23] These remarks reflect China's enduring sensitivities over the Indian state of Arunachal Pradesh, which shares a 640-mile (1,030-kilometre) unfenced border with Tibet.[24]

These developments do not augur well for peace and tranquility on the border. Retired Major General Eustace D'Souza, after visiting Arunachal Pradesh, expressed a strong apprehension of China's takeover of Tawang by launching an assault from Tibet. He wrote: 'The intelligence apparatus should be stepped up to give early warning of any possible Chinese intrusions and for this both the locals and the Tibetan diaspora should be involved.'[25] He has suggested that India should work out a sound plan to improve defence, communications, and intelligence in order to thwart any future attack by China.

At the same time, Prime Minister Singh urged the media not to amplify the persisting differences between India and China on the border issue. On 16 October 2009, following recent exchanges with China on the disputed areas, the Indian government sought to lower the temperature by stating that both sides would continue discuss the border issue as well as other areas to find resolutions to their differences.[26] India brought China's strategic activism in PAK out into the open in order to register its protest that there cannot be different standards on disputed areas.[27] These unpalatable developments are clear signals that China might indulge in provocative acts. The ball is in China's court to ensure that the functional relationship between India and China does not allow such ripples to hinder a fair, reasonable, and mutually acceptable solution to the boundary problem.

The Pakistan Factor

Deterioration in Sino-Indian relations following the 1962 war provided a propitious opportunity for Beijing and Islamabad, as India's adversaries, to forge a strategic understanding on containing India in fulfilment of their respective national interests. Interestingly, Sino-Pakistan relations, characterized as an 'all-weather' friendship, have remained consistently firm and stable since the conclusion of the border agreement between Beijing and Islamabad in March 1963. It merits mention that under this agreement Pakistan gave away to China more than five thousand kilometres of land in the disputed area of PAK. Since then, the China–Pakistan military and strategic nexus has been a major source of irritants between New Delhi and Beijing. Allen S. Whiting observes:

> Pakistan's geopolitical situation ha attracted China's support since the early 1960s. It was a useful counterweight against India, perceived both as a neighbouring threat and a client of the Soviet Union. In addition, the proximity of Kashmir to the disputed Sino-Indian border area took on strategic importance with a nearby road from Xinjiang through western Tibet serving essential military logistic needs.[28] China assisted Pakistan in its nuclear and missile building programmes in order to 'help Pakistan to keep its option open'.[29]

In this respect, Mohan Malik observes:

> Since the Sino-Indian border war of 1962, China has aligned itself with Pakistan and made heavy military and strategic investments in that country to keep the common enemy, India, off balance. Interestingly, China's attempts to improve ties with India since the early 1990s have been accompanied by parallel efforts to bolster Pakistani military's nuclear and conventional capabilities vis-à-vis India. It was the provision of a Chinese nuclear and missile shield to Pakistan during the late 1980s and 1990s that emboldened Islamabad to wage a 'proxy war' in Kashmir without fear of Indian retaliation.[30]

In the early 1990s, China supplied short-range M-11 missiles and their components to Pakistan, including surface-to-air missiles (SAM) and anti-tank missiles. Further, Pakistan's Hatf-1, Hatf-2, and Shaheen missiles were developed with Chinese assistance. According to *Jane's Intelligence Review*:

> Indian defence analysts claim that while North Korea supplied Pakistan with the Ghauri II, the guidance systems for both the

> Ghauri I and II originated in China. In addition, due to the short length of its serial production before the launch, the Shaheen missile appears to have been based on a proven design, most likely the Chinese M-9. The Shaheen may be produced in the factory near Rawalpindi, which was reportedly designed and equipped by China.[31]

On 5 February 1996, *The Washington Times* first disclosed the intelligence report that the Chinese National Nuclear Corporation, a state-owned corporation, transferred five thousand ring magnets to the A. Q. Khan Research Laboratory at Kahuta in Pakistan, which does not operate under IAEA safeguards. These ring magnets can be used in gas centrifuges to enrich uranium. According to the report, the ring magnets provided to Pakistan are used in special suspension bearings at the top of rotating cylinders in the centrifuges. The *New York Times* of 12 May 1996 reported that the shipment, worth seventy thousand dollars, was made after June 1994. In that deal, China's Nuclear Energy Industry Corporation—a subsidiary of the China National Nuclear Corporation—was directly involved. Further, the State Department's report on non-proliferation efforts in South Asia (21 January 1997) confirmed that 'between late 1994 and mid-1995, a Chinese entity transferred a large number of ring magnets to Pakistan for use in its uranium enrichment programme'.[32]

Indisputably, India–China relations will continue to be adversely affected by China's supply of military hardware and nuclear technology to Pakistan. The underlying motivation behind it is the geopolitical and geostrategic containment of India.[33] However, a greater cause of anxiety to India is not so much the unresolved boundary dispute as China's extensive support to Pakistan's development of nuclear weapons and missiles. The ongoing Chinese support, from India's viewpoint, has introduced a permanent element of instability in the South Asian region. India's former ambassador to China, C. V. Rangnathan, holds a similar view that China's assistance to Pakistan to develop nuclear and missile technology, in addition to its being Pakistan's biggest supplier of conventional military weapons, is an obstacle to building trust between the PRC and India.[34]

Needless to say, China's intensified military and strategic cooperation with Pakistan has prompted India to intensify defence and strategic cooperation with the United States.[35] The US policy is to encourage India's emergence as a global power by providing it with military, technological, and nuclear assistance in order to contain China's ability to dominate the Asian region.[36]

Moreover, China is beefing up its defence expenditure for the modernization and expansion of its nuclear and missile development, which India sees as a potential danger to its security. In comparison to the seventy-one billion dollars China spent on defence, India spent on defence approximately twenty-nine billion dollars in fiscal year 2009–10, reflecting a 24 per cent hike in the aftermath of 26/11/08.

China's projection of power in the Indian Ocean and its expanding strategic presence in Southeast and South Asia are of serious concern to India. In this regard, G. Parthasarthy, India's former high commissioner to Pakistan, writes:

> As China strengthens its navy with acquisition of aircraft carriers and nuclear submarines, India will soon find that unless it combines the boosting of its maritime muscle with imaginative diplomacy in its Indian Ocean neighbourhood and on China's Pacific shores, it will be strategically marginalized and outflanked by an assertive and expansionist China, which appears bent on exploiting the high costs of imperial overreach by the Americans in recent years. Given the manner in which China has joined hands with Pakistan to sabotage India's quest for permanent membership of the UN Security Council and the devious role played by China in the Nuclear Suppliers Group to undermine moves to end global nuclear sanctions against India, we should have no doubt that 'strategic containment' of India will remain the cornerstone of Chinese foreign policy in the foreseeable future.[37]

The China Institute of Strategic Studies, run by the Foreign Ministry, warned that China could firmly support Pakistan in the event of war. It further added: 'While Pakistan can benefit from its military cooperation with China while fighting India, the People's Republic of China may have the option of resorting to strategic military action in Southern Tibet (Arunachal Pradesh) to thoroughly liberate the people there.'[38]

During the past three years, China's strategic activities in PAK have been on the increase. It has undertaken several projects in PAK, which include upgrading the Karakoram Highway under a deal signed between Islamabad and Beijing in 2006. The Karakoram highway runs from the trading city of Kashgar in China's far western Xinxiang region to Gilgit in Pakistan and on to Islamabad. Once the project is completed, the transport capacity of the strategically significant highway will have increased threefold.[39] China is also building a 7,000 MW hydropower project in Bunji and is likely to assist in developing hydel and thermal projects in PAK. India has conveyed its concerns to China about the ongoing projects in the contested territory of PAK. In response, Chinese President Hu Jintao said that it was for 'India and Pakistan to resolve' and that China had 'no reason to change its policies on Kashmir'.[40]

From a long-term perspective, China's assistance to Pakistan in developing projects in the disputed territory will have a negative spillover on the India–China bilateral relationship. It is also more than certain that India will be unable to make China reverse its policies in PAK.

China and Bangladesh

China was among those few countries that had opposed the independence of Bangladesh, mainly because of Beijing's friendly ties with Islamabad. Although China does not share direct land borders with Bangladesh, strategic considerations have been a factor in China's policy to come closer to Bangladesh. Vinod C. Khanna observes, 'Further, as China looks at the possibilities of a naval presence in the Indian Ocean, the port of Chittagong—where it is developing a container port facility—and the long Bangladesh coastline along the Bay of Bengal offer enticing possibilities.'[41]

China is also exploiting to its advantage the anti-India image in Bangladesh. To Beijing, the best route to strengthen its ties with Dhaka is to use military aid as a political weapon because Bangladesh is heavily dependent on Chinese military hardware to meet its defence requirements. China supplies weapons to Bangladesh to serve its political, economic, strategic, and diplomatic interests in South Asia and to weaken India's influence in the region as well as to encircle it strategically.

As reported, China also transfers missiles to Bangladesh. According to strategic affairs experts, the C-802A missile is a modified version of the Chinese Ying Ji-802 (the Western version is SACCADE) with its weight reduced from 815 kilograms to 715 kilograms to increase its strike range from 42 kilometres to 120 kilometres. Bangladesh has already established a missile launch pad near Chittagong Port with assistance from China. Its missile programme is a recent one; the maiden missile test was conducted on 12 May 2008 with the active participation of a group of Chinese experts. It successfully test-fired the anti-ship cruise missile C-802A with a strike range of 120 kilometres from the frigate BNS *Osman* near Kutubdia Island in the Bay of Bengal.[42]

China and Bangladesh are fast expanding their defence cooperation to solidify their bilateral ties, which serves their respective national interests. In April 2008 Chinese Foreign Minister Yang Jiechi and Bangladeshi army chief, General Moeen U. Ahmed, held intensive discussions in Dhaka on defence and security affairs, resulting in the signing of several agreements that included the supply of upgraded military hardware and small arms to Bangladesh. It is no secret that China is Bangladesh's biggest supplier of small firearms, which are easily accessible to jihadi elements with negative implications for India's internal security and stability.

Although China has denied the charge that the transfer of arms to Bangladesh is directed against India, the South Block in New Delhi has urged its Chinese counterparts to stop supplying small arms including missiles to Bangladesh in order to improve conditions for peace in the region. Chinese leaders, however, have outright glossed over India's security concerns, given the fact that Chinese-made small arms are flooding the arms bazaar in Bangladesh. India's fear is that the easy accessibility of these weapons to terrorist outfits operating in Bangladesh poses a grave threat to both internal and intraregional security and stability. Further, if no serious effort is made to stop the supply of small arms originating from China, the entire region may be transformed into a megamarket of small arms.

Further, China trains Bangladeshi forces under the Defence Cooperation Agreement signed between Bangladesh and China in 2002 and assists in the development of Bangladesh's nuclear technology. Mansi Mehrotra noted:

> China is providing training to Bangladesh's armed forces and is shaping Dhaka's security apparatus. Recently, China has assured to help Dhaka in developing peaceful use of nuclear technology for the implementation of Rooppur nuclear power plant. China has also built six 'friendship bridges' across various rivers in the country. In addition, China has been making huge investments in the Bangladesh economy as it realizes the importance of untapped resources of Bangladesh.[43]

Bangladesh has offered to set up a special economic zone for China. To enhance trade and people-to-people contact, ambitious plans have been formed to build a road linking Bangladesh with China through Myanmar.[44]

In fact, China is exploiting the psychology of the Bangladeshi ruling elite to advance and consolidate its multiple security and strategic interests by supplying military hardware to Bangladesh. Moreover, it promotes its commercial interests by dumping cheap goods into Bangladesh. New Delhi has taken a diplomatically passive position, taking no appropriate measures to wean Bangladesh from China's influence. Rather, India's lack of strategic activism indirectly encourages China to expand its strategic choices in the region.

China and Sri Lanka

Sino-Sri Lankan relations have a special place in the South Asian regional security structure. Strategically located in the Indian Ocean, Sri Lanka has remained a central focus of imperial and great powers over the centuries. China is not an exception. Its growing influence in South Asia has whetted its appetite for carving out a greater strategic space in the Indian Ocean for a host of reasons, but specifically to counter India's growing influence in the region. In this respect, China is feverishly engaged in India's strategic encirclement by garnering the military and strategic support of countries such as Pakistan, Bangladesh, and Sri Lanka whose anti-India postures are well known.

Sri Lanka is now emerging as China's soft target. China began cultivating its military ties with Sri Lanka in the 1990s by supplying weapons and providing training to Sri Lankan forces when India and the United States had denied military assistance to Colombo in its offensive against the LTTE. As *Times Online* reported, 'Sri Lanka's imminent victory over the Tamil Tigers owes much to a badly needed injection of arms and aid from China, as well as robust Chinese support at the United Nations, ever since the Government began its new offensive in 2007.'[45]

The *Times Online* further elaborated that in the year 2007

> China started building a $1 billion (£660 million) port at Hambantota on Sri Lanka's southern coast, that many military analysts suspect it plans to use as a refuelling and docking station for its navy. Beijing says that Hambantota is purely commercial, but US and Indian military planners see it as a part of a 'string of pearls' strategy under which China is also building or upgrading ports at Gwadar in Pakistan, Chittagong in Bangladesh and Sittwe in Burma.[46]

Jane's Defence Weekly noted:

> Sri Lanka signed a classified $37.6 million deal to buy Chinese ammunition and ordnance for its army and navy. More significantly, however, China then gave Sri Lanka, apparently free of charge, six F7 jet fighters last year, according to the Stockholm International Peace Research Institute. The Sri Lankan Air Force urgently needed the aircraft after a daring raid by the Tigers' air wing destroyed ten military planes in 2007. Since 2007, China has also encouraged Pakistan to sell weapons to Sri Lanka and to train Sri Lankan pilots to fly the Chinese fighters, according to Indian security sources. In addition, China has provided crucial diplomatic support in the UN Security Council, blocking efforts to put Sri Lanka on the agenda. It has also boosted financial aid to Sri Lanka, even as Western countries have reduced their contributions.[47]

From the above-mentioned facts, it can be deduced that Chinese military aid has substantially contributed to enhancing China's political, diplomatic, and strategic influence over Sri Lanka vis-à-vis India, which is a disturbing sign for peace and stability in South Asia in the longer term. In the future, China–Sri Lanka strategic tie-ups are likely to expand further.

It is also reported that China might have clinched a deal with the Maldives to build a naval facility capable of hosting submarines on the island of Marao, forty kilometres away from the capital, Male. According to the Israeli Web site DEBKA, the deal may have been signed and sealed in May 2005 during Premier Zhu Rongji's visit to Male. It will allow China to lease the island for twenty-five years and develop it, which means jobs for the locals. Pakistan was apparently instrumental in 'persuading' the Maldives to lease the island to the Chinese. The island will be operational in 2010. It is not clear how India, given its excellent relations with the Maldives, allowed this deal to go through.[48]

Given China's increased strategic intrusion in the region, India will need to embark upon a multifaceted and a multilayered strategy to counter China in order to preserve its security and strategic interests in South Asia and the Indian Ocean. These include coordination among the three branches of its military services, and the fast modernization and upgrading of its naval arm to offset any threat from China whose interests in the Indian Ocean are second only to the United States.

Also, India will need to attach the highest priority to strengthening the Indian Coast Guard to ensure the country's maritime security.

Emerging Trends

The balance of power between India and China in South Asia, unlike in Southeast Asia, has not yet shifted in Beijing's favour; it is still in India's favour. As regards the issues concerning counter-terrorism, climate change, and the Doha Round of Development, there will be broad continuity in the perceptions and approaches of New Delhi and Beijing. Nevertheless, their serious differences on the Sino-Pakistani military and strategic nexus, and on the question of China's expanding military and strategic role in South Asia and the Indian Ocean may exacerbate tension between New Delhi and Beijing.

If viewed from a holistic perspective, Sino-Indian relations may undergo a new phase of conflict and confrontation as suggested by the current trend of China's highly sensitive activities inside India's borders to undercut Indian sovereignty over Arunachal Pradesh. If one recalls, China had tried to block a $2.9 billion Asian Development Bank loan to India because some of the money was earmarked for an irrigation project in the state of Arunachal Pradesh.[49] This apart, China's strategic encirclement of India in South Asia through its strengthened relations with India's key neighbours—Bangladesh, Nepal, and Sri Lanka—will be a major source of irritation between New Delhi and Beijing, thus amplifying the trust deficit on both sides.

The current trend also suggests that though India–China relations will continue to be guided by the two countries' perceptions of core national interests, China's grand strategic design to reshape in its favour the balance of power in the region may provoke a sharp 'collusion and confrontation' between New Delhi and Beijing. In this game plan, New Delhi will be the main loser unless it charts out an appropriate policy course. China's next strategic move, although not yet precisely known, will depend on two factors: India's nuclear-deterrence capability and the future of the India-United States strategic partnership. Even then, China might continue to focus on weakening the strategic partnership between New Delhi and Washington by exploiting the Obama administration's shift from the policy of its predecessor on the NPT and CTBT.

Be that as it may, India and China are still gripped by the old mindsets of the 1962 Sino-Indian war. Both countries will need more time to dispel persisting mutual distrust, and overcome past reservations. In fact, there is no magic rod that can transform their deeply etched psyche of mutual suspicion into mutual trust. Yet, despite the persistence of mutual distrust, New Delhi and Beijing have come to realize that the current international environment is propitious for strengthening mutual ties to fulfil their shared interests. It is also a positive sign that they have inherently recognized the imperative of working together to offset the hegemony of a single power in the Asia–Pacific region. From this perspective, the possibility of a triangular relationship between India, China, and Russia is credible. At least theoretically, China has endorsed this idea. It might mature into reality, albeit depending on a host of factors. Nonetheless, there is a shared perception among New Delhi, Beijing, and Moscow of the desirability of the triangular relationship to help reshape the current international system on the principles of sovereignty, equality, and fairness. To what extent it can be translated into reality is a matter of speculation.

As regards the border dispute, nothing suggests that India and China will be able to resolve it in near future. This is partly rooted in topographical complexity, and partly attributed to their contradictory legal claims over the demarcation of borders. It will, however, be in their long-term national interests if they can continue to upgrade measures to build confidence and security, irrespective of their divergent views and contradictory claims on the boundary issue. Zhang Yan, Chinese Ambassador Extraordinary and Plenipotentiary in New Delhi, has hinted that the boundary question is 'sensitive and complicated' and not easily resolved because it has a long history.[50] He has, therefore, counseled 'more patience and wisdom' in order to resolve it amicably.

Given the hardboiled realities of international globalizing, both India and China have enormous opportunities to cooperate in those areas in which they have no direct clashes of interests. They need to explore the possibility of accommodating each other's concerns and exigencies without being swayed by the political impulse to outsmart each other in an inevitably interdependent political and economic world order.[51]

Conclusion

As the current trends suggest, the future relationship between India and China will largely depend on personal rapport between the top leadership of both sides. Neither euphoria nor pessimism will deliver the goods.

If India and China focus on accelerating economic development and addressing common internal problems, they will be able to resuscitate the classical principle of peaceful coexistence. Such a focus will not only free both countries from the foibles of the past and the narrow strategic thinking of the present, but will also enable them to play a vital role in reshaping the new balance of power in the Asia–Pacific region. It will be an uphill task for many plausible reasons. First, in order to maintain its privileged position in the architecture of Asian security, the United States is unlikely to abandon its proactive diplomacy designed to prevent China and India from coming closer to each other politically, militarily, strategically, and diplomatically. Second, India and China are likely to clash in their mutual ambition of becoming global power, which may hinder their chances of working closely to shape a new balance of power in the Asia–Pacific region.

As far as India is concerned, it is important for New Delhi to assess how its long-term national interests would be served by cementing strategic ties with Washington, and how Sino-Indian strategic cooperation could be a stabilizing factor in the region. Moreover, India needs to be hyper-alert on its borders in view of China's frequent incursions into Tawang in the Indian state of Arunachal Pradesh. India also needs to take note of China's incremental defence and strategic presence in the Indian Ocean. One Indian commentator writes, 'China's incremental efforts to build a "string of pearls" along the Indian Ocean rim symbolize its fourth strategic corridor—and the advent of a challenge to India from the south.'[52]

Given the trust deficit between New Delhi and Beijing, India and China need to be 'pragmatic realists'. It would be an egregious strategic blunder on the part of China if it entertains the wild idea of invading India in near or distant future. Perhaps, China understands well that today's India is not the India of 1962 when it suffered a humiliating defeat at Chinese hands. India's naval and air power is capable of making a befitting response to any misfortune China may bring on India in the future, although China is much ahead of India in nuclear and missile capabilities. India, therefore, will need to upgrade its missile system accordingly. Further, India will also be required to formulate a long-term strategy to counter China's expanding strategic intrusion in and around South Asia in order to ensure regional stability and peace. If India fails to respond in a timely manner to Chinese strategic designs in the region, Beijing's strategic encirclement of India may intensify.

CONCLUSION

The new South Asia, punctuated by profound domestic upheavals, offers novel challenges to and opportunities for creating a secure and stable region.The emerging security architecture in the region is grappling with a host of dilemmas. One of the most troubling is whether India and Pakistan, as de facto nuclear-weapons states, will be able to enter into a no-first-use agreement in view of Pakistan's obsession with India as a potential threat to its national security and survival. It is a patent fact that the region has been hamstrung by the antagonistic psychology of the ruling elites of India and Pakistan since the partition of British India in August 1947. The entire region has been held hostage to the enduring hostility between New Delhi and Islamabad on the interconnected issues of Kashmir and cross-border terrorism, which are subject to the geopsychological impulses of each government's public-policy makers as they seek to justify their respective positions. Unless the deeply entrenched geopsychology of mutual hostility is properly addressed, cooperative threat-reduction measures will remain a mirage.

II

Cooperative security between India and Pakistan is realizable provided that they cultivate mutual respect for each other's security concerns, and economic and strategic interests, given the fact that both countries are beset with territorial conflict and profound internal security problems. However, cooperative security is an important tool for improving the worsening security scenario in a fast-globalizing world order.

Undoubtedly, it is an uphill task for India and Pakistan to undertake cooperative security measures unless their divergent geopsychological perceptions of national security are narrowed down. Further, convergence on security is essential to advance the dialogue on the imperative of developing common security architecture to deal with common security threats. Both parties also need to prepare their respective political constituencies in favour of cooperative security in order to realize their respective national interests as well as to ensure regional security and economic development through productive dialogue and civic engagement. Unfortunately, each country is feverishly engaged in projecting an image of the other as a threat out of proportion to reality. Therefore, it is futile to expect that India and Pakistan can embark on a cooperative security path.

III

Scholars of South Asian studies have no doubt endeavoured to locate sources of conflict and cooperation within the analytical framework of geopolitics. This study suggests that geopsychology is likely to replace geopolitics and geoeconomics as a global analytical framework in the face of current non-traditional threats such as terror, environmental degradation, and ethnoreligious conflicts worldwide. In particular, in volatile regions such as South Asia, the ruling classes' understanding of geopsychology is indispensable for conflict management.

The findings of this study suggest that South Asian security problems are rooted in the psycho-cultural divergences of ruling elites who can find no common ground on security and strategic issues. Even if the bilateral political dialogue registers some progress, its gains are diluted by any regime change, especially with reference to Pakistan. When, for instance, India and Pakistan began a composite dialogue in 2004, both A. B. Vajpayee and Pervez Musharraf raised high hopes that the instrumentality of composite dialogue would enable them to transcend the bitterness of the past to resolve outstanding problems amicably. Under the CBMs, bus and rail services were started between the two countries. However, these and several other measures failed to stop the recurrence of militant activities against India. Given the geopsychological framework of fixed beliefs, values, and tenets, CBMs at best make a marginal difference in moderating their age-old, negative, and stereotypical attitudes toward each other. M. K. Bhadra Kumar supports this assumption. He writes: 'Islamism runs into the Pakistani military and $700 million [committed by the Obama administration, my emphasis added] cannot dilute deep-rooted beliefs and tenets. Nor can it be overlooked that is not in one's power to change Pakistan's strategic assessment of its own security interests.'[1] This is further reinforced by the perception of US Joint Chiefs Chairman Admiral Mike Mullen that

US pressure will not work on a Pakistani military drenched in Islamic ideology. To quote Admiral Mullen: 'My experience is that knocking them [Pakistani generals] hard isn't going to work. The harder we punish, the further away they get.'[2]

There is a widely shared geopsychology among Pakistan's ruling elites that India poses a threat to their country's security. The heat subsides when some atmospheric changes are visible, which seem to reflect a change of heart among Pakistani leaders. It became manifest in President Zardari's recent public utterances that India is not a 'real threat to his country'; the threat is an internal one that, he underlined, must be eliminated. However, such pronouncements are hardly relied upon by India.

In fact, India's morbid and moribund policy on regional security has placed it in a serious dilemma. New Delhi is neither in a position to use its strategic assets to thwart future threats from militants, nor has it a distinct policy to deal with the situation emanating from the tripartite partnership of Afghanistan, Pakistan, and the United States under the Obama administration.

IV

President Barack Obama is endeavouring to recast US policy in a different strategic mould to prove that his predecessor's militarist and unilateralist approach in the post 9/11 world order was basically flawed.[3]

Undoubtedly, President Barack Obama is faced with the gargantuan challenge of the resurgence of the Taliban. The latter's strategic hold beyond Afghan borders was clearly manifest in its establishment of territorial control over the Swat Valley, although a Pakistani army operation flushed them out. Moreover, the security situation in Afghanistan and Pakistan is fast deteriorating with grave security implications for India, in particular, and for South Asia in general, given the persisting nexus in Pakistan between mullahs and military elites who virtually rule the roost. The democratically elected leaders—Zardari and Gilani—find themselves helpless to conduct Pakistan's policy freely toward India except to toe the ISI and military generals' line of asking India to resolve the Kashmir issue as a precondition to mending fences with Pakistan.

As one commentator has rightly observed, 'Pakistan's elected government has been embattled from the start. It enjoys *de jure* power, but it cautions about testing its actual authority over the military.'[4] So far as the question of resuming the peace dialogue is concerned, it will depend on whether Pakistan delivers on India's major demand to bring the militants to book and dismantle the infrastructure of terror on its soil. But Pakistan's leaders are reluctant to take concrete action against militants unless the troika—the political leadership, military, and mullahs—speaks with one voice to exterminate home-grown militants and jihadi elements once for all.

V

Kashmir will remain a festering wound between India and Pakistan. No one has a precise and definitive answer to the question of whether resolution of the Kashmir issue will usher in a durable peace in South Asia. However, both the countries need to realize the imperative of restarting the composite dialogue process—stalled since the 26/11/08 Mumbai attacks—in the larger interest of regional peace and stability.

Furthermore, if there is any possibility of nuclear exchange in South Asia, Pakistan will probably be the first one to employ nuclear weapons against India. Although such a possibility does not exist at the moment, India needs to be hyper-alert and should rid itself of the illusion that Pakistan has no valid reason to employ nuclear weapons against it. As past history bears testimony, Islamabad will not hesitate for a moment to use weapons of mass destruction if it rightly or wrongly perceives that India might go to war against it. At the same time, Pakistan fully understands that India, unlike Israel, lacks the courage and stamina to undertake bold steps to threaten Pakistan's security, as is evident from India's inability to take any measures against Pakistan after the deadly Mumbai attacks. Therefore, Pakistan is fully convinced that India is too politically reluctant, mentally ill-prepared, and morally weak to risk a war against it.

On the question of nuclear proliferation in South Asia, the United States' influence over Pakistan's nuclear programme is waning. Washington has limited options to reduce the risk of nuclear proliferation in South Asia. So long as the Obama administration is preoccupied with the task of rooting out the Taliban and al-Qaeda, it cannot risk penalizing Pakistan for its incremental nuclear programme.

On the other hand, India and the United States have a high stake in ensuring a peaceful and stable South Asia. If the United States is really serious about ensuring the security of its citizens in South Asia and protecting its business and investment interests in India, it will need to provide counter-terrorist technology and equipment to India to help serve the national interests of both countries.

VI

In the new South Asia, India will have major stakes and interests. Pakistan and small South Asian countries will remain a critical factor in reshaping South Asia's security architecture. Without their strategic cooperation and political support, one cannot imagine a stable and peaceful South Asia, nor can India boost regional economic integration. It is, therefore, incumbent upon India to pursue patient and prudent diplomacy to revive the peace dialogue with Pakistan so that India–Pakistan relations can get back on track. This apart, India's foreign policy establishment and strategic community ought to grasp the fundamental reality that Pakistan enjoys strategic leverage over India. Further, Pakistan is capable of dealing with the United States and the outside world through its well-crafted and a well-articulated diplomacy. Moreover, Pakistan's strategic diplomats have made the Obama administration realize that the United States cannot decimate the Taliban and al-Qaeda without Pakistan's wholehearted support. That is why the Obama administration avoids antagonizing Pakistan on the question of Islamabad's expanding nuclear-weapons programme and on the diversion of American funds to the procurement of weapons against India. Pakistan has been able to bamboozle the United States into thinking that Islamabad is its reliable ally in the global war on terror. This logic has prompted the Obama administration to funnel more economic and development aid to Pakistan. In this scenario, it will be futile for India to ask the United States to use its influence with Pakistan to permanently end cross-border terrorism.

VII

This study suggests India needs to re-evaluate its entire gamut of relationships with South Asian states that, excepting Bhutan, look upon it with scepticism. In the perception of the small countries of South Asia, India does not treat them as equal partners on the issue of peace and stability in the region. Indian Prime Minister Manmohan Singh acknowledged in June 2009 that India was 'living in a neighbourhood of great turbulence'.[5]

Further, India needs to improve and upgrade its coastal security in the wake of 26/11/08, which blatantly exposed India's maritime unpreparedness even though India is cognizant of the threat emanating from highly modernized, highly motivated, and superbly trained militants. Although India is planning to spend Rs 20,000 crore on research in the defence sector to modernize its forces, it needs to be wary of China's well-calculated strategic plans to encircle it in South Asia and in the Indian Ocean.

VIII

It is also a patent fact that in certain respects, the new South Asia is hardly different from the old South Asia as far as concerns the policies and perspectives which South Asian countries employ in their dealings with one another. The old mindsets of regional leaders have undergone no fundamental transformation. However, regional leaders are increasingly realizing that they must embrace economic globalism and regionalism if their respective countries are to achieve economic progress and prosperity. But no positive change is manifest in these leaders' perceptions of security and strategy that could advance mutually friendly relations among South Asian states. Rather, India's relations with its neighbours are more troubled than ever before.

It is also a flawed assumption among influential US think tanks that a transition to democracy in countries such as Nepal, Bhutan, and Pakistan will herald a better future for South Asia. This view is hardly sustainable, given the age-old anti-India posturing of Pakistan on the Kashmir issue, Nepal's grouse about India's reluctance to amend the 1950 treaty, and Sri Lanka's distancing itself from India in the wake of India's refusal to provide the cutting-edge weaponry to defeat the LTTE. More importantly, civilian leaders in a nascent democratic Pakistan are bent upon exploiting the Kashmir dispute more vigorously than ever by blaming India for having deadlocked the composite dialogue since 26/11/08.

Both India and Pakistan have lost moral authority over their people by sidetracking developmental priorities while putting a premium on their arms build-up. The leadership's contempt for a serious dialogue on curtailing defence expenditures demonstrates their lack of ardour for peace and development in the region. If the graph of defence expenditures continues to go up, it will not be possible to dispel the fear developed and solidified over the past six decades. It is a misconception that nuclear deterrence is an absolute guarantee to India and Pakistan's national securities. Only so long as they opt never to be the first to strike, can they continue to enjoy the deterrent value of nuclear weapons.

Both countries can coexist by maintaining a proper balance between the no-first-use doctrine and nuclear deterrence. Although India has already declared its no-first-use policy, it can ill-afford to maintain it indefinitely unless there is a bilateral treaty on no-first use between India and Pakistan, and between India and China. The chances are bleak that India and Pakistan will enter into such a treaty. The fundamental reason for this is that it is not geopolitics but geopsychology and geoculture that shape and dominate India and Pakistan's decision-making processes. Also, Pakistan may be further emboldened by the recent disclosure of K. Santhanam, senior scientist and DRDO representative at the Shakti-98 project Pokhran II tests in 1998 under the Shakti-98 project, that the yield for the thermonuclear test was much lower than had been claimed.[6] If Santhanam's contention were to be taken at face value, its repercussions would be fatal because India's top military brass must know the truth about the potency of India's nuclear weapons.

On Sino-Indian relations, the trust deficit between India and China is widening, given China's frequent incursions into Indian territory in Arunachal Pradesh, and the unresolved boundary dispute, including the military and security nexus between China and Pakistan. India will need to counter China's projection of power and its growing interventionist profile in South Asia and the Indian Ocean through subtle diplomatic means Further, India needs to narrow down the military gap vis-à-vis China by modernizing its defence systems.

Delays in procurement procedures have further compounded India's defence problems. India's policymakers and strategic planners need to reshape India's neighbourhood policy, securing maritime borders against threats from non-state actors, and ensuring defence integration and coordination among the three defence services.

NOTES

Chapter One

1 See Paul Hirst and Grahame Thompson, *Globalization in Question*, Cambridge, UK: Polity, 1996; Robert O. Keohane and Joseph S. Nye, Jr., *Power and Interdependence,* New York: Longman, 2000.

2 See B.M. Jain, *Global Power: India's Foreign Policy, 1947–2006*, Lanham, MD: Lexington Books, 2006, p.4.

3 B.M. Jain, 'Regional Security in South Asia', in Hussein Solomon (ed.), *Challenges to Global Security: Geopolitics and Power in an Age of Transition*, London: I.B.Tauris, 2008, p.90.

4 Berger: 'Foreign Policy', p.29.

5 Sherle R. Schwenninger, 'Revamping American Grand Strategy', *World Policy Journal* (Fall 2003), p.25.

6 Michael T. Klare, 'Tithing at the Crude Altar', *The National Interest* (July/August 2009), pp. 20–29.

7 Robert S. Litwak, *Regime Change: U.S. Strategy through the Prism of 9/11*, Washington, D.C.: Woodrow Wilson Centre for Scholars, 2007, p.46.

8 Joseph S. Nye, Jr., 'Limits of American Power', *Political Science Quarterly*, Vol. 117, No.4 (2002–2003), p.552.

9 Litwak: *Regime Change*, p.27.

10 G. John Ikenberry, Liberal *Order and Imperial Ambition*, Cambridge, UK: Polity Press, 2006, p.3.

11 For details of this part, see *Ibid.*, pp.65–72.

12 See Peter J. Katzenstein, *A World of Regions: Asia and Europe in the American Imperium,* Ithaca, NY, Cornell University Press, 2005.

13 For a study of the related aspect as to how environment and space affects one's "psychological state of mind", see, M.A. Persinger, 'Geopsychology and geopsychopathology: Mental processes and disorders associated with geochemical and geophysical factors', *Cellular and Molecular Life Sciences* Vol. 43, No. 1 (January 1987), pp.92–104.

14 See Willy Hellpach, *Geopsyche*, Berlin, 1935.

15 www.questia.com/PM.qst?a=o&d=26121562, accessed on 7 July 2008; see also Hellpach's collective work Klima, Wetter, Mensch, Berlin, 1938.
16 See Ahmar Moonis, (ed.), *Paradigms of Conflict Resolution in South Asia*, Dhaka: The University Press, 2003.
17 See Alexander L. George, 'The Causal Nexus between Cognitive Beliefs and Decision-Making Behaviuor: The "Operational Code" Belief System,' in Lawrence S. Falkowski (ed.), *Psychological Models in International Politics*, Boulder: Westview, 1979, pp.95–124.
18 For a perceptive analysis, see Zafar Iqbal Cheema, 'Pakistan's Nuclear Policy under Z.A. Bhutto and Zia-ul-Huq: An Assessment', *Strategic Studies* (Summer 1992), pp.5–20.
19 A strong pro-weapon lobby developed in Pakistan during the 1960s and early 1970s, see Ashok Kapur, *Pakistan's Nuclear Development*, London: Croom Helm, 1987.
20 In order to explain the potency of perception and misperception in decision-making process of international actors, see Robert Jervis, *Perception and Misperception in International Politics*, Princeton: Princeton University Press, 1976; also Yaacov Y. I. Vertzberger, *The World in Their Minds: Information Processing, Cognition, and Perception in Foreign Policy Decision-making*, Stanford, CA: Stanford University Press, 1990.
21 James H.K. Norton, *India and South Asia*, N.Y.: McGraw-Hill/Dushkin, 2003.
22 B.M. Jain, 'India-Pakistan Engagement with the Greater Middle East: Implications and Options', *Perspectives on Global Development and Technology Journal*, Vol. 6, Nos. 1–3 (special issue, 2007), pp.459–82.
23 In this connection see, Stephen Peter Rosen, *Societies and Military Power: India and its Armies*, Ithaca, N.Y.: Cornell University Press, 1996.
24 See George K. Tanmah, 'Indian Strategic Thought: An Interpretive Essay', in Kanti Bajpai and Amitabh Mattoo (eds.), *Securing India: Strategic Thought and Practice*, New Delhi: Manohar, 1996, pp.28–111.
25 For a critique of cultural relativism, see Alastair Iain Johnston, *Cultural Realism: Strategic Culture and Grand Strategy*, Princeton, N.J.: Princeton University Press, 1995.
26 Robbie Robertson, *The Three Waves of Globalizaton: A History of a Developing Global Consciousness*, London: Zed Books, 2003, p.143
27 *Asia Source*, Interview with Henry Kissinger, 22 February 2006, http://www.asiasource.org, accessed on 15 July 2008.
28 T.V. Paul (ed.), *The India-Pakistan Conflict: An Enduring Rivalry*, Cambridge, UK: Cambridge University Press, 2005; Baldev Raj Nayar and T.V. Paul, *India in the World Order: Searching for Major-Power Status*, Cambridge, UK: Cambridge University Press, 2004.

29 Hamid Ansari, 'The OIC and India: Signals of a Rethink', *The Hindu,* 30 January 2006.

30 Pervez Hoodbhoy, 'India & Pakistan: case for common defence', *The Hindu*, 28 November 2009.

31 *Ibid.*

32 Ashley Tellis, 'The Strategic Implications of a Nuclear India,' *Orbis* (Winter 2002), pp.13–45.

33 See Mahendra Lawoti, Anup Kumar Pahari (eds.), *The Maoist Insurgency in Nepal: Revolution in the Twenty-first Century,* London: Routledge, 2009; S.D. Muni, *Maoist Insurgency in Nepal: The Challenge and the Response*, New Delhi: Rupa and Company, 2004.

34 See Ashok K. Mehta, *India-Nepal Relations: The Challenge Ahead*, New Delhi: Rupa and Co. 2004.

35 Jain: 'Regional Security', p.91.

36 *The Hindu,* 10 September 2007.

37 *Ibid.*

38 For details, see *The Hindu,* 13 March 2009.

39 *The Times of India,* 4 March 2009.

40 *The Hindu*, 6 September 2009.

41 Anil Bhatt, 'Dhaka Mutiny Timing Ominous for India', www.deccanchronicle.com/.../dhaka-mutiny-timing-ominous-india-343, accessed on 15 September 2009.

42 www.satp.org/satporgtp/countries/bangladesh, accessed on 4 July 2009.

43 For details, see *The Times of India*, 4 March 2009.

44 *The Tribu*ne, 4 March 2009.

45 *Ibid.*

46 For details, see *Sri Lanka Guardian*, 29 September 2009.

47 Sudha Ramachandran 'China Moves into India's Backyard', *Asia Times*, 13 March 2007. Christina Y. Lin has also warned about the consequences of China's increasing strategic intervention in different parts of Asia. He writes: Having established key "pearls" of WMD client states of Iran in the Middle East, Pakistan in South Asia, and DPRK in East Asia, China is procuring additional pearl nodes along the Indian Ocean (e.g., Sri Lanka, Burma, Bangladesh, etc.) and establishing naval ports, electronic surveillance, military cooperation, nuclear technology and bio-chemical weapons cooperation with these nodes. In that situation, Sri Lanka might also jeopardise its own security, including of India and South Asia, from a long term perspective. In other words, Chinese strategic presence in Sri Lanka cannot be comforting to India. Once China strengthens and stabilizes its strategic role in the region, as it is already doing with the help of Colombo and Islamabad, the region will hardly remain tension free. Christina Y. Lin, 'Militarization of

China's Energy Security Policy–Defence Cooperation and WMD Proliferation Along its String of Pearls in the Indian Ocean', (se2.isn.ch/serviceengine/Files/ESDP/56390/.../StringPearls.pdf, accessed on 10 June 2009.

48 www.hvk.org/articles/0202/70.html, accessed on 10 June 2009.

49 Hoodbhoy: 'India & Pakistan.'

Chapter Two

1 Robert S. Litwak, *Regime Change: U.S. Strategy through the Prism of 9/11,* Washington, D.C.: Woodrow Wilson Centre for Scholars, 2007, p.16.

2 For a perceptive analysis, see Joseph S. Nye, Jr., 'Redefining the National Interest', *Foreign Affairs* (July–August 1999), pp.22–35.

3 For an in-depth analysis of the multi-dimensional character of the concept of geopolitics, see Patrick O' Sullivan, *Geopolitics*, London: Croomhelm, 1986; Filip Tunjic, 'War and Geopolitics, Really Together?', *Strategic Digest*, Vol. XXV, No.1 (January 2000), pp.20–34.; J. Mathews, 'Poor Shift', *Foreign Policy* (January–February1997), pp.50–60.

4 B.M. Jain, 'India-Pakistan Relations: The Need for Psycho-cultural Prophylaxis,' in Ramakant (et al., eds.), *Contemporary Pakistan: Trends and Issues*, Vol. II, Delhi: Kalinga Publishers, 2001, pp.187–99.

5 For an analytical framework pertaining to this part, see Barry Buzan, *People, State and Fear: An Agenda for International Security Studies in the Post-Cold War Era*, London: Harvester Wheatsheaf and Boulder: Lynne Rienner, 1991.

6 See B.M. Jain and E.M. Hexamer (eds.), *Nuclearisation in South Asia: Reactions and Responses*, Jaipur and New Delhi: Rawat, 1999; B.M Jain, *Nuclear Politics in South Asia: In Search of an Alternative Paradigm*, New Delhi: Rajat, 1994.

7 For an insightful analysis of this part, see Lee Feinstein, 'Avoiding Another Close Call in South Asia', Arms Control Today (July–August 2002), www.armscontrol.org/print/1080, accessed on 19 April 2009.

8 See Anthony H. Cordesman, working draft on 'Iranian Weapons of Mass Destruction', 6 November 2008, *csis.org/files/media/csis/pubs/081106_iranwmdnuclear.pdf,* accessed on 9 August 2009.

9 See Jasjit Singh (ed.), *Kargil 1999: Pakistan's Fourth War in Kas*hmir, Delhi: Knowledge World and IDSA, 1999.

10 See Press Release of the Cabinet Committee on Security and Operationalization of India's Nuclear Doctrine, 4 January 2003, in Arvind Gupta, Mukul Chaturvedi and Akshay Joshi (eds.), *Security and Diplomacy, Essential Documents*, New Delhi: Mans Publications, 2004, pp.19–20.

11 For a detailed analysis of this part, see B.M. Jain's essay, 'Indo-Pakistan Relations: Sources of Estrangement', Washington, DC: The Henry Stimson Centre, 1997.
12 See Saira Khan, *Nuclear Weapons and Conflict Transformation*, London: Routledge, 2008.
13 For a detailed exposition, see Tariq Ruff, 'The 2000 NPT Review Conference,' *The Nonproliferation Review* (Spring 2000), pp. 146–61.
14 For the related part, see George Perkovitch, 'Think Again: Nuclear Proliferation,' *Foreign Policy* (Fall 1998), pp.12–13.
15 *The Hindu*, 9 June 2003.
16 See http://armscontrol.org/aca/midmonth/2004/October/F16.asp, accessed on 18 January 2009.
17 See B.M. Jain, 'India-China Relations', *The Round Table* (April 2004), pp.253–69.
18 For a detailed analysis, see B.M. Jain, 'India and Russia: Reassessing the Time Tested Ties,' *Pacific Affairs*, Vol. 76, No. 3 (Fall 2003), pp. 375–97.
19 For details, see BM Jain, *Global Power: India's Foreign Policy, 1947–2006*, Lanham, MD: Lexington Books, 2008, pp.122–24.
20 On the Kargil tragedy, see Ashley J.Tellis (et al., ed.) *Limited Conflicts Under the Nuclear Umbrella: Indian and Pakistani Lessons from the Kargil Crisis*, Santa Monica: Rand Corporation, 2001.
21 Ahmad Faruqui, 'Beyond Strategic Myopia in South Asia,' *Strategic Review*, Vol. XXIX, No.1 (Winter 2001), pp.18–25.
22 See Joseph S. Nye, Jr., 'Limits of American Power,' *Political Science Quarterly*, Vol. 117, No.4 (2002–03), pp.545–59.
23 For a detailed analysis of its historical backdrop, see Sumit Ganguly, *The Crisis in Kashmir: Portents of War, Hopes of Peace*, Cambridge: Cambridge University Press, 1997.
24 *The Indian Express*, 25 September 2009.
25 *Ibid.*
26 See Ashley J. Tellis, 'The Strategic Implications of a Nuclear India,' *Orbis* (Winter 2002), pp.13–45.
27 For a critique of paradigm shifts in the globalization and regionalization, see B.M. Jain, 'Globalization and Regionalization in International Relations and Foreign Policy: A Critique of Existing Paradigms', *Journal of Diplomacy and Foreign Relations* (September 2001), pp.86–101.

Chapter Three

1 Mushirul Hasan (ed.), *Nehru's India: Selected Speeches,* New York: Oxford University Press, 2007.

2 B.M. Jain, *Nuclear Politics in South Asia: In Search of an Alternative Paradigm*, Jaipur and New Delhi: Rawat Publishers, 1994.

3 For a perceptive analysis of this part, see Haider K. Nizamani, *The Roots of Rhetoric: Politics of Nuclear Weapons in India and Pakistan*, Westport, CT: Greenwood Publishing Group, 2000.

4 Zia Mian, 'A Story of Leaders, Partners, and Clients', *Foreign Policy in Focus* (FPIF), 27 September 2005, www.fpif.org/fpiftxt/819, accessed on 20 July 2009.

5 For a perceptive analysis of Nehru's foreign policy approach, see Rahul Sagar, 'State of Mind: What Kind of Power will India Become?', *International Affairs* ,Vol. 85. No. 4 (2009), pp. 801–16.

6 *Constituent Assembly Debates,* 6 April 1948, pp. 3333–34.

7 Quoted in *Brochure* 'National Nuclear Energy Programme', New Delhi: Lok Sabha Secretariat, 1985, p.3.

8 *Ibid.*, p. 4.

9 *Ibid.*

10 *Ibid.*, p.7.

11 *Ibid.,* Speeches of Prime Minister Lal Bahadur Shastri, July 1964–May 1965, Delhi, 1965, p.16.

12 For a critical analysis of Indira Gandhi's personality and her style of conducting the foreign policy, see Pranay Gupte, *Vengeance: India After the Assassination of Indira Gandhi,* New York: W.W. Norton & Co., 1985, pp. 71–72, 83–86.

13 For the views of Indira Gandhi on these aspects, see *Prime Minister Indira Gandhi's Statements on Foreign Policies,* January–March 1982, New Delhi: External Publicity Division, Ministry of External Affairs, Government of India, 1982.

14 Onkar Marwah, an expert on defence and foreign affairs, observes that 'the decision to undertake the nuclear test was a direct consequence of the appearance of United States Task Force 74, led by the nuclear armed aircraft carrier `Enterprise' in the Bay of Bengal in the closing stages of the 1971 Indo-Pakistan War.' Onkar Marwah, 'The Nonproliferation Policies of Non-Nuclear Weapon States', in David B. Dewitt, *Nuclear Non-Proliferation and Global Security,* London and Sydney: Croom Helm, 1987, p.113.

15 Indira Gandhi, *On Peoples and Problems,* London: Hodder and Stoughton, 1982, p.200.

16 *Ibid.,* p.35.

17 Quoted in Baldev Raj Nayar, *American Geopolitics and India,* New Delhi: Manohar, 1976, p.158.

18 *Annual Report* 1983–84, New Delhi: Ministry of External Affairs, Government of India, New Delhi, pp.37–38.

19 *Ibid.,* p. 38.

20 *Ibid.,* p. 45.

21 *Performance Budget* of *the Department of Atomic Energy, 1984–85*, Government of India, New Delhi, p.2.

22 *Ibid.*

23 *Ibid.*

24 *Ibid.*, p.3.

25 *Ibid.,* p.4

26 *Ibid.,* p.43.

27 *Annual Report 1987–88*, Ministry of External Affairs, Government of India, New Delhi, p.41.

28 *Ibid.,* p.50.

29 *Annual Report 1988–89*, Ministry of External Affairs, Government of India, New Delhi, p.52.

30 *Ibid.*, pp.52–3.

31 *Ibid.*, p.53.

32 *Annual Report 1987–88*, p.52.

33 *The Times of India,* 18 May 1994.

34 *Ibid.*

35 *Ibid.*

36 *Ibid.,* 20 May 1994.

37 *Ibid.*

38 See *The Times of India,* 19 May 1994.

39 *Ibid.*

40 See K. Subrahmanyam, 'Narsimha Rao and the Bomb', *Strategic Analysis,* Vol.28, No.4 (2004), www.idsa.in/publications/strategic-analysis/2004/oct/K%20Sub.pdf, accessed on 20 July 2009.

41 Rebecca Johnson, *Unfinished Business: The Negotiations of the CTBT and the End of Nuclear Testing,* New York and Geneva: United Nations, 2009, p.126

42 *Ibid.*

43 *Ibid.*, quoted, p.139.

44 *Ibid.*, p.140.

45 See P.R. Chari, 'India's Nuclear Doctrine: Confused Ambitions', *The Non-Proliferation Review* (Fall–Winter 2000), pp.122–35.

46 *Strategic Digest*, Vol. 37, No. 3 (March 2007), p.362.

47 UPA Government Report to the People 2004–2008, http://pmindia.nic.in/upa_en_2004-08.pdf, accessed on 18 September 2009.
48 *The Hindu*, 3 August 2009.
49 *Ibid.*
50 *Ibid.*
51 *The Hindu*, 5 December 2008.
52 *Ibid.*
53 *The Hindu*, 17 June 2009.
54 *Ibid.*
55 www.dae.gov.in/pmstmt.htm, accessed on 10 April 2009.
56 Quoted in Mani Shankar Aiyar, 'Towards a Nuclear-Weapons-Free and Non-violent World Order', www.gsinstitute.org/pnnd/pubs/AIYAR_RajivGandhi.pdf, accessed on 20 July 2008.
57 *Ibid.*
58 *The Hindu*, 27 July 2009.
59 *Ibid.*
60 Sagar, 'State of Mind', p.805.
61 See Michel Krepon, *Better Safe Than Sorry: The Ironies of Living with the Bomb*, Palo Alto, CA: Stanford University Press, 2009, pp.133–73.

Chapter Four

1 B.M. Jain, *Global Power: India's Foreign Policy, 1947–2006*, Lanham, MD: Lexington Books, 2008, p.149.
2 In India, it is referred to as Pakistan-occupied Kashmir(PoK) since the Kashmir Valley was invaded and occupied by the Pakistani army in October 1947. For a detailed and critical discussion on the related aspect, see T.V. Paul, 'Causes of the India-Pakistan Enduring Rivalry', in T.V. Paul (ed.), *The India-Pakistan Conflict: An Enduring Rivalry,* Cambridge, UK: Cambridge University Press, 2005, pp.1–24.
3 See Ashok Kapur, 'Major Powers and Persistence of the India-Pakistan Conflict', in TV Paul, p.133.
4 www.indianembassy.org/.../Pakistan/suomoto_jsingh_feb261999.html, accessed on18 June 2009.
5 *Ibid.*
6 See Shaira Khan, 'Nuclear Weapons and the Prolongation of the India-Pakistan Rivalry', in T.V. Paul (ed.), pp.176–7.
7 For details, see *Daily Times*, 3 December 2008.
8 *The Hindu*, 10 December 2008.
9 *Ibid.*
10 *Ibid.*

11 *The Hindu*, 12 December 2008.

12 *Ibid.*; see also Philip Jenkins, 'The Roots of Jihad in India', *The New Republic*, 24 December 2008, http://www.tnr.com:80/toc/story.html?id=f1dba11c-0b2d-4e10-b2fc-2416a7fb2f7b&k=1784; George Packer, 'Risk Factors', *The New Yorker*, 25 December 2008, http://www.newyorker.com/talk/comment/2008/12/15/081215taco_talk_packer ; C.Raja Mohan, 'Re-mapping India', *The Indian Express*, 22 December 2008, http://www.indianexpress.com/news/remapping-india/401262/

13 *NDTV*, 5 January 2008.

14 *The Hindu*, 9 January 2009.

15 Editorial, *The Hindu*, 1 September 2009.

16 *Ibid.*

17 In this regard, see Praveen Swami, 'Understanding Pakistan's response to Mumbai', *The Hindu*, 26 January 2009.

18 *The Hindu,* 6 February 2009

19 See *The Hindu,* 12 September 2009.

20 *Ibid.*

21 Sreeram Chaulia and Stephan Richter, 'Transforming India-Pakistan Relations', *The Globalist*, 23 February 2009, http://www.sreeramchaulia.net/IndPak.pdf, accessed on 18 June 2009.

22 *Ibid.*

23 *The Hindu*, 17 June 2009.

24 Rama Laxmi, *The Washington Post*, 17 July 2009.

25 *Ibid.*

26 Quoted, *The Hindu*, 6 July 2009.

27 See Raj Chengappa *Weapons of Peace: The Secret Story of India's Quest to a Nuclear Power,* New Delhi: Harper Collins Publishers, 2000; Akhtar Ali, *Pakistan's Nuclear Dilemma: Energy and Security Dimensions*, Karachi: Economic Research Unit, 1984.

28 See R. Rajaraman, 'Nuclear Posture', *The Hindu,* 7 February 2003.

29 Jain, *Global Power*: 169.

30 Ahmed Rashid,' Waziristan or Bust', *The Times of India*, 26 October 2009.

31 http://www.isn.ethz.ch/isn/Current-Affairs/Security-Watch/Detail/?lng=en&id=109228 / accessed on 7 November 2009.

32 See Jain, *Global Power*: 182.

33 *Ibid.,* p.185.

Chapter Five

1 In this regard, Madhukar Shumshere J.B. Rana, former finance minister and special advisor, Ministry of Foreign Affairs of Nepal, observes: a bilateral strategic divide arose, for the first time, when King Mahendra assumed

direct rule in 1961 and in 1962, during the Sino-Indian border war. He took a bold and far-reaching decision to allow China to build the north-south or Arniko highway to link Lhasa to Kathmandu, which was started in 1963 and completed in 1965. This divide arose prominently, once again, when India adamantly refused to recognize King Birendra's 'zone of peace' concept. The genesis of this policy lay, most probably, in the annexation of Sikkim by India in 1975 as a part of the Indian union. The policy was reinforced by the fear of 'Bhutanization' (or de facto protectorate status) of Nepal given the rise of India as a nuclear power under the leadership of an authoritarian, aggressive Indira Gandhi—both internally and externally. Madhukar Shumshere J.B.Rana, 'Indo-Nepal Strategic Partnership for the Asian Century: From Dependency to Interdependence, Landlocked to Transit State, and Buffer to Bridge State', unpublished paper.

2 *Ibid.*

3 *The Trend*, 19 April 1995.

4 See M.R. Josse, 'Nepal's Strategic Balancing', *South Asian Journal* (January-March 2004), www.southasianmedia.net/Magazine/.../nepal_strategic.htm, accessed on 18 July 2009.

5 news.indiamart.com/news.../prachanda-visit-indi-19863.html, accessed on 24 November 2008.

6 *The Hindu*, 23 August 2009.

7 *Ibid.*

8 See B.M. Jain, *India's Defence and Security: Intra-regional Dimension*, Jaipur: Ina Shree, 1998.

9 *Annual Report 2007–08*, New Delhi: Ministry of External Affairs, Government of India, p.13.

10 Pushpita Das, 'Demarcate the India-Border Dispute', IDSA Strategic Comments, 31 August 2009, www.idsa.in/publications/.../PushpitaDas310809.htm, accessed on 10 September 2009.

11 For details see, Jain: *India's Defence and Security,* pp.80–81.

12 banglapedia.search.com.bd/HT/G_0023.htm, accessed on 20 April 2009.

13 *Annual Report*, 2007–08, p.4.

14 See Harsh V. Pant, 'India and Bangladesh: A Relationship Adrift', in Manas Chatterji and B.M. Jain (eds.), *Conflict and Peace in South Asia*, London: Emerald Publishing Group, 2008, p. 238.

15 *Ibid.*, p. 241.

16 See *The Hindu*, 17 September 2004.

17 *Annual Report 2007-08,* p.4.

18 *South Asia Intelligence Review Weekly*, Assessments & Briefings, Volume 6, No. 29 (28 January 2008), www.satp.org/satporgtp/sair/Archives/6_29.htm, accessed on 15 February 2009.

19 *The Hindu*, 16 December 2008.
20 *Ibid.*
21 For details, see K. Subrahmanyam's reporting, *The Times of India,* 20 April 2001.
22 *Strategic Digest* (June 2005), pp.807–8.
23 *The Hindu*, 7 August 2005.
24 See *The Indian Express*, 3 January 2009.
25 *Ibid.*
26 *Ibid.*
27 Shamsur Rabb Khan, 'Towards Better India-Bangladesh Relations', IDSA Comment, 9 January 2009, http://www.idsa.in/idsastrategiccomments/TowardsBetterIndiaBangladeshrelations_MSRKhan_090109, accessed on 15 June 2009.
28 See *The Hindu*, 26 July 2004.
29 http://nation.ittefaq.com/issues/2009/07/07/all0599.htm, accessed on 4 August 2009.
30 *Ibid.*
31 *Strategic Digest*, Vol. 35, No. 2 (February 2005), p.179.
32 *The Hindu,* 7 August 2005.
33 news.indiamart.com/news-analysis/natwar-visit-to-dhak-10059.html, accessed on 14 April 2009.
34 For greater details see Syed Jamaluddin, 'Bangladesh-India Economic Relations', *The Financial Express*, 29 July 2009, www.thefinancialexpress-bd.com/2009/07/26/74259.html, accessed on 10 August 2009.
35 Jain: *India's Defence and Security*, p.110.
36 http://sundaytimes.lk/090524/News/sundaytimesnews_28.html, accessed on 16 June 2009.
37 *Ibid.*
38 *Annual Report, 2007–08*, p.5.
39 *The Hindu,* 17 October 2008.
40 *Ibid.*
41 *Daily Mirror,* 24 July 2007.
42 See *The Hindu*, 19 May 2009.
43 *Ibid.*
44 *The Hindu*, 21 May 2009.
45 *Ibid.*
46 *Ibid.*
47 D.B.S. Jeyaraj, 'Sri Lankan Tamils in a post-war scenario', *The Hindu*, 21 May 2009.

Chapter 6

1 Howard B. Schaffer, 'U.S. Interests in South Asia', in Rafiq Dossani and Henry S. Rowen (eds.), *Prospects for Peace in South Asia*, Stanford, CA: Stanford University Press, 2005, p.329.

2 See B.M. Jain, *India and the United States, 1961–1963*, Delhi: Radiant, 1987.

3 See Henry A. Kissinger, *The White House Years*, Boston: Little Brown & Co, 1979.

4 See Zalmay Khalilzad and Daniel Byman, 'Afghanistan: The Consolidation of a Rogue State', *The Washington Quarterly* (Winter 2002), www.twq.com/winter00/231Byman.html, accessed on 10 May 2009.

5 See Harsh V. Pant, 'The U.S.-India Nuclear Deal, Iran, and India's Future,' *The Asia-Pacific Journal: Japan Focus*, www.japanfocus.org/-Harsh_V_-Pant/2100, accessed on 10 June 2009.

6 B.M. Jain, *Global Power: India's Foreign Policy, 1947–2006*, Lanham, MD: Lexington Books, 2008.

7 Lee H. Hamilton, 'The Bush Doctrine–An Evaluation', www.wilsoncenter.org/about/director/docs/Hamilton_Bush_Doctrine.doc, accessed on 10 June 2009.

8 http://www.nytimes.com/2001/09/22/international/22RESP.html, accessed on 13 April 2009.

9 www.rediff.com/news/2006/dec/18ndeal3.htm, accessed on 10 June 2009

10 For a chronology of the India-USA Nuclear Deal See *Outlook*, news.outlookindia.com/item.aspx?618693, accessed on 10 June 2009.

11 *Zee News*, 6 September 2008.

12 *Asia Pacific Defence Forum*, Vol. 34, No.1 (2009), pp. 24–25.

13 *Ibid.*

14 explorer.altopix.com/map/1ahjlb/295/232/Gwadar_Port.htm, accessed on 9 June 2009.

15 Editorial, 'Secretary Clinton Goes to India', *The New York Times*, 18 July 2009, p.A2o; http://www.nytimes.com/2009/07/18/opinion/18sat1.html?_r=1&hpw, accessed on10 August 2009.

16 *Ibid.*

17 Sumit Ganguly, 'Hillary, India and The New York Times', *Forbes,* http://www.forbes.com/2009/07/21/new-york-times-india-clinton-climate-nuclear-opinions-contributors-sumit-ganguly.html, accessed on 24 July 2009.

18 *Christian Science Monitor*, 21 July 2009.

19 *The Hindu*, 19 July 2009.

20 *Ibid.*

21 For details, see *The Times of India*, 22 July 2009.

22 See *The Hindu,* 20 July 2009.

23 *Ibid.*

24 For a detailed critique see G Parthasarathy, 'Post-Clinton visit, the key issues', *The Hindu Business Line*, 6 August 2009, http://thehindubusinessline.com/2009/08/06/stories/2009080650270800.htm, accessed on 18 September 2009.
25 www.cfr.org/.../global_nuclear_nonproliferation_regime.html, accessed on 28 September 2009.
26 *The Hindu*, 21 July 2009.
27 Ashok Parthasarathi, 'Concerns over a pernicious agreement', *The Hindu*, 6 August 2009.
28 *Ibid.*
29 *Ibid.*
30 Joshua Kucera, 'Bush Administration Reluctance to Recalibrate Pakistan Policy Draws Criticism from Democrats', www.eurasianet.org/departments/insight/articles/eav022808a.shtml, 28 February 2008, accessed on 14 June 2009.
31 Karen De Young, 'Taliban Advance, Pakistan's Wavering Worry Obama Team', *The Washington Post*, 24 April 2009. www.washingtonpost.com/wpdyn/content/article/2009/04/23/AR2009042304114.html?wpisrc=newsletteraccessed on 18 July 2009.
32 Mark Mazzetti and Eric Schmitt, 'Afghan Strikes by Taliban Get Pakistan Help, U.S. Aides Say', *The New York Times*, 25 March 2009.
33 *Ibid.*
34 *Ibid.*
35 "The War in Afghanistan: Say You're Staying Mr. President," *The Economist*, 28 March 2009, p. 18.
36 http://www.afghanistan-un.org/2009/05/presidents-meetings-with-president-karzai-of-afghanistan-and-president-zardari-of-pakistan/, accessed on 16 June 2009.
37 For a detailed note on this aspect, see the reporting of Peter Spiegel and Jay Solomon, *The Wall Street Journal*, 6 May 2009, http://online.wsj.com/article/SB124156465200189381.html, accessed on 16 June 2009.
38 *Ibid.*
39 www.guardian.co.uk/world/2009/apr/14/sharia-law-in-pakistans-swat-valley, accessed on 20 April 2009.
40 See *The Times of India*, 31 March 2009.
41 *Voice of India Rajasthan TV Channel*, 30 March 2009.
42 *The Economist*, 26 March 2009.
43 *The Hindu*, 22 November 2007.
44 *Ibid.*
45 *The Indian Express*, 6 June 2009.
46 *Ibid.*

47 *The Times of India*, 7 June 2009, http://timesofindia.indiatimes.com/World/Pak-used-US-aid-against-India/articleshow/4624601.cms, accessed on 7 June 2009.

48 http://hsgac.senate.gov/public/index.cfm?FuseAction=Files.View&FileStore_id=a70ad531-01a9-43d7-94ad-da531046d824, accessed on 18 October 2009.

49 *Ibid.*

50 http://www.stimson.org/pub.cfm?ID=785, accessed on 18 October 2009.

51 See Craig Cohen (with Frederick Barton, Karin Von Hippel), *A Perilous Course: U.S. Strategy and Assistance to Pakistan*, Washington, D.C.: Centre for Strategic and International Studies, 2007.

52 www.america.gov/.../20090504164618esnamfuak0.845669.html&disti=ucs, accessed on 20 July 2009.

53 *The Hindu,* 3 May 2009.

54 *Ibid.*

55 rupeenews.com/.../gen-kiyanis-rejects-us-plan-for-pakistan-army-impact/, accessed on 12 July 2009.

56 *The Hindu*, 24 April 2009.

57 *Ibid.*

58 washingtonindependent.com/36143/obama-strategy-deepens-us-committment-to-afghanistan-pakistan, accessed on 14 April 2009.

59 *The Atlantic Politics*, 26 March 2009.

60 Michael Krepon, 'The U.S.-Pakistan Strategic Relationship', hsgac.senate.gov/public/_files/KreponTestimony.pdf, accessed on 14 April 2009.

61 *Ibid.*

62 *Ibid.*

63 www.heritage.org/Research/asiaandthepacific/tst062707.cfm, accessed on 9 January 2009.

64 *Ibid.*

65 http://74.125.153.132/search?q=cache:PSsoSXh075cJ:www.cnn.com/2009/POLITICS/12/01/obama.afghanistan/index.html+obama+has+decided+to+send+30,000+additional+troops+to+Afghanistan&cd=3&hl=en&ct=clnk&gl=in, accessed on 2 December 2009.

66 Emily Wax's news despatch, *The Washington Post*, 26 September 2009.

Chapter Seven

1 *The Wall Street Journal*, 24 June 2009.

2 Samuel S. Kim, 'China and the World in Theory and Practice', in Samuel S. Kim (ed.), *China and the World, Chinese Foreign Relations in the Post-Cold War Era,* Boulder, CO: Westview Press, 1994, p. 23.

3 See Gerald Segal, 'Does China Matter?', *Foreign Affairs*, Vol. 75, No. 5, (September/October 1999), pp. 24–36.
4 See Kim: '*China and the World*', p. 146.
5 For this part, see Pieter Bottelier, 'Twenty Five Years of China's Economic Reforms', *Perspectives*, Vol.5, No. 4 (31 December 2004), pp. 45–64.
6 For a perceptive analysis, see Zhao Hongwei, *Political Regime of Contemporary China,* Lanham: University Press of America, 2002, chapter 2, pp. 46–58.
7 Mel Gurtov and Byong-Moo Hwang, *China's Security: The New Role of the Military*, Boulder: Lynne Rienner Publishers, 1998, p.57.
8 Kim: '*China and the World*', p.15.
9 William T. Tow, *Asia-Pacific Strategic Relations,* Cambridge: Cambridge University Press, 2001.
10 Kim: '*China in the World*', p.48.
11 See Stuart Harris, 'Introduction: Reading the Chinese Leaves', in Stuart Harris and Gary Klintworth, *China as Great Power: Myths, Realities and Challenges in the Asia-Pacific Region*, New York: St Martin's Press, 1995, pp.3-6.
12 Wei He, "Military Budget increase normal, not aggressive," *China Daily,* 3 September 2009, http://www.chinadaily.com.cn/opinion/2009-03/09/content_7553122.htm, accessed on 10 October 2009.
13 Luke T. Chang, *China's Boundary Treaties and Frontier Disputes*, London/New York: Oceana Publications, 1982, p.41.
14 *Ibid.,* p.9.
15 *FY04 Report to the Congress on PRC Military Power*, Pursuant to the FY2000 National Defense Authorization Act, www.dklin.why3s.us/Articles%20and%20Documents/PRC%20military/d20040528PRC.pdf, accessed on 18 October 2008.
16 Prasant Sen Gupta, *China's Belief Systems and Sino-Indian Relations: The Maoist Era*, Calcutta, Minerva Associates Pvt. Ltd., 1998, p.5.
17 Quoted, *Ibid.*, p.4.
18 See Subramanian Swamy, *India's China Perspective*, New Delhi: Konark Publishers, 2001; see also Yaacov Vertzberger, *Misperceptions in Foreign Policy Making: The Sino-Indian Conflict, 1959–1962*, Boulder: Westview Press, 1984.
19 See Mohan Guruswamy and Zorawar Daulet Singh, *India China Relations: The Border Issue And Beyond,* New Delhi: Viva Books Pvt. Ltd., 2009.
20 B.M. Jain, 'India-China Relations', *The Round Table* (April 2004), pp.253–69.
21 For a detailed analysis of the multi-dimensional border issue, see Garver, John W, 'The Restoration of Sino-Indian Comity Following India's Nuclear Tests,' *The China Quarterly* (December 2001), pp. 686–88.
22 *Xinhua News Agency*, 18 January 2002.
23 www.dailynews365.com/.../china-expresses-dissatisfaction-on-manmohan-singhs-arunachal-visit/, accessed on 20 October 2009.

24 *Ibid.*

25 "Are we heading towards the 1962 Repeat" in *Freedom First Magazine* (September 2009).

26 *The Hindu*, 17 October 2009.

27 *Ibid.*

28 Allen S. Whiting, 'The Future of Chinese Foreign Policy', in Kim: '*China and the World*', p. 264.

29 *Ibid.*

30 Mohan Malik, 'China's Southern Discomfort', *Asia Times Online*, 11 July 2002.

31 *Jane's Intelligence Review,* 5/99, p.3.

32 Shirley A. Kan, 'CRS Brief for Congress, IB92056: China's Proliferation of Weapons of Mass Destruction and Missiles', *Current Policy Issues*, 16 May 2001, www.ncseonline.org/nle/crsreports/international/inter-73.cfm, acc essed on 15 October 2008.

33 Pertaining to this aspect, see Zbigniew Brzezinski, 'A Geostrategy for Eurasia' *Foreign Affairs*, Vol. 76, No.5 (Sept/Oct 1997), p.58.

34 C.V. Rangnathan, 'The China Threat: A View From India', in Herbert Yee and Ian Storey, *The China Threat: Perceptions, Myths and Reality,* London: Routledge, 2002, p.294.

35 Garver: 'The Restoration of Sino- Indian Comity,' pp. 865–89.

36 See Daniel Twining, 'America's Grand Design in Asia', *The Washington Quarterly* (Summer 2007), p.79.

37 G. Parthasarathy, 'India faces growing Chinese hostility after 26/11', *BUSINESSLINE*, 19 March 2009, http://www.thehindubusinessline.com:80/2009/03/19/stories/2009031950270800.htm, accessed on 15 September 2009.

38 Quoted, *Ibid.*

39 *The Hindu*, 16 October 2009.

40 *Ibid.*

41 www.india-seminar.com/2008/584/584_vinod_c_khanna.htm, accessed on 7 January 2009.

42 Muhammad Javed Iqbal, 'India: Bangladesh missiles part of China's encirclement', newsgroups.derkeiler.com/Archive/Soc/soc.culture.pakist an/2008-09/msg00170.html, accessed on 10 February 2009.

43 Mansi Mehrotra, 'Bangladesh's Economic Relations with India, Pakistan and China: An Overview', www.weeklyblitz.net/index.php?id=211, accessed on 4 June 2009.

44 *Ibid.*

45 www.timesonline.co.uk/tol/news/world/asia/article6297463.ece,16 May 2009, accessed on 4 June 2009.

46 *Ibid.*

47 *Ibid.*

48 www.tamilnation.org/intframe/indian_ocean/index.htm, accessed on 18 May 2009.

49 For details see Jeremy Kahn, 'Why India Fears China?' www.newsweek.com/id/217088?from=rss, accessed on 1 November 2009.

50 Zhang Yan, 'Trend of China-India friendship irreversible', *The Hindu*, 12 October 2009.

51 See *Global Times,* Editorial, http://www.globaltimes.cn/www/english/opinion/editorial/2009-06/436174.html, 11 June 2009.

52 http://chellaney.spaces.live.com/Blog/cns!4913C7C8A2EA4A30!249.entry, accessed on 6 November 2009.

Conclusion

1 M.K. Bhadra Kumar, 'India must energise regional diplomacy', *The Hindu*, 15 May 2008, p.8

2 Quoted, *Ibid.*

3 See Richard Falk, 'Barak Obama's historic victory and his foreign policy challenges', http://www.stwr.org/united-states-of-america/barack-obamas-historic-victory-and-his-foreign-policy-challenges.html, accessed on 12 November 2008.

4 *The Hindu*, 5 December 2008.

5 *Business Standard*, 10 June 2009

6 *The Times of India,* 27 August 2009.

BIBLIOGRAPHY

Abraham, Itty (ed.), *South Asian Cultures of the Bomb: Atomic Publics and the State in India and Pakistan*, Bloomington: Indiana University Press, 2009.

Ahmad, Qazi Shakil, 'Pakistan-India Relations: Some Geostrategic Considerations', *Pakistan Horizon*, Vol. 57, No. 3 (July 2004): 13–19.

Ahmad, Ishtiaq, *The Nuclear Danger: Moving Down to Minimum Deterrence*, Islamabad: National Book Foundation of Pakistan, 1996.

Akbar, M.J., *The Siege Within*, New Delhi: Penguin Books, 1985.

———, *Nehru: The Making of India*, London: Viking, 1998.

Alagappa, Muthiah (ed.), *The Long Shadow: Nuclear Weapons and Security in 21st Century*, Palo Alto, CA: Stanford University Press, 2008.

Ali, Akhtar, *Pakistan's Nuclear Dilemma: Energy and Security Dimensions*, Karachi: Economic Research Unit, 1984.

Alikhan, Shafique, *Two Nation Theory*, Karachi: Royal Book Company, Pakistan, 1988.

Allison, Graham, 'How to Stop Nuclear Terror', *Foreign Affairs,* Vol. 83, No.1 (January/February 2004).

Ayoob, Mohammed, 'South Asia's Dangers and U.S. Foreign Policy,' *Orbis*, Vol. XLV, No. 1, (Winter 2001): 128–33.

Balz, Dan, 'U.S. Urges Pakistan to Forgo Tests,' *Washington Post*, 18 May 1998.

Baral, Lok Raj (ed.), *Nepal, Quest for Democracy*, New Delhi: Adroit publishers, 2006.

Basrur, Rajesh M., *South Asia's Cold War: Nuclear Weapons and Conflict in Comparative Perspective*, London: Routledge, 2008.

Berger, Samuel R., 'Foreign Policy for the Global Age', *Foreign Affairs*, Vol. 79, No. 6 (November/December 2000): 22–39.

Bertsch, Gary K., Seema Gahlaut, and Anupam Srivastava (eds.), *Engaging India: US Strategic Relations with the World's Largest Democracy*, New York: Routledge, 1999.

Bhadrakumar, M.K., 'U.S. draws India into the Afghan war, *The Hindu*, 25 December 2008.

Bose, Sugata and Ayesha Jalal, *Modern South Asia: History, Culture, Political Economy*, London, New York: Routledge, 1998.

Brass, Paul R., *India, Pakistan, Bangladesh, Sri Lanka, and Nepal*, London: Routledge, 2009.

Brown, Michel E. (ed.), *Grave New World, Security Challenges in the 21st Century*, Washington, D.C.: Georgetown University Press, 2003.

Castles, Stephen, *Ethnicity and Globalization*, London: Sage Publications, 2000.

Chambers, Michael R. (ed.), *South Asia in 2020: Future Strategic Balances and Alliances*, Carlisle Barracks, PA: Strategic Studies Institute, U.S. Army War College, 2002.

Chapman, Graham P., *The Geopolitics of South Asia: From Early Empires to the Nuclear Age*, Burlington, VT: Ashgate, 2003.

Chari, Chandra, *War, Peace and Hegemony in a Globalized World: The Changing Balance of Power in the Twenty-first Century*, London: Routledge, 2008.

Chari, P.R., Pervaiz Iqbal Cheema, and Stephen P. Cohen, *Four Crises and a Peace Process*, Washington: Brookings Institution Press, 2007.

—— (eds.), *Perception, Politics, and Security in South Asia: The Compound Crisis of 1990*, New York, NY: Routledge, 2003.

Chatterji, Manas and B.M. Jain (eds.), *Conflict and Peace in South Asia*, London: Emerald Group Publishing Ltd., 2008.

Chengappa, Raj, *Weapons of Peace: The Secret Story of India's Quest to a Nuclear Power*, New Delhi: Harper Collins Publishers, 2000.

Chellaney, Brahma, Nuclear *Proliferation: The US-India Conflict,* New Delhi: Orient Longman Ltd, 1993.

Cheema, Zafar Iqbal, 'Pakistan's Nuclear Policy under Z. A. Bhutto and Zia-ul-Haq: An Assessment,' *Strategic Studies* (Summer 1992): 5–20.

Chopra, Pran, *India, Pakistan and the Kashmir Tangle*, New Delhi: Harper Collins, 1994.

Clary, Christopher, 'A.Q. Khan and the limits of the non-proliferation regime,' *Disarmament Forum*, No. 4 (2004): 34–41.

Cohen, Stephen, 'A New Beginning in South Asia,' *Policy Brief*, No. 55 (January 2000), Washington DC: Brookings Institution.

Cohen, Stephen P., *India: Emerging Power*, Washington, D.C. Brookings Institutions, 2001.

Council on Foreign Relations, *A New U.S. Policy toward India and Pakistan: Report of an Independent Task Force*, New York, N.Y.: Council on Foreign Relations, 1997.

Craig, Baxter, *Bangladesh: A New Nation in an Old Setting*, Boulder, C.O.: Westview Press, 1984.

Dahal, Dev Raj and Nischal Pandey (eds.), *Comprehensive Security in South Asia*, New Delhi: Manohar Publishers and Distributors, 2006.

Das, Veena (ed.), *Mirrors of Violence: Communities, Riots and Survivors in South Asia*, New Delhi: Oxford University Press, 1994.

Dash, Kishore C., 'The Challenge of Regionalism in South Asia,' *International Politics*, Vol. XXXVIII, No. 2 (June 2001): 216–17.

Deora, M.S., *India and the Freedom Struggle of Bangladesh*, New Delhi: Discovery Publishing House, 1995.

Dittmer, Lowell (ed.), *South Asia's Nuclear Security Dilemma*, Armonk NY: M.E. Sharpe 2005.

Dixit, J.N., *Across Borders: Fifty Years of India's Foreign Policy*, New Delhi: Picus Books, 1998.

——, *Liberation and Beyond: Indo-Bangladesh Relations*, New Delhi: Konark Publishers, 1999.

Durrani, Mahmud Ali, *India and Pakistan: The Cost of Conflict and the Benefits of Peace*, Karachi: Oxford, 2001.

Dutta, Sreeradhar, 'Indo-Bangladesh Relations: An Overview of Limitations and Constraints,' *Strategic Analysis*, Vol. 26, No. 3 (July-September 2002): 427–440.

Farmer, B.H., *An Introduction to South Asia*, London: Routledge, 1983.

Faruqui, Ahmad, 'Beyond Strategic Myopia in South Asia,' *Strategic Review*, Vol. XXIX, No. 1 (Winter 2001): 18–25.

Flanagan, Stephen J., James A. Schear (eds.), *Strategic Challenges: America's Global Security Agenda*, Washington, D.C.: National Defense University Press, 2008.

Frankel, Francine, *Bridging the Non-proliferation Divide: The United States and India*, New Delhi: Konark Publishers, 1995.

Gandhi, Indira, *The Years of Endeavour,* New Delhi: Government of India, 1975.

Ganguly, Sumit, *Conflict Unending: India-Pakistan since 1947*, Washington, DC: Woodrow Wilson Centre Press, 2001.

——, 'America and India at a Turning Point,' *Current History* (March 2005): 120–24.

——, *The Origins of War in South Asia,* Boulder, CO: Westview, 1994, 2nd edition.

——, *Conflict Unending: India-Pakistan Tensions Since 1947*, New York: Columbia University Press, 2002.

——, 'The Kashmir Conundrum', *Foreign Affairs,* Vol. 85, No. 4 (July/August 2006): 45–57.

Ganguly, Sumit and Brian Shoup, 'Nepal: Between Dictatorship and Anarchy', *Journal of Democracy*, Vol. 16, Number 4 (October 2005): 129–45.

Garver, John W, 'The Restoration of Sino-Indian Comity Following India's Nuclear Tests,' *The China Quarterly* (December 2001): 686–88.

——, 'Sino-Indian Rapprochement and the Sino-Pakistan Entente,' *Political Science Quarterly*, Vol. 111, No. 2 (1996): 323–47.

Gilboy, Georg and Eric Heginbotham, 'China's Coming Transformation', *Foreign Affairs*, Vol. 80, No. 4 (July/August 2001): 26–39.

Glaser, Bonnie S., 'China's Security Perceptions,' *Asian Survey*, Vol. 33, No. 3 (March 1993), pp. 252–71.

Goldstein, Avery, 'The Diplomatic face of China's Grand strategy: A Rising Power's Emerging Choice', *The China Quarterly* (December 2001): 835–64.

Gordon, Sandy, *India's Rise to Power in the Twentieth Century and Beyond*, New York: St. Martin's Press, 1995.

Gould, Harold A., and Sumit Ganguly (eds.), *The Hope and the Reality: U.S.-Indian Relations from Roosevelt to Reagan*, Boulder, C.O.: Westview Press, 1992.

Gries, Peter Hays, 'A China Threat?: Chinese Face Nationalism', *World Affairs*, (Fall 1999), pp.63–75.

Gujral, I.K., *A Foreign Policy for India*, New Delhi: Ministry of External Affairs, Government of India, 1998.

Gupta, Shekhar, 'Nuclear Weapons in the Subcontinent', *Occasional Paper* No. 21 (May 1995), Washington, D.C.: The Henry L. Stimson Centre: 34–5.

Gupte, Pranay, *India: The Challenge of Change*, London: Mandarin-Mathuen, 1989.

Guruswamy, Mohan and Zorawar Daulet Singh, *India-China Relations: The Border Issue And Beyond*, New Delhi: Viva Books Pvt. Ltd., 2009.

Hagerty, Devin T. (ed.), *South Asia in World Politics*, Lanham, MD: Rowman & Littlefield, 2005.

——, *The Consequences of Nuclear Proliferation: Lessons from South Asia*, Cambridge, Mass.: MIT Press, 1998.

Hainfa, Aziz, 'Pakistan has lost presumption of innocence', *India Abroad*, Vol. XXXVI, No. 46 (18 August 2006).

Harrison, Selig, *China, Oil and Asia: Conflict Ahead*, New York: Columbia University Press, 1992.

Harshe, Rajen, and K.M. Sethi (eds.), *Engaging with the World: Critical Reflections on India's Foreign Policy*, New Delhi: Orient Longman, 2005.

Hasan, Askari Rizvi, 'Pakistan's Strategic Culture,' in Michael R. Chambers (ed.), *South Asia in 2020: Future Strategic Balances and Alliances,* Washington, D.C.: Strategic Studies Institute, 2002.

Hasan, Sibte, *Pakistan*, Karachi: Pakistan Publishing House, 1989.

Hersh, Seymour M., 'On the Nuclear Edge', *The New Yorker*, 29 March 1993, pp.56-67.

Hewitt, Vernon, *Toward the Future? Jammu and Kashmir in the 21st Century*, London: Cambridge, 2001.

Hoffman, Steven, *India's China Crisis,* New Delhi: Oxford University Press, 1991.

Huq, Muhammad Shamsul, *Bangladesh in International Politics: The Dilemmas of Weak States*, Dhaka: Dhaka University Press Limited, 1993.

Husain, Ross Massod, 'Promotion of Inter-Government, Inter-People and Inter-Institutional Understanding in South Asia,' *South Asian Survey*, Vol. 2, No. 2 (1995): 185–200.

Hussain, Mushahid, 'Pakistan-China Defence Co-operation: An Enduring Relationship,' *International Defence Review* (February 1993), pp.108–11.

Hussain, Rifaat, 'Pakistan's Relations with Azad Kashmir and the Impact on India-Pakistan Relations', in Rafiq Dossani and Henry S. Rowen (eds.), *Prospects for Peace in South Asia*, Stanford, CA: Stanford University Press, 2005:109–40

Jain, B.M., *Global Power: India's Foreign Policy, 1947–2006*, Lexington Books: Lanham, MD, 2008.

——, 'India-China Relations', *The Round Table*, Vol. 93, No. 374 (April 2004): 253-69.

——, 'India-Pakistan Relations,' in David Levinson and Karen Christensen (eds.), *Encyclopedia of Modern Asia*, New York: Charles Scribner's Sons, 2002: 20–33.

——, 'Non-offensive Defense in South Asia: Psycho-cultural Dimension,' *Indian Journal of Asian Affairs,* Vol. 7, No. 2 (December 1994): 1–10.

——, *India's Defence and Security: Intra-regional Dimension,* Jaipur: Ina Shree Publishers, 1998.

——, 'India-Pakistan Relations: The Need for Psycho-cultural Prophylaxis' in Ramakant (ed.), *Contemporary Pakistan: Trends and Issues*, Vol. II, Delhi: Kalinga Publishers, 2001: 187–99.

——, *Nuclear Politics in South Asia: In Search of an Alternative Paradigm*, Jaipur and New Delhi: Rawat, 1994.

Jain, B.M., and E.M. Hexamer(eds.), Nuclearisation in South Asia: Reactions and Responses, Jaipur and New Delhi: Rawat Publications, 1999.

Jamwal, N.S., 'Border Management: Dilemma of Guarding the India-Bangladesh Border,' Strategic Analysis, Vol. 28, No.1 (January–March 2004): 5–36.

Jehangir, Karamat, 'Missile Acquisition by Pakistan: Military Strategic Imperatives,' *South Asia Survey,* Vol. 11, No. 2 (2004):171–76.

Jeyaraj, D.B.S., 'Sri Lankan Tamils in a Post-War Scenario', *The Hindu*, 21 May 2009.

Johnson, Rebecca, *Unfinished Business: The Negotiations of the CTBT and the End of Nuclear Testing*, New York and Geneva: United Nations, 2009.

Johnson, Rob, *A Region in Turmoil: South Asian Conflicts Since 1947*, London: Reaktion Books, 2005.

Kalam, A.P.J. with Y.S. Rajan, *India 2020: A Vision for the New Millennium*, New Delhi: Viking, Penguin India, 1998.

Kapur, Ashok, Y.K. Malik, Harold A Gould and Arthur G. Rubinoff (eds.), *India and the United States in a Changing World*, New Delhi: Sage, 2002.

Kapur Ashok, *Pakistan in Crisis*, London: Routledge, 1991.

——, *India-From Regional to World Power,* London: Routledge, 2006.

——, *Pakistan's Nuclear Development*, London: Croom Helm Press, 1987.

Kapur, Harish, *India's Foreign Policy, 1947–1992: Shadows and Substance*, New Delhi: Sage, 1994.

Karat, Rajesh S., *Foreign Policy of Bhutan*, New Delhi: Manak, 2005.

Karnad, Bharat, 'Peril of a Tight Embrace: India, US, Kashmir and Non-Proliferation Issues', *Strategic Analysis,* Vol. 26, No. 3 (July–September 2002): 329–40.

Karnad, Bharat, *India's Nuclear Policy: Credible Minimum Deterrence*, New Delhi: Pentagon Press, 2008.

Kaul, Triloki Nath, *A Diplomat's Diary, 1947–99: China, India, and USA: The Tantalizing Triangle,* Delhi: Macmillan India, 2000.

Khan, Abdul Wali, *Facts are Facts: The Untold Story of India's Partition*, New Delhi: Vikas, 1987.

Khan, Jamshed Ayaz, 'Weapons of Mass Destruction: Pakistan's Perspective', *Regional Studies,* Vol. XXIII, No. 2 (Spring 2005): 3–13.

Khan, Saira, *Nuclear Weapons and Conflict Transformation*, London: Routledge, 2008.

Khosla, I.P., 'India-Bangladesh Relations', *South Asian Journal* (January–March 2005): 65–81.

Kissinger, Henry, *The White House Years*, Boston: Little Brown & Co., 1979.

——, *Does America Need a Foreign Policy? Toward a Diplomacy for the 21st Century*, New York: Simon Schuster, 2001.

Klare, Michael T., 'Tithing at the Crude Altar', *The National Interest* (July/August 2009): 20–29.

Kothari, Rajni, *State Against Democracy: In Search of Human Governance*, New Delhi, Ajanta, 1989.

Krepon, Michael, *Better Safe Than Sorry: The Ironies of Living with the Bomb*, Palo Alto, CA: Stanford University Press, 2009.

Krepon, Michael and Chris Gagne (eds.), *Nuclear Risk Reduction in South Asia*, Washington D.C.: Henry L. Stimson Centre, 2003.

Krishna, Ashok, and P.R. Chari (eds.), *Kargil: The Tables Turned*, New Delhi: Manohar, 2001.

Krishnaswamy, S, 'We are totally offensive power', *Frontline* Vol. 20, No. 25 (19 July–1 August 2003).

Kumar, B.B. (ed.), *Illegal Migration from Bangladesh*, New Delhi: Concept Publishing, 2006.

Kutty, B.M., 'Pakistan-India Relations: Non-governmental Initiatives', *Pakistan Horizon,* Vol. 57, No. 3 (July 2004): 41–53.

Kux, Dennis, *The United States and Pakistan: 1947–2000*, Karachi: Oxford University Press, 2001.

——, *Estranged Democracies: India and the United States, 1941–1991,* New Delhi: Sage Publications, 1993.

Lamb, Alastair, *Kashmir: A Disputed Legacy, 1946–1990*, Karachi: Oxford University Press, 1992.

——, *Incomplete Partition: The Genesis of the Kashmir Dispute, 1947–48*, Karachi: Oxford University Press, 1997.

Lampton, David M., *Same Bed, Different Dreams: Managing U.S.-China Relations, 1989–2000*, Berkeley, CA: University of California Press, 2001.

Leifer, Michael, 'Chinese Economic Reform and Security Policy: The South China Sea Connection', *Survival,* Vol. 37, No. 2 (1996), pp. 44–59.

Leventhal, Paul L., Sharon Tanzer and Steven Dolley, *Nuclear Power and the Spread of Nuclear Weapons*, New Delhi: Manas Publications, 2005.

Limye, Satu P, *U.S.-Indian Relations: the Pursuit of Accommodation,* Boulder, C.O.: Westview Press, 1993.

Ludden, David, *India and South Asia: A Short History*, Oxford, England: One World Publications, Ltd., 2002.

Malik, Mohan, 'The China Factor in the India-Pakistan Conflict,' *Occasional Paper*, Honolulu: Asia-Pacific Centre for Security Studies, November 2002.

——, 'China's Southern Discomfort', *Asia Times Online*, 11 July 2002.

Malik, Iffat, *Kashmir: Ethnic Conflict, International Dispute*, Karachi: Oxford University Press, 2002.

Malik, V. P and Jorg Schultz (eds.), *The Rise of China: Perspectives from Asia and Europe*, New Delhi: Pentagon Press, 2008.

Mansingh, Surjit, *India's Search for Power: Indira Gandhi's Foreign Policy 1966–1982,* New Delhi: Sage Publications, 1984.

—— (ed.), *Indian and Chinese Foreign Policies in Comparative Perspective,* New Delhi: Radiant Publishers, 1998.

Mathew, Joseph C., *Ethnic Conflict in Bhutan*, New Delhi: Nirala Publications, 1999.

Mearsheimer, John J., *The Tragedy of Great Power Politics*, New York: W.W. Norton & Company, 2001.

Mehta, Ashok K., *India-Nepal Relations: The Challenge Ahead*, New Delhi: Rupa and Co., 2004.

Mehta, Pratap Bhanu, "Still Under Nehru's Shadow? The Absence of Foreign Policy Frameworks in India", *Indian Review,*Vol. 8,No. 3 (July–September 2009): 209-33.

Menon, Raja, *A Nuclear Strategy for India*, Thousand Oaks, CA: Sage Publications, 2000.

Mich, Hsin-Huang, Hsin-Huang Michael Hsiao, Xinhuang Xiao, Cheng-yi Lin, Zhengyi Lin, *Rise of China: Beijing's Strategies and Implications for the Asia-Pacific* , London: Taylor & Francis, 2009.

Mohan, C. Raja, *Crossing the Rubicon: The Shaping of India's New Foreign Policy*, New York: Palgrave, 2004.

——, 'A Paradigm Shift Towards South Asia,' *Washington Quarterly*, Vol. XXVI, No.1 (Winter 2002–03): 141–55.

——, 'Re-mapping India', *The Indian Express*, 22 December 2008.

Moonis, Ahmar (ed.), *Paradigms of Conflict Resolution in South A*sia, Dhaka: The University Press, 2003.

Muni, S.D., *Maoist Insurgency in Nepal: The Challenge and the Response*, New Delhi: Rupa & Co., 2004.

Mustafa, Zubeida (ed.), *The South Asian Century, 1900–1999*, Karachi: Oxford University Press, 2001.

Nanda, Ravi, *Evolving Indo-US Relations*, New Delhi: Lancers Books, 2004.

Nayar, Baldev Raj and T.V. Paul, *India in the World Order: Searching for Major-Power Status*, New York: Cambridge University Press, 2002.

Nawaz, Shuja, *Crossed Swords: Pakistan, Its Army, and the Wars Within*, New York: Oxford University Press, 2008.

Norton, James H.K., *India and South Asia*, N.Y.: McGraw-Hill/Dushkin, 2003.

Nye, Joseph S. Jr., *Understanding International Conflicts: An Introduction to Theory and History*, New York: Pearson Longman, 2007.

——, *Soft Power: The Means to Success in World Politics*, New York: Public Affairs, 2005.

——, *The Paradox of American Power: Why the World's Only Superpower Can't Go It Alone,* New York: Oxford University Press, 2003.

Pandey, Nischal Nath, *Nepal's Maoist Movement and Implications for India & China*, New Delhi: Manohar Publishers and Distributors, 2005.

Parekh, Bhiku, *Rethinking Multiculturalism: Cultural Diversity and Political Theory,* Houndmills, Basingstoke, Hampshire: Macmillan Press, 2000.

Paul, T.V. (ed.), *The India-Pakistan Conflict: An Enduring Rivalry*, Cambridge: Cambridge University Press, UK, 2005.

Perkovich, George, *India's Nuclear Bomb: The Impact on Global Proliferation*, Berkeley: University of California Press, 2001, paperback edition.

——, 'Nuclear Third Way in South Asia,' *Foreign Policy* (Summer 1993): 85–104.

Pillsbury, Michael (ed.), *Chinese View of Future Warfare*, New Delhi-Lancers Publishers, 1997.

Raghavan, V.R, *India-China Relations: A Military Perspective*, New Delhi: Gyan Publishing House, 1998.

Rahman, Rita D., and Jose Miguel Andreu, *China and India, Toward Global Economic Supremacy*, New Delhi: Academic Foundation, 2006.

Rajan, Krishna V., 'Nepal-India Relations', *South Asian Journal* (January–March 2005): 82–90.

Rajaraman, R., 'Nuclear Posture', *The Hindu*, 7 February 2003.

Rizal, Dhurba and Yozo Yokota, *Understanding Development, Conflict and Violence, The cases of Bhutan, Nepal, North-East India and the Chittagong Hill Tracts of Bangladesh*, New Delhi: Adroit Publishers, 2006.

Robertson, Robbie, *The Three Waves of Globalizaton: A History of a Developing Global Consciousness*, London: Zed Books, 2003.

Russett, Bruce, Harvey Starr and David Kinsella, *World Politics: The Menu for Choice*, Belmont, California: Wadsworth Publishing, 2005.

Sahadevan, Neil Devotta, *Politics of Conflict and Peace in Sri Lanka*, New Delhi: Manak Publications, 2006.

Sangar, David E., *Inheritance: The World Obama Confronts and the Challenges to American Power,* New York: Random House 2009.

Sardesai, Damodar, and Raju G.C. Thomas (eds.), *Nuclear India in the 21st Century*, New York: Palgrave 2002.

Schaffer, Teresa C., 'Building a New partnership with India', *The Washington Quarterly* (Spring 2002), http://www.lexis.com/research/retrieve (accessed on 18 September 2006.

Schmitt, Eric, and David E. Sanger, 'U.S. Accuses Pakistan of Altering Missile', *The New York Times*, 29 August 2009.

Schofield, Victoria, *Kashmir in the Crossfire*, New York: I.B.Tauris, 1996.

Schulz, John J., 'Riding the Nuclear Tiger: The Search for Security in South Asia', *Arms Control Today* (June 1993): 3–8.

Schwenninger, Sherle R., 'Revamping American Grand Strategy', *World Policy Journal* (Fall 2003):25

Shambaugh, David (ed.), *The Modern Chinese State*, Cambridge: Cambridge University Press, 2000.

Sharma, Shalendra D., *China and India in the Age of Globalization: A Comparative Political Economy*, New York: Cambridge University Press, 2009.

—— (ed.), *Asia in the New Millennium: Geopolitics, Security and Foreign Policy*, Institute of East Asian Studies, UC Berkeley, 2000.

Shih, Chih-Yu, *Collective Democracy, Political and Legal Reform in China*, Hong Kong: The Chinese University Press, 2000.

Singh, Jasjit (ed.), *Kargil 1999: Pakistan's Fourth War in Kashmir*, Delhi: Knowledge World and IDSA, 1999.

Singh, Jaswant, *Defending India*, New York: Macmillan, 1999.

Singh, L P., 'India's Bottom Line: A Minimal Deterrent', *The Pioneer* (July 1998).

Shobhan, Farooq, *Dynamics of Bangladesh-India Relations: Dialogue of Young Journalist Across Border*, Dhaka: Dhaka University Press, 2005.

Sobhan, Rehman, *Bangladesh: Problems of Governance*, New York: Cambridge University Press, 1993.

Singh, Waheguru Pal and Jing- Dong Yuan, *China and India: Cooperation and Conflict*, Boulder, CO: Lynne Rienner, 2003.

Smith, R. Jeffrey, 'Chinese Missile Launchers Sighted in Pakistan,' *The Washington Post*, 6 April 1991.

Spector, Leonard S., *Nuclear Ambitions,* Boulder, CO: Westview Press, 1992.

Srinivas, Chary, M., *The Eagle and the Peacock: U.S. Foreign Policy toward India since Independence*, Westport, Conn.: Greenwood Press, 1995.

Storey, Ian, 'Indo-US Strategic Ties on the Upswing,' *Jane's Intelligence Review* (March 2003): 42.

Subedi, Surya P., *Dynamics of Foreign Policy and Law: A Study of Indo-Nepal Relations*, New Delhi: Oxford University Press, 2005.

Subramanyam, Adluri (ed.), *India-Sri Lanka Partnership in the 21st Century*, New Delhi: Kalpaz Publications, 2007.

Swaine, Michael D., *Interpreting China's Grand Strategy: Past, Present, and Future*, Santa Monica, CA: Rand Corporation, 2000.

Swamy, Subramanyam, *Sri Lanka in Crisis: India's Options*, New Delhi: Har-Anand Publications, 2007.

Talbott, Strobe, *Diplomacy, Democracy, and the Bomb*, Washington, DC: Brookings Institution Press, 2004.

Tan, Tai Yong, Gyanesh Kudaisya, *The Aftermath of Partition in South Asia*, London: Routledge, 2000.

Tellis, Ashley J., (et al.), *Limited Conflicts under the Nuclear Umbrella: Indian and Pakistani Lessons from the Kargil Crisis,* Santa Monica: RAND Corporation, 2001.

——, 'The Strategic Implications of a Nuclear India,' *Orbis* (Winter 2002): 13–45.

——, *India's Emerging Nuclear Posture: Between Recessed Deterrent and Ready Arsenal*, Santa Monica: RAND, Project Air Force, 2001.

——, *India as a New Global Power: An Action Agenda for the United States*, Washington, D.C.: Carnegie Endowment for International Peace, 2005.

Thakur, Ramesh, *The Government and Politics in India*, New York: St. Martin's Press, 1995.

Thapa, Deepak and Bandita Sijapati, *A Kingdom Under Siege: Nepal's Maoist Insurgency, 1996-2003*, Kathmandu: Printhouse, 2003.

Thomas, Raju, *Democracy, Security and Development in India*, New York: St. Martin's Press, 1996.

Tien, Hung-mao and Tun-jen Cheng (eds.), *The Security Environment in the Asia-Pacific*, Armonk, NY: M.E. Sharpe, 2000.

Varadarajan, Siddharth, 'Pokhran as Pandora: Remapping the Geography of Power,' *The Times of India*, 16 May 1998.

Wignaraja, Ponna and Akmal Hussain (eds.), *The Challenge in South Asia*, Karachi: Oxford University Press, 1989.

Wilson, A.J. and Dennis Dalton, *The States of South Asia, Problems of National Integration*, New Delhi: Vikas, 1982.

Wirsing, Robert G., *Kashmir in the Shadow of War: Regional Rivalries in Nuclear Age*, New York: M.E. Sharpe, 2003.

Yasmeen, Samina, and Aabha Dixit, 'Confidence-building in South Asia', *Occasional Paper* No. 23 (September 1995), Washington, D.C.: Henry L. Stimson Centre.

Zhang, Ming, *China's Changing Nuclear Posture: Reactions to South Asian Nuclear Tests*, Washington DC: Carnegie Endowment for International Peace, 1999.

INDEX